P9-BZT-833

MAKING MONTE CARLO

A History of Speculation and Spectacle

MARK BRAUDE

Simon & Schuster
New York   London   Toronto   Sydney   New Delhi

FOR LAURA

Simon & Schuster
1230 Avenue of the Americas
New York, NY 10020

First Simon & Schuster hardcover edition April 2016

SIMON & SCHUSTER and colophon are registered trademarks
of Simon & Schuster, Inc.

For information about special discounts for bulk purchases,
please contact Simon & Schuster Special Sales at 1-866-506-1949
or business@simonandschuster.com.

The Simon & Schuster Speakers Bureau can bring authors to your live event.
For more information, or to book an event, contact the Simon & Schuster Speakers
Bureau at 1-866-248-3049 or visit our website at www.simonspeakers.com.

Interior design by Lewelin Polanco
Cartography by Erik Steiner, Spatial History Project,
Center for Spatial and Textual Analysis (CESTA), Stanford University

Manufactured in the United States of America

1 3 5 7 9 10 8 6 4 2

Library of Congress Cataloging-in-Publication Data

Braude, Mark.
Making Monte Carlo : a history of speculation and spectacle /
Mark Braude.—First Simon & Schuster hardcover edition.
pages cm
Includes bibliographical references.
1. Monte-Carlo (Monaco)—History—20th century. 2. Monte-Carlo (Monaco)—
Social life and customs—20th century. 3. Gambling—Monaco—Monte-Carlo—
History—20th century. 4. Casinos—Monaco—Monte-Carlo—History—20th century.
5. Celebrities—Monaco—Monte-Carlo—Biography. 6. Upper class—Monaco—
Monte-Carlo—Biography. 7. Rich people—Monaco—Monte-Carlo—Biography.
8. Monte-Carlo (Monaco)—Biography. I. Title.
DC946.B73 2016
944.9'49—dc23 2015008580

ISBN 978-1-4767-0969-7
ISBN 978-1-4767-0971-0 (ebook)

I.

Culture follows money.

—F. Scott Fitzgerald, Letter to Edmund Wilson

II.

We'd been in Monte Carlo for a little while before. We'd seen all the same people there that we'd seen in the winter in St. Moritz and that we'd seen in the fall in Venice . . . they weren't just the "international crowd"— they were like a whole new nationality. A nationality without a nation.

—Andy Warhol, *The Philosophy of Andy Warhol*

CONTENTS

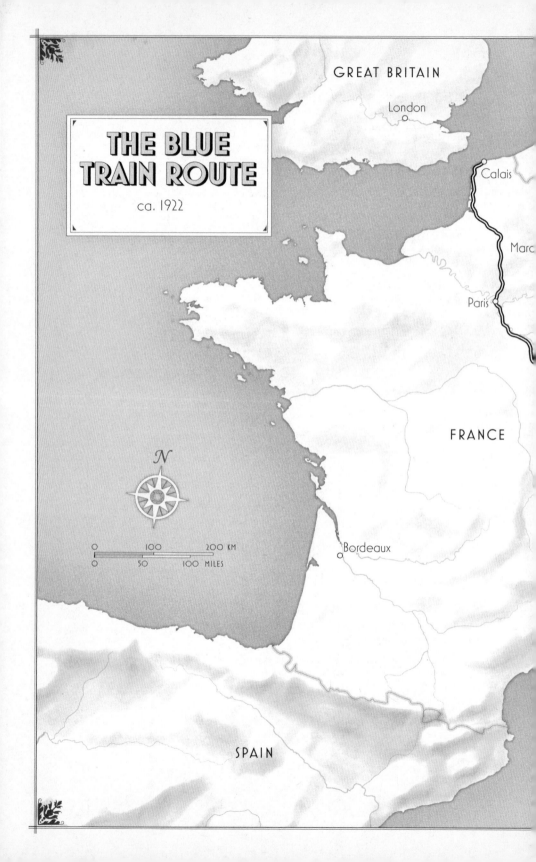

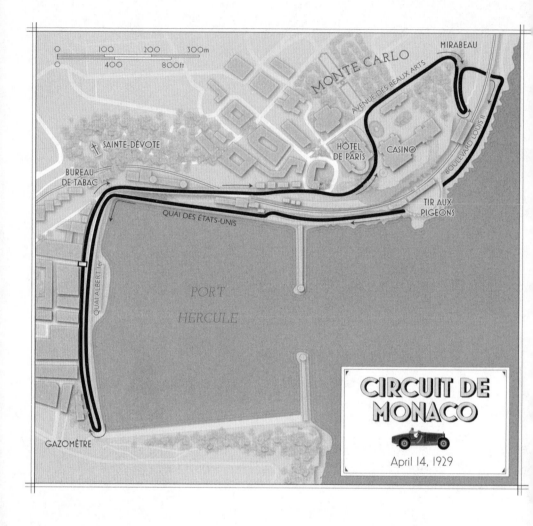

MONTE CARLO

MIRABEAU

AVENUE DES BEAUX ARTS

SAINTE-DÉVOTE

HÔTEL
DE PARIS

CASINO

BOULEVARD LOUIS II

BUREAU
DE-TABAC

TIR AUX
PIGEONS

QUAI DES ÉTATS-UNIS

QUAI ALBERT 1er

PORT
HERCULE

GAZOMÈTRE

0   100   200   300m
0   400   800ft

CIRCUIT DE MONACO

April 14, 1929

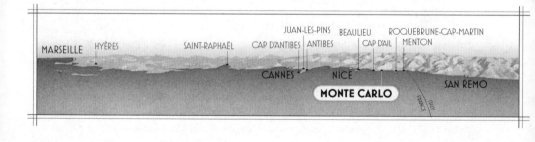

MARSEILLE   HYÈRES   SAINT-RAPHAËL   CAP D'ANTIBES   JUAN-LES-PINS   ANTIBES   BEAULIEU   CAP D'AIL   ROQUEBRUNE-CAP-MARTIN   MENTON

CANNES   NICE

MONTE CARLO

SAN REMO

FRANCE   ITALY

MONTE CARLO STORIES

It came vividly to Selden on the Casino steps that Monte Carlo had, more than any other place he knew, the gift of accommodating itself to each man's humour.

—Edith Wharton, *The House of Mirth*

IN 1863 WORK BEGAN on a new town at the eastern edge of the tiny principality of Monaco. By the close of the next decade the Monte Carlo casino-resort had emerged as the world's gambling playground of choice.

In the same era, the color poster gained favor as a form of mass advertising. Posters could be printed cheaply and distributed widely, and they came out as glossy and disposable as the attractions they sold. Designed to grab the attentions of passersby hurrying through crowded urban spaces, they seduced by offering glimpses into the forbidden. Posters advertising Monte Carlo promised a town without shadows, where sun-kissed lives played out on clay courts and under canvas sails. They featured fast men and fast women doing fast things in fast machines. Only rarely did the posters show the casino that funded their production.

People critiqued the new resort and its preferred advertising medium in similar terms. Both were deemed garish and vulgar, overly sexualized and superficial. Both pandered to the vain, venal, and selfish. Both brazenly put culture in the service of commerce.

The first visitors to the gambling town found it looked nothing like the one in the posters. Accustomed as they were to wax museums and phantasmagorias and other pleasant lies of the age, they wouldn't have been particularly upset by this deception. They hadn't taken the long and costly trip to the coast to emulate the people in the posters. They'd come to Monte Carlo because it was the only place for hundreds of miles to legally play at cards, dice, and wheels. Among those first visitors, any trace of glamour or luxury would have been understood merely as a nice touch, an added bonus.

Later, after enough people had passed through and lost enough money, the real Monte Carlo started to look better than the one in the posters. Now you came for the glamour and the luxury. Now the gambling was the nice touch, the added bonus.

This second act was in many ways harder to pull off than the first.

———

At the time of its debut in 1911, the Monte-Carlo Golf Club was one of four full courses on the European continent. It was a spectacular venue, perched up on a mountainside nine hundred meters above the sea. Sheep wandered onto the fairways. Built to please the Riviera's British expats, it was paid for by Monaco's largest developer: the Société Anonyme des Bains de Mer et du Cercle des Étrangers à Monaco (the Sea Bathing and Foreigners' Circle Company of Monaco, hereafter SBM). This same company owned the Monte Carlo casino and a host of other attractions in the principality. The SBM also maintained the local roads and harbor, and provided the people of Monaco with water, gas, garbage collection, and so many other services that a *Guardian* reporter suggested that the company was the "real, subtle, subterranean, but omnipresent power and influence" in Monaco, "the State within a State."

In 1928 the SBM built another dazzling attraction for its international clientele, the Monte-Carlo Beach hotel, which stood on a crescent-shaped stretch of shoreline twenty minutes walk from the main casino. With terra-cotta roofing and thatched breezeway lined with palms, its design nodded to the Mediterranean as much as it did to Hollywood or Palm Beach. This makes sense, since the hotel was the brainchild of the American press agent Elsa Maxwell, who'd recently been hired as the SBM's publicist. As Maxwell liked to tell it, when she asked that the hotel's Olympic-size swimming pool be placed right at the edge of the ocean, the French contractor in charge was so puzzled he "held up work until a clause was inserted in his contract guaranteeing him full payment in the event I later was proved to be mentally incompetent."

Apart from their both being funded by gambling losses, the Monte-Carlo Golf Club and the Monte-Carlo Beach hotel share another common trait: neither one is located in Monte Carlo, or even in Monaco. The Golf Club covers a slope of Mont-Agel in France, while the Beach hotel sits a quarter mile to the east of Monaco in Roquebrune, also on French soil. Monaco, fabled land of luxury and sun, lacks the tableland suitable for an eighteen-hole course, as well as any decent natural beachfront.

When Alfred Hitchcock's Riviera thriller *To Catch a Thief* opened in American theaters in the summer of 1955, the print campaign featured a shot of Grace Kelly and Cary Grant superimposed onto a scene of Monaco's harbor twinkling in the night, with a tagline that promised: "When They Meet in Monte Carlo Your Emotions Are in for a Pounding!" But in the film Kelly and Grant's characters meet at the Carlton in Cannes, and very little of *To Catch a Thief* takes place in Monte Carlo. Hitchcock shot most of the footage that does feature the resort stateside on the studio lot, using rear projection.

And it wasn't while making *To Catch a Thief* in 1954 that Kelly met her future husband, Prince Rainier, as is sometimes claimed, but rather the following year, while she was a guest of the organizers of the nascent Cannes Film Festival. That couple's first meeting—the prince offered the movie star a tour of his palace—had been a carefully staged photo opportunity, arranged by an editor of the illustrated weekly *Paris Match*.

While this book offers a history of a gambling town, it is less concerned with gambling than with tracing how a small group of men and women discovered that what was bought and sold in a casino could be something greater than the turn of a card or the spin of a wheel. Above all, this is a book about how we create places largely through the stories we tell about them, and about how places can in turn be made to suit those stories, rebelling against some and trading on others as needed. In other words, any accurate history of Monte Carlo must also include a history of the inaccuracies spun about Monte Carlo.

1

THE CUNNING AND THE EASILY DUPED

WHEN THE GAMBLING IMPRESARIO François Blanc arrived in Monaco in the spring of 1863, he would have seen three churches, a poorly built hotel next to a modest two-story casino, five paved roads, and a dozen alleyways, the whole scene enveloped in a light haze of dirt and dust whipped up by the cold northwesterly winds known as the mistral. From a distance, the prince's palace perched up on the Rock of Monaco may have impressed, but a closer look would have spoiled the illusion. Inside, many of the walls were bare. The paintings that had once adorned them had recently been sold off, along with jewels and other family treasures amassed over six centuries of rule.

A Monégasque glimpsing Blanc would have been equally unimpressed by the sight of a jowly man in poor health, with a tonsure of unkempt white hair, wearing clothes that despite their obvious expense hung awkwardly on his small frame. This Blanc was no match for the one who populated the fantastic stories that had preceded his arrival: stories about the wild vagabond and exile, the card sharper, the prodigy, the charmer and showman with the pretty German wife nearly three decades his junior, the man richer than even their own Prince Charles III.

Any tales told about François Blanc were unlikely to have fazed the Monégasques. The idea that someone born so low could have gained so much by entirely legal methods would have struck them as laughable. As one of the most astute chroniclers of the age had put it, behind a great fortune there often hides "a crime which has been forgotten, because it was committed cleanly." Honoré de Balzac's words appeared in 1835, the same year Monte Carlo's future founder was carrying off his boldest swindle yet.

———————

In the village of Courthézon that lies in the Rhone Valley, famed for its luscious wines, Marie-Thérèse Blanc gave birth to identical twins. Her husband, Claude, a minor tax official, had died while his sons were in the womb. Perhaps as compensation for their humble beginnings, the widow Blanc gave her boys kingly names; the firstborn was Louis-Joseph, the younger Louis-François. It was December 12, 1806.

Though seemingly ill starred, the twins were born lucky in their own way. They entered the world at the opening of a century when more so than ever before, starting life poor and obscure in the provinces didn't automatically mean ending it the same way. Louis-François, who went by François to distinguish himself from his brother, was the brighter of the two. He could do things with numbers that puzzled his village teachers. Having no family trade or plot to inherit, François and Louis left the valley as soon as they were old enough to care for themselves. There is no record indicating that the Blanc brothers ever returned to Courthézon, or that François offered any inspiring speeches about his humble beginnings once he'd achieved worldwide fame.

The brothers drifted from town to town in the centuries-old style of the *compagnons*, workers who crisscrossed the country on *tours de France* to apprentice under several masters. They took whatever jobs they could find, while François honed his own kind of craft in the boisterous back rooms of the inns and taverns they frequented in their travels. There he'd stake his and Louis's wages on games of cards and dice, and was soon winning enough to support them both. In those years, professional gamblers rarely relied on luck alone. Most were skilled in a variety of useful arts, from bottom-dealing, to sharping cards, to manipulating rigged dice. And someone with François's facility with numbers could have offered trumped-up odds to his opponents without much risk of getting caught, as the still novel concept of probability would have been unknown to most if not all of his opponents.

Winning the wages of hapless *compagnons* made for a lucrative business and by 1833 the Blancs had enough money to open a small bank in Bordeaux. The term bank applied loosely, as the depositors of that town merely provided the necessary float for the brothers to pursue their true interest, which was speculating on the bourse, the Parisian exchange. If half a dozen clients had ever tried withdrawing their accounts on the same day, the Banque Blanc would have folded.

François and Louis understood the bourse as an arena where skill and artfulness could trump luck. As with any contest, it could be fixed. For traders out in the provinces like themselves, the trick was getting information out of Paris before one's competitors, and then buying or selling according to how the exchange had performed, before other traders caught up. This was a time when news still traveled slowly and inconsistently, just before the wide adoption of the wireless telegraph changed everything. The Blancs had heard stories about the Rothschild banking family and their continent-wide network of agents, all supposedly communicating with the help of specially trained carrier pigeons. The brothers also learned of harebrained schemes involving windmills: a miller on the outskirts of Paris opened his shutters to show a rise in stocks for the day and his neighbor did the same, and so on down the line until the message reached a trading house miles away; but these systems proved more maddening than profitable, as a single distracted miller could undo the whole chain.

Traders at that time coveted a bit of French ingenuity known as the *télégraphe aérien* (aerial telegraph). The genius of this state-run network lay in the simplicity of its semaphore system. An official in Tower A held a written message aloft for another official in Tower B to spy though his telescope and pass along in the same way to the next tower. Paris was connected to all the major cities in France in such a manner, but the network could only be used to relay official messages and private citizens were forbidden from building their own towers. So the Blancs devised a plan to profit from the *télégraphe aérien* as straightforward as the technology itself: they bribed as many telegraph officials as they could.

Their operation, focusing on the Parisian bond market, worked as follows: Messieurs Gormand and Franck were the Blancs' two agents in Paris. Each trading day, one of them sent a package by morning mail coach to an official named Guibout, who ran the *télégraphe* atop City Hall in Tours, roughly halfway between Paris and Bordeaux. If bonds were up, Guibout received a pair of gloves; if bonds were down he got stockings, or sometimes a cravat. The same package included the day's code, a random letter of the alphabet. Guibout would insert a typo into an official telegram, followed by the day's code letter and then an H for *hausse* (rise), or a B for *basse* (fall). Conspirators at other towers recognized the code and passed it along with the erratum uncorrected. The final insider, working the Bordeaux tower, ran the message to the Blancs and they traded accordingly. Over the months the codes grew more complex, with specific colors of clothing indicating the magnitude of the day's rise or fall. The mail carriers of France could be forgiven for thinking that Gormand and Franck of Paris and Guibout of Tours were engaged in some kind of intricate courtship ritual, or perhaps contemplating a move into the garment business. The Parisians sent more than 100 packages to Guibout between the summer of 1834 and the spring of 1836, during which time the Blancs netted about 100,000 francs.

The problem was that Guibout couldn't man the Tours telegraph at all hours, so the Blancs brought on another confederate, named Lucas, to cover the post. This led to their undoing. When Lucas fell ill in the spring of 1836, a telegraph worker named Cailteau saw him through his last days and Lucas, wanting to pass along his good fortune to his caregiver, told him about the arrangement with the Blancs. He promised that Cailteau needed only to say the word to Guibout and he'd be set up to take his place. When Lucas died a few days later, Cailteau went straight to the director of the Tours telegraph, who launched an investigation. A package was intercepted; it contained a pair of yellow gloves and a note bearing only a single letter of the alphabet; a search of Guibout's papers confirmed that codes had been transmitted. The French authorities arrested the Blancs and charged them with corrupting government officials. Guibout and his wife were also placed under arrest. The record is silent as to the fate of Gormand and Franck, the two Parisian agents.

———————

At ten o'clock in the morning of March 11, 1837, guards opened the doors of the Palais-de-Justice in Tours to let in the gathered crowd, whose members were eager to have all of their worst suspicions about crooked financiers confirmed. They'd waited for hours to see how the "*Affaire des télégraphes*" would unfold. When the brothers entered, the court reporter could tell them apart only because François wore white glasses and Louis wore blue ones. The

brothers were both dressed tastefully in black suits. The proceedings revealed that people who'd met the twins during their years of
vagabondage hadn't been left with any memories that could attest
to lives dedicated to probity or hard work. A Marseillaise recalled
seeing the Blancs forcibly ejected from a club there called Le Salon.
At a café in Lyon, François had been spotted over a two-day stretch
winning at cards with alarming consistency and he'd also attended
a course in "prestidigitation" in the same town. At a private gambling club in Paris, after winning considerable amounts, the brothers were asked not to return, on suspicion of fraudulent methods.
In Brussels, François had gone by the name Leblanc and had made
inquiries about how one might build a private network of telegraph
towers.

The brothers didn't deny any of the charges against them. Louis
testified, with what the court reporter described as "a kind of dignity" in his voice, that they'd only "met their adversaries on equal
terms." Every smart trader, said Louis, employed his own method
to attain secret information—that was how the game worked. He
described the use of windmills and of carrier pigeons. He pointed
to the methods employed by the Rothschilds, whom he noted were
well respected and received by royalty, a comment that prompted
hoots and whistles from the gallery. François, in his testimony,
added that even with what little information they did attain, they
still often lost huge sums.

Since the bourse was in truth little more than "an infamous
gambling-hell," argued counsel for the defense, the methods employed by his clients, while undeniably callous, only epitomized the
kind of shrewdness and ingenuity one needed to survive in the modern marketplace. "An idea occurred to the Blanc Brothers," he told
the court, "which could not have occurred to me, or to you either,
for ordinary people who do not frequent the Stock Exchange would
be simply incapable of conceiving such a thing. . . . If you want to
play on the Exchange you must keep up your guard, because there

you will only meet two kinds of people, the cunning and the easily duped, and if you don't want to be a dupe than you had better be cunning."

It was hard to argue with such clear logic, and no law had yet been written to adequately address the practice of insider trading. The court acquitted Guibout's wife outright, and though the Blanc brothers and Guibout were found guilty, they received only small fines to cover court costs. François and Louis left town for Paris, to try their hand at a different kind of speculation.

———————

Any gambler newly arrived to Paris at that time would have soon found his way to the Palais-Royal, the city's hub for vice and intrigue of all sorts. The four-story palace complex occupied an entire block in the heart of the first arrondissement, just across the Rue de Rivoli from the Louvre. It had served as the Parisian residence of the Orléans dynasty until the twilight of the ancien régime, when the cash-strapped duc d' Orléans, Louis Philippe Joseph, rented out the top floors as apartments and partitioned the adjoining arcades into 180 leasable units for commercial use. The palace gardens were opened to the public and, as forces conspired to turn the once influential duc into a hated enemy of the Revolution, city officials lost interest in policing this potent reminder of aristocratic excess. Few other sites in Paris attracted such a wild mix of people. Loan sharks, flâneurs, pamphleteers, musicians, and hawkers of wares both fine and flimsy gathered in the salons, theaters, restaurants, bookstores, and brothels of the palace arcades. A curious visitor might be shown the café table the journalist Camille Desmoulins mounted on the eve of the Revolution to make a fiery speech that stoked a citywide riot, or the shop a few steps away where the young Charlotte Corday bought the knife she used to assassinate the ferocious Jean-Paul Marat after the Revolution turned to Terror.

Amid the upheaval of the 1790s, the stipulations the duc d'Orléans had laid out in the original commercial leases came up for some creative reinterpretation. After a series of transfers and subleases (and some well placed bribes), gambling houses opened in the arcades in 1791, with winking approval from the state. For the first time in the city's history, working Parisians could legally play the same games that members of the aristocracy had at court, in a public and open setting. Soon more than one hundred gambling operations populated the Palais-Royal and its vicinity.

In 1793 the Revolutionary Government declared the Orléans palace and its arcades national property. The duc d'Orléans had by then fallen to the guillotine (though not before trying to buy time by reinventing himself as the reform-minded "Philippe Égalité"), and the people of France weren't especially keen on debating the intricacies of his will. Nor did the new owners of the Palais-Royal see any reason to change established practices, and so gambling continued there as before, though the myriad small operations gradually consolidated into fewer houses. By the time the Blancs arrived in Paris, the arcades held only five clubs.

The French called these clubs *enfers* (hells)—with love or disdain depending on the speaker. Balzac set the opening of his first hit with the reading public, *La Peau de chagrin* (*The Wild Ass's Skin*), at the gates of the hell at N° 36. Inside, "the paper on the walls is greasy to the height of your head, there is nothing to bring one reviving thought. There is not so much as a nail for the convenience of suicides. The floor is worn and dirty. An oblong table stands in the middle of the room, the tablecloth is worn by the friction of gold, but the straw-bottomed chairs about it indicate an odd indifference to luxury in the men who will lose their lives here in the quest of the fortune that is to put luxury within their reach."

The novelist didn't have to do much exaggerating to conjure such a description; the *Palais* enfers could indeed be raucous and inhospitable. People joked about how perfectly these hells were located since the Seine flowed just a short walk away, should you suffer an unlucky streak that could only be cured by throwing yourself in. Still, even the most austere of the Palais houses exuded a rough kind of glamour, particularly for new arrivals to Paris who relished the proximity to big-city decadence and the thrill of potential ruin. Each *enfer* had its particular flavor: N° 36 barred entrance to women and served no strong spirits; people with strong royalist sympathies favored N° 50; and if one wanted a quiet game, best avoid the crowded N° 154 and head instead to the decrepit N° 113. This had been the most popular of the *enfers* in the time of Bonaparte, but had more recently fallen off, supposedly the victim of a curse, as many suicides had been committed there.

As François and Louis sampled the attractions of the arcades they formed a friendship with the city's reigning gambling authority, a former lawyer named Jacques Bénazet. A few years earlier, while leading an arbitration case involving the two officials then tasked with overseeing the Palais *enfers*, Bénazet had talked his way into holding the position himself. It is testament to his great charm as much to the vagaries of Parisian politics that in the course of his official duties Bénazet had also managed to acquire majority shares in two of the most profitable clubs, Frascati's and the Cercle des Étrangers. Bénazet strode through the arcades togged out in the finest silks; it was said that people "held their breath when his name was mentioned, it seemed to spell gold and things that glittered."

Bénazet liked the twins and started sharing the secrets of his trade with them, grooming François, whom he recognized as the shrewdest of the pair, to one day oversee his own club. François had already mastered how to win steadily at the games played in Bénazet's clubs—écarté, roulette, trente et quarante, faro, and baccarat—but dealing and banking these games required a different set of skills altogether. Bénazet offered instruction in casino security, financial forecasting, and publicity. François learned the time-tested rule that while anyone can make some money being the smartest gambler in the house, the surest way to make a lot of it was to become the house itself.

———————

The tutorials didn't last long. Just weeks after the Blancs arrived in Paris, the reigning Louis-Philippe I declared that all public gambling would be abolished effective January 1, 1838. It was a controversial move, since the Parisian clubs had provided his treasury with between 6 million and 9 million francs of yearly revenue. Even Napoleon, who hated gambling, had made special allowances for the Palais *enfers*, recognizing their legal status just as he was restricting gambling across the rest of his empire. The Palais-Royal may have had special meaning for Bonaparte; he lost his virginity to a Breton prostitute he met in the Palais gardens on a cold November night in 1787.

Louis-Philippe, son of the guillotined duc d'Orléans, had his own attachments to the place, and Parisians whispered that he'd decided to clamp down on gambling only out of embarrassment that his ancestral home had become the country's most notorious landmark. In fact, the change in law formed part of a wider set of social reforms ushered in by the July Monarchy, and kept in line with the prevailing mood, as gambling prohibitions spread across much of Europe and the United States.

On New Year's Eve 1837, the final day of play in France, Bénazet had to call in national guardsmen to restore order to the arcades. At three in the afternoon a workman killed himself at the sinister N° 113, and Bénazet closed it on the spot. A few hours later another man shot himself, outside one of Bénazet's own clubs, after realizing that he couldn't possibly win enough to pay back the debts he'd accrued over the course of the day. The first dawn of 1838 found the Palais-Royal in chaos, with blood in the arcades and an unruly mob jeering and whistling at the bleary-eyed gamblers with no place left to play. The authorities struggled to clear the lot of them from the grounds.

———————

Ultimately Louis-Philippe's law did little to curb the French love for gambling. Now people just played more discreetly than they once had, or they traveled to places where gambling was still legal. About this mass exodus of former Palais-Royal customers, the French satirist Joseph Méry wrote:

> *Nous avons détruit*
> *Frascati, le Salon, le coin de Marivaux,*
> *Pour enricher les bains de trois pays rivaux.*

> *We've destroyed*
> *Frascati, le Salon, le coin Marivaux [three Palais clubs]*
> *To enrich the spa towns of three rival countries.*
> *[Presumably Belgium, Switzerland, and the German states.]*

And Méry was right; the change in law did in fact enrich other countries, whose rulers recognized the value in standing firm against the growing tide of reform. Several Palais operators left to head up casinos in spa towns along the Rhine, in the small German-speaking territories where play went on unabated. Bénazet acquired the exclusive right to run the concession in Baden-Baden, which was then one of Europe's most fashionable thermal resorts. With the capital from their Bordeaux adventures dwindling, the Blanc brothers set off from Paris as well, eager to open a hell of their own.

2

THE ART OF MISDIRECTION

THE BLANCS BRIMMED WITH ideas about how to beat their mentor at his own game, but unlike Bénazet they lacked the money to buy a concession in one of the more reputable spa towns. Instead they opened a small private club in Luxembourg. François met an Alsatian woman there, Magdeleine-Victoire Huguelin, with whom he would have two sons, Camille and Edmond (though whether in wedlock or out remains unclear). Domestic pleasures ended up being the only kind Luxembourg could offer the Blancs, as their club folded after less than a year of operation. The brothers, Magdeleine-Victoire, and the children headed for the German village of Bad Homburg (pop. 2,500). François had seen a newspaper advertisement announcing that the local ruler, the landgrave Ludwig of Hessen-Homburg, was willing to sell the exclusive right to offer gambling in his territory. Not mentioned in the ad were Ludwig's mounting debts, or that he'd already been trying to set up a casino in Bad Homburg for nearly a decade.

Aside from the landgrave's castle and the few hundred houses gathered round it like clouds, little recommended Bad Homburg to potential visitors. A single inn, the Adler, catered to the few Frankfurters who came in the summers to drink the waters of a nearby mineral spring, but that was about it. The Blancs promised to make the place a bustling resort. In exchange for the right to the concession they agreed to build a *Kurhaus* ("cure house") that they would hand over to the landgrave, who would then rent it back to the Blancs for a thirty-year term. Construction began in the spring of 1841, while the brothers meanwhile ran a few roulette tables out of a gloomy back room in the Adler. As a small jab at Bénazet, they hired one of his former Palais-Royal favorites as their croupier. Things moved along slowly and the brothers struggled to make payroll on more than one occasion. Laborers would pound on the door of the makeshift office the brothers had set up in the Adler, until François came out to placate them with vague promises of raises and of permanent employment once construction was completed. The landgrave helped out with small loans, but being somewhat of an armchair entrepreneur, rarely without first advising his partners on how to better manage their affairs.

———————

Though they faced bleak prospects in Bad Homburg, the Blancs had started out in the casino business at a crucial turning point in both the histories of the gaming industry and of the spa industry. While gambling and spa life had long been interrelated, no one had yet fully realized the profits that lay in more closely combining the two pursuits.

Adept as they were at the practice of doing nothing, members of the European nobility had been frequenting thermal resorts for centuries. Especially de rigueur in the seventeenth century was the Belgian town of Spa, which lent its name to any place offering similar natural attractions. In theory, one visited a spa resort to "take the cure," which meant submitting oneself to a strict medical regimen of bathing and drinking mineral waters pumped from a local source. But the spa experience was always as much about fashion as it was about health. People settled in at their favored sites for weeks and months at a time, returning each year like pilgrims. Since neither the journey nor the cure came cheaply, those wanting to be seen among the right social set or hoping to secure a fortuitous marriage appreciated the concentration of "quality" these enclaves encouraged. Finding one's name on the lists of spa town arrivals and departures that ran in metropolitan newspapers became a mark of distinction. Yet, while expensive to reach, the spa towns were also still a relatively good deal, especially for down-at-the-heel nobles who could put on a show of mixing among high society while living more frugally than they might otherwise in a country manor or a city home full of servants.

As the resorts filled with people in perfectly good health, spa speculators built other diversions to keep their clients occupied and loyal. There were splendid pump rooms and theaters and sprawling gardens for promenading, racetracks and casinos as well, gambling being an especially pleasant way to while away the languid hours. Some of the larger spa towns built dedicated gaming houses, but most offered games in a few rooms of existing social halls. Traveling professionals also worked the resort circuit, sweeping in with their own (usually rigged) wheels, tables, and dice, and leaving a few weeks later after purses had been sufficiently lightened.

The strange thing about spa gambling was how little money, or at least the gaining of it, seems to have figured into the practice. Instead, this wagering formed part of a larger and more elaborate social ritual of aristocratic privilege. By playing for high stakes in the spa casinos, members of the European nobility mimicked the patricians of old, who had used contests to display what the Greeks called *arete* and the Romans *virtus*: the ability to bear unforeseen events with a stoicism that revealed one's inner fortitude, a valued asset for anyone charged by noble birth to protect the populace. Finding fewer opportunities than their ancient forebears to display honor on the battlefield, the nobility had turned to waging proxy wars on the green felt, and any games that pitted gamblers against each other in head-to-head combat, such as whist and *hasard*, proved especially popular at the spas.

For a fading class clinging to the idea of its own relevance, here was an opportunity to show disdain for the vulgarities of earned wealth and for the values of the hated bourgeoisie. One could dismiss huge losses at the tables with a shrug. The insults and debts that arose from these gambling battles inevitably gave rise to duels, also a fine way to evince one's noble standing. Thackeray made sure to include a gambling-debt duel when recounting the rituals of spa life in *The Luck of Barry Lyndon*. Parents even hired "gaming masters" to instruct their children, lest they one day be shunned by their peers for lacking dexterity at the tables. "Being a gambler gives a man position in society," wrote Montesquieu. "It is a title which takes the place of birth, wealth and probity. It promotes anyone who bears it into the best society without further examination."

We can add spa life to the long list of things that changed drastically with the introduction of rail travel in the nineteenth century. As the costs and lengths of trips to the resorts fell, spa owners scrambled to meet the needs of their expanding clientele. By the time the Blancs were setting up in Bad Homburg, the once relatively humble spa casino trade was quickly morphing into a modern industry. The future lay in economies of scale, mathematical accuracy, and steady and predictable flows of profit. Spa speculators trained their croupiers in complicated oddsmaking, set stricter betting limits, and added new layers of management and security.

The remnants of the European nobility, now made to sit elbow to elbow with anyone who could afford a train ticket, grew somewhat disenchanted with the spa casinos. Playing for high stakes would never lose its charm for the bored and wealthy, but aristocratic gamblers now bet less boldly than they once had, and spa casino owners could no longer count on a few wealthy addicts to see them through the season.

As resort operators devoted ever more funds to publicizing their wares to clients newly freed by the railway to hop from resort to resort, their expenses swelled. And with more importance placed on the idea of fair and regulated games, buying and maintaining gaming materials also ate up a huge part of annual budgets. A reputable spa casino needed roulette wheels as finely crafted as any luxury good, and a single wheel could cost several times the annual salary of the man whose job it was to spin it. The time when inexperienced entrepreneurs like the Blancs could open a casino without first securing a great deal of outside investment was coming to an end.

It took someone as well versed in the social intricacies of spa life as he was in the perilous thrills of the Parisian *enfers* and the backroom games of provincial taverns to navigate this sea change. What other casino operators lamented as the death of a golden age, François Blanc recognized as the start of something bigger and better: a new contest, with new rules to be learned and then bent to suit his needs.

Blanc spotted how tastes for particular games were shifting alongside the changes in the makeup of his clientele. He predicted that the coming wave of middle-class gamblers would prefer playing for longer periods of time and for lower stakes, since they were less interested in the quick bursts of adrenaline that had marked the adversarial gambling of the previous era. The new spa gamblers were more intent on lining their pockets than they were in flirting or in putting on airs. Rather than setting out to battle their peers, they would enjoy communal table games, where everyone played against the faceless house. Blanc could also see the inherent weakness in games like faro, piquet, and écarté, which were then the mainstays of spa casinos. These were "banking" games, where each player had a turn to act as the "bank" and stake the round, meaning that most of the money passed back and forth between gamblers, while the house took only a small commission. Profits from banking games were steady, but too slim for Blanc's liking.

Blanc got rid of all banking games at Bad Homburg. It was an unprecedented move. He focused instead on two games: roulette and trente et quarante, which was a simple counting game that, as with roulette, had players squaring off only against the house. Blanc tried another relatively novel ploy by banishing the double-zero from all his roulette tables. Though it might have seemed foolish to start a new casino by first cutting the era's most popular games as well as one's margins, Blanc had closely calculated how much these moves would cost him in the short term, and he was prepared to wager that amount against the projected gains these changes would bring in terms of efficiency and publicity.

The single-zero roulette tables caused a furor right away. Serious players started talking about the little *Kurhaus* in Bad Homburg with the best odds in all of Europe.

As the first customers trickled in, Blanc took another risk by putting whatever they spent back into anything that might encourage them to stay for longer and want to return for more: wilder parties, bigger orchestras, and flashier advertising. He offered horses and guns for hunting in the nearby woods, free of charge. The landgrave meanwhile encouraged the brothers to exploit Bad Homburg's mineral springs, granting them exclusive right to drill for any new sources. François paid some scientists from the Sorbonne to analyze the quality of Bad Homburg's mineral waters and, not surprisingly, these were found to possess many curative properties. He also wooed the famed chef Chevet away from his trendsetting Palais-Royal eatery, sealing the deal with the promise of a restaurant crafted to Chevet's exact specifications. The official "Garden Director-General" of the Royal Prussian court was brought in to landscape the casino's entrance. The famed violinist Niccolò Paganini—who counted music, women, and gambling as his three great loves—was hired for a command performance and Blanc gave him a healthy stipend to spend on roulette, hoping to amuse other gamblers with the spectacle of the great musician at play. With Bad Homburg gaining a reputation as a center of high culture, patrons who might have been embarrassed by their pleasure-seeking could justify their trips to the casino as more than mere gambling sprees.

Blanc's architect Louis Jacobi outfitted the casino in the finest silks and Morocco leather. While whetting gamblers' appetites with such showy displays of luxury, decorating the gaming rooms so lavishly was also meant to reassure clients that the house had the wherewithal to pay out any big winnings. This was already common practice across the Atlantic, where even the lowliest fly-by-night operators outfitted their backroom gambling dens with gold and velvet; these were known in American parlance as "first-class hells."

The numbers of visitors to Bad Homburg grew steadily but slowly. In 1839 there had been 829 of them; by the time the *Kurhaus* opened three years later that figure had more than doubled and by 1847 more than five thousand visitors to Bad Homburg were recorded, beating out that year's total at the rival spa town of Bad Ems. The Blancs now felt confident enough to offer stock in their enterprise and issued shares at five hundred florins apiece, the first ever instance of a casino being incorporated. They did make sure that no one shareholder could acquire enough to give him more than five votes at the general meetings, guaranteeing that the Blancs alone would always set company policy.

As with the other spa towns in Northern Europe, Bad Homburg's peak seasons were the spring and summer. François Blanc tried to scoop regular clients from competing resorts by staying open through the winters, when many of the other Rhine spas closed. This took a heavy financial toll, especially in the early years, but helped Blanc grow a particular following that would remain very faithful to him: members of the Russian aristocracy, who were keen to escape the freeze of Saint Petersburg.

One of Bad Homburg's most beloved figures was the Russian countess Sophie Kisselev, who haunted the roulette tables propped up in her custom-made chair surrounded by servants, astrologers, and spiritualists who divined the most suitable numbers for the old woman to play. One wit said that she only gambled once a day, from eleven in the morning to eleven at night. Another story held that Kisselev had visited the pope to be cured of her gambling addiction and that he had obliged her with a prayer, though the benediction had only temporary effect. Blanc often gave Kisselev cash advances, just as he did with most players who bore noble names, since they in return introduced him in salons across Europe, where he talked up the wonders of his fledgling resort.

Another Russian who gambled in Bad Homburg as avidly as the countess though with far less money to do so was Fyodor Dostoyevsky, who amassed huge debts in the 1860s in no small part thanks to his time at Blanc's tables. Desperate to make some quick money to pay off these debts, he took a large advance from his publisher while agreeing to terms that bordered on extortion: if Dostoyevsky failed to produce a book within a few weeks of the contract's signing he'd forfeit the rights to all his previous books for a nine-year period. Under that pressure he produced a novella, *The Gambler*, in a matter of days. It unfolds in a spa town along the Rhine, "Roulettenburg," whose casino attracts, among others, "Grandmother," an eccentric and wealthy Russian with a passion for roulette. Producing *The Gambler* may not have exorcised Dostoyevsky's roulette demons, but it did bring him together with the young woman taking his dictation, Anna Grigoryevna, one of the first female philatelists in Russia; Dostoyevsky married her shortly after completing the book. Later, at a roulette table in Baden-Baden, he lost all the money he'd just acquired by pawning every item of clothing Anna owned.

Today we would label both *The Gambler*'s central character, Alexis, and his creator as compulsive gamblers. Freud thought along such lines; in an essay on themes of parricide in Dostoyevsky, he diagnosed the novelist as a neurotic and a latent homosexual, with an Oedipus complex thrown in for good measure. Freud believed Dostoyevsky gambled obsessively as an attempt at self-castration, driven by his guilt over his desire to kill his overbearing father— the same guilt, according to Freud, that caused the writer's epilepsy. Castration fantasies aside, it is certain that for some players the potential for ruin offers as great a thrill as that of winning; in Walter Benjamin's words: "The fascination of danger is at the bottom of all great passions. There is no fullness of pleasure unless the precipice is near. It is the mingling of terror with delight that intoxicates. And what more terrifying than gambling?"

————

At Bad Homburg's tables, the social gulf separating the Kiselevs of the world from its Dostoyevskys was beginning to narrow. In the crowded gaming rooms one couldn't always distinguish one's table-mates according to traditional markers of class, country, or métier. A German writer recalled seeing millionaires dancing with actresses at Bad Homburg, while aristocrats mingled with ballerinas; he promised his readers that nowhere on earth offered "a more colorful confusion, a more mixed society." Indeed Blanc wanted the Bad Homburg spectacle to enchant the widest audience possible and he worked to make resort and casino function in perfect symmetry, their combined pleasures available to anyone able to reach his town.

François Blanc wasn't alone in foreseeing that the quantity of his clientele would eventually provide steadier and greater profits than its so-called quality, but he became the most successful gambling impresario of the nineteenth century because he so deftly adapted the older theatrical appeals of aristocratic gambling to suit the needs and tastes of the modern age. Even as it grew more crowded with bodies, he continued to sell Bad Homburg as a kind of enclosed dream-space of privilege, yet he did so hoping to make it more crowded still. The future of his industry, Blanc saw clearly, lay less in merely providing games of chance at a casino and more in making people feel as though they'd gained entry into an elite group simply by being in the resort where the casino was housed. One as mathematically inclined as Blanc might have said that he simply took an established equation and reversed the signs: his predecessors had built casinos to complement the natural attractions of their existing spa resorts, while he started with a casino and invented the resort to surround it.

───────────

Louis Blanc watched from the background as his brother's boldness began to pay dividends, just as it had at a much smaller scale in Bordeaux, and on their *tours de France* before that. Content to stay out of the limelight, Louis had nonetheless played a vital role in making the family's fortune—seeing that accounts were in order and offering a steadying influence for François, who in minutes could swing from the highest ecstasies to the darkest melancholia. And so it was disastrous when, in 1852, François lost both Louis and Magdeleine-Victoire to early deaths.

Blanc was left with two young sons. He hired a governess. Her name was Marie Hensel, and though born to a humble cobbler and his wife in Friedrichsdorf, she spoke decent French. She told François that her line traced back to his home country, as she hailed from exiled Huguenots. With marriage in mind, François sent Marie to finishing school to learn to carry herself as a woman of privilege. The couple wed in a small ceremony in Paris in 1854; she was twenty-one and he forty-eight. Five months after the wedding, Marie gave birth to a daughter, Louise.

Marie Blanc worked keenly alongside her husband and soon took Louis's place as his trusted business partner. A son, Edmond, and another daughter, Marie-Félix, were born. Bad Homburg grew and prospered alongside the family. Even though the numbers of annual visitors never grew massive, usually hovering within the 5,000 to 10,000 range, the casino took in healthy profits, and by 1862 the Blancs' company stood valued at 12 million florins.

As an adviser to Monaco's Prince Charles III later remarked, François Blanc in Bad Homburg "showed himself to be a master of the art of hiding the green felt behind a veil of luxury and elegant pleasures." Magicians and cardsharps call this kind of thing the art of misdirection, the drawing of an audience's eyes in one direction while hands work busily elsewhere. Blanc would perfect the technique far from Bad Homburg, in a place of his own conjuring.

3

THE ANTECHAMBER OF DEATH

Small nations. The concept is not quantitative; it describes a situation; a destiny: small nations haven't the comfortable sense of being there always, past and future; they have all, at some point or another in their history, passed through the antechamber of death; always faced with the arrogant ignorance of the large nations, they see their existence perpetually threatened or called into question; for their very existence is a question.

—Milan Kundera, *Testaments Betrayed*

STATES GROW RICHER AND stronger as they grow larger. This is a dominant narrative in the history of the last two and a half centuries, a blood-soaked tale of conquest, annexation, and unification (sometimes willingly, but usually not) of disparate populations under a single flag. Historians of nation-building have shown how new forms of media and new modes of travel helped people to imagine themselves as small but vital pieces within a greater whole, bound to others whom they might never see face-to-face, but with whom they purportedly shared the same passions, the same tongues, the same histories, and the same visions for the future.

The history of Monaco does not fit neatly into this narrative. The growth of its population over the centuries can be counted in thousands, not millions. And its territory spans only 499 acres, making it about half the size of Central Park. Of the world's sovereign states, only the Vatican is smaller. Yet despite having little in the way of natural resources, Monaco has become one of the wealthiest places on the planet, recently outranking the United States in per capita GDP. The history of a principality hemmed in on three sides by French territory and by the Mediterranean to its south has not been one of expansion, but of contraction. Not only did the Grimaldi princes and princesses keep their territory from being swallowed up by a stronger neighbor amid the great sweep of nineteenth-century nation-building, they grew rich precisely by trading on the restrictive size and weakness of their state. There are few moments of conquest, annexation, or unification in Monaco's history; there is only the shock of loss, followed by a desperate cycle of reinvention.

Monaco lies roughly halfway between the busy ports of Marseille and Genoa. It boasts a natural harbor and three flanks protected by mountains. For centuries, the leaders of competing Mediterranean powers coveted this fortuitous combination of trading hub, fortress, and safe haven. The Phoenicians are believed to have settled the region around 1600 BCE; they built a temple by the sea devoted to the sun god Melqart. The Greeks who followed the Phoenicians identified Melqart with their own Heracles, who, according to legend, landed in the area on the way to complete his Tenth Labor; the Greeks dubbed the harbor Portus Heraklis Monoeki ("the Port of Heracles Alone"), as no one else could be worshipped in a temple devoted to this jealous demigod.

Next came the Romans and the Via Aurelia, the great Mediterranean land route that provided one of the empire's crucial arteries for four centuries, built clinging to the sides of hills to prevent an ambush. Julius Caesar so valued the shelter of Monaco's harbor—by that time known as the Port of Hercules—that he gathered his fleet there before launching battle against Pompeii. After the Roman

Empire fell, various Germanic and Arabic tribes occupied the region, which may have stood completely abandoned from the tenth to the twelfth century, when the Holy Roman Emperor granted the Republic of Genoa possession of the land, stipulating that the Genoese fortify it against piracy. They built the four-towered fortress atop the Rock of Monaco in 1215, which still stands at the center of the Princely Palace complex.

The roots of the present Grimaldi dynasty stretch back to the violent feuds involving the Holy Roman Emperor Frederick II and Pope Innocent IV that divided thirteenth-century Genoa into two warring factions: the Ghibellines, who supported the crown, and the Guelphs, who supported the papacy. The wealthy Grimaldi clan, headed by a roguish seaman named Francesco, backed the Guelphs and was driven out of Genoa. The clan settled in nearby Ventimiglia and eyed the fortress of Monaco, held by the enemy Ghibellines.

On the night of January 8, 1297—which in Monégasque memory is as dark and stormy as nights come—Francesco Grimaldi and his followers called at the Ghibelline fortress, having first disguised themselves as Franciscan monks seeking shelter from the inclement weather. After being let behind the gates they revealed the swords hidden in their long robes and cut down the entire garrison. Not for nothing do the Monégasques refer to Francesco as *il Malizia*, "the Cunning One," sometimes translated as "the Spiteful One." The words Francesco was said to have shouted during the killing spree, *"Deo Juvante"* (It is God's will), provided Monaco's official motto (and, later, the name for one of Prince Rainier's and Grace Kelly's yachts). Today a bronze statue of a sword-wielding monk stands watch over the scene of that long-ago slaughter, while Monaco's coat of arms features two friars brandishing their weapons. That *monaco* means monk in Italian is a misnomer; rather, Monaco's moniker mines *Monoeki*, the shorthand of its Greek name.

The Grimaldi line does not actually descend directly from Francesco, who held the Monaco fortress for only a few years, but rather from his cousin, Rainier I. Still, as far as origin stories go, the tale of *il Malizia* is a fitting one. Generations of Grimaldi rulers kept control over Monaco only by being as brutally sly as their adopted patriarch. The dynasty survived by lending out its subjects, harbor, and fortress to stronger neighbors, most often France, in exchange for protection and guarantees of noninterference. Grimaldi lords perfected the art of playing on their guardians' fears that they might shift allegiance to another protector at any given moment. The family lived mainly from the traditional *droit de mer* that gave it the right to levy a 2 percent tax on all goods traded in the Port of Hercules.

While the Grimaldi were unabashed in their striving, their subjects were a relatively unambitious lot. They said so themselves—what else could be expected from people living in a place so poorly suited to farming? "I am Monaco upon a rock," went the words of a local saying, "I neither sow nor reap. But all the same I want to eat." The Monégasques made their way by fishing and shepherding, and by tending to a few olive and lemon trees.

The situation brightened in the fourteenth century when, as a reward for help fighting the English, France granted the Grimaldi control of two communes to the east of Monaco. Mentone and Roccabruna (in French, Menton and Roquebrune), lay on fertile land and their citrus harvests soon provided the bulk of the principality's economy. Locals liked to say that "Menton and Roquebrune paid; Monaco profited." The citrus trade, along with the dividends from the port tax, landholdings in France, and some good marriages, provided the Grimaldi a comfortable lifestyle and years of favor at Versailles.

Prosperity ended in 1789. Galvanized by revolution, the people of Monaco, Mentone, and Roccabruna declared their lands free republican cities and called for the dethronement of the reigning Honoré III. The French National Assembly's abolition of feudal rights stripped the prince of all his lands and Monaco was briefly absorbed into France. Looters pillaged the Grimaldi palace and members of the dynasty were imprisoned. Honoré III's daughter-in-law,

Françoise-Thérèse, whose husband, Joseph, had taken up arms against the revolutionaries, was sentenced to death for aiding enemies of the republic. She died on the same day of the Thermidorian Reaction that saw Robespierre executed along with twenty-one of his allies, just hours after she'd met the blade. All other members of the Grimaldi dynasty managed to pass through the period with their heads still attached to their bodies.

With Napoleon's rise, the Grimaldi sensed an opportunity to recoup their losses, and family members held prominent positions under the emperor. Yet only after Bonaparte's defeat did the Grimaldi regain dominion over their land, when Talleyrand and the other diplomats redrawing the map of Europe decided that a sovereign Monaco could serve as a check against rising Sardinian influence in the south. But the coalition changed course after Bonaparte's disastrous Hundred Days and now the Sardinians were allowed to occupy the principality as punishment for French excesses. Monaco's prince, Honoré V, had seen most of his family's fortune melt away in the span of a generation. He tried establishing a lace-making factory, but it failed. A perfumery folded as well, as did a distillery, a hatmaking workshop, and a plant for making false teeth.

When Honoré V died in 1841, leaving no legitimate heir, his epitaph read: "Here lies one who wished to do good." He was succeeded by his brother, Prince Florestan I, who spent most of his reign in Paris or in his country estate, more interested in the theater than in high politics. Meanwhile, agents for the liberal-leaning Sardinians began to foment a secessionist movement in Mentone and Roccabruna and things came to a head amid the larger European revolutions of 1848. The people of the two territories again declared their freedom and called for the dethronement of the Grimaldi. Unlike in their first go-round, they now pledged allegiance to the Sardinian king, rather than to France. Only the few hundred subjects living in Monaco proper remained loyal to Florestan, and then just barely so.

With the loss of Mentone and Roccabruna, so went the citrus trade and 80 percent of Monaco's territory. Florestan could hardly cover his clothing budget, let alone care for his subjects. He sold off much of the family's jewelry and art. The playwright Victorien Sardou later satirized Florestan's troubles with the character of Rabagas, ruler of a comic-opera principality who describes himself as "an unhappy little sovereign, crushed between two fat neighbors, who argue over nothing but the sauce with which they will devour my States."

It was Florestan's wife, Princesse Caroline, who ensured that Monaco too would one day grow fat and happy. An accomplished stage actress in her day, she had far more savvy than did her husband. Caroline had heard of the landgrave of Hessen-Homburg growing rich from his casino and saw no reason why something that worked in one small and sovereign territory couldn't work in another. In the spring of 1855 she secretly dispatched her closest adviser, a Parisian lawyer, whom we know only by his last name, Eynaud, to Bad Homburg. He came back beaming about yearly revenues in the hundreds of thousands of francs, saying that people "spent money there like water."

It was clear that the most valuable mercenary service the Grimaldi could now provide was to transform their land into a pleasure zone for the rest of Europe. So while the nineteenth century may have seen a vast swath of humanity placed under the control of some form of national power structure, the case of Monaco reminds us that the same forces that fostered the creation of modern nations also helped microstates to flourish by allowing people to escape their home communities in ways never before possible.

————

A few weeks after Eynaud's return, and with much convincing from his wife, Prince Florestan legalized gambling in Monaco. Sanctioned casino gambling could at that time be found in the spa towns of Belgium, Switzerland, and some of the German-speaking territories, as well as in Northern Spain. Monaco stood alone in offering gambling along the southern coast of Europe. But by legalizing a widely banned practice Florestan was thumbing his nose at the same neighboring protectors that had guaranteed Monaco's independence. Pushed too far, one or all of them might choose to annex the principality for good. He was risking losing the same control over his territory and subjects he'd hoped to protect in the first place.

Eynaud formulated a solution. The nearby towns of Cannes and Nice were gaining renown as coastal resorts that might one day rival the inland spa towns. Eynaud counseled the prince that Monaco could similarly be promoted as a modern spa resort—one that so happened to have the only legal casino for hundreds of miles. "The bathing establishment," he told Florestan, "should in a sense act as a façade for the gambling establishment."

In September of 1855, prince and adviser drew up plans to form a new company to oversee the gambling concession in Monaco, showing their hand by giving it the grandly aquatic name of Société Anonyme des Bains de Mer et du Cercle des Étrangers à Monaco (the Sea Bathing and Foreigners' Circle of Monaco Company). The document outlining the SBM's founding statutes to potential concessionaires mentioned the right to provide games of chance only as the fourteenth of twenty-one articles.

No sooner was the document signed than Eynaud went searching for a candidate to buy the concession. The news traveled quickly to Bad Homburg, though it wouldn't be François Blanc who opened the first casino in Monaco.

4

COMPLETE DISORDER REIGNS

FOR SOMEONE WHO MADE his fortune exploiting people's misguided beliefs that luck could be swayed in their favor, François Blanc was absurdly superstitious, a man who saw signs and omens wherever he looked. He was convinced that relatives and top managers were conspiring against him. Each day Blanc read the papers from the major European metropolises, wanting to know of even the slightest tremors in the halls of power, lest they come to make the earth quake in Bad Homburg.

Forward thinking though he was, Blanc had a blind spot when it came to Monaco. "It would be such a doubtful venture that no one would undertake it," he told an associate. Bad Homburg too had been a doubtful venture at first, but at least it had been close to other spa towns in Northern Europe and to the burgeoning rail network. Reaching Monaco entailed a nauseating three-hour carriage ride from Nice along the narrow Corniche mountain road, littered with highwaymen, followed by an hour's walk down rocky hills. The other option was a two-hour trip aboard a shaky craft called the *Palmaria*, which seemed to sail only as often as the captain was sober and willing.

Blanc deemed Monaco's political situation too unstable for the concession to merit his interest. Its territory had been slashed barely a decade earlier. And the Italian Risorgimento was gathering steam to the east, throwing the whole region into upheaval. Worst of all was the presence of garrisoned soldiers from Sardinia. The Sardinian penal code forbade games of chance, yet Monaco's weakling prince openly defied the laws of his occupier. Blanc's opinion did not surprise Eynaud, who advised Florestan that they would fail to find a decent investor until the prince could show definitively that no neighboring state would force him to overturn his decree.

Yet there were other speculators—hungrier than Blanc and confident they could repeat the feat he'd pulled off in Bad Homburg—who were more willing to take on Monaco's obvious risks. Two fast-talking suitors came down from Paris with plans to build a grand casino and hotels. Hundreds of miles away, Blanc already knew more about the pair—a businessman named Napoléon Langlois and a journalist named Albert Aubert—than did anyone in Monaco; Langlois had only two hundred thousand francs at best, and this only on credit, while Aubert was penniless. Neither of them had any casino experience.

But the Parisians dazzled Florestan and Eynaud, and they were granted a thirty-five-year concession for the exclusive right to run a bathing establishment in Monaco and to offer "distractions of all kinds, notably balls, concerts, performances, and games of chance, such as Whist, Écarté, Piquet, Pharaon, Reversi, Roulette with one or two zeroes, and Trente-et-Quarante." In return, the pair pledged to build spa facilities and a hotel with surrounding gardens, and to establish a regular omnibus service connecting Nice and Monaco.

Florestan died in July 1856, shortly after the agreement was reached. The throne passed to his son Charles-Honoré, who reigned as Prince Charles III (or Carlo III, in the local dialect). At that time, one could have crossed Carlo's principality on foot in under an hour, heading eastbound from the palace out to the barren plateau at the edge of the territory that the *Monégasques* called Les Spélugues, which can be translated either as "the grottoes" or "the disreputable haunts." The locals tended to avoid the area. Bandits were spotted there from time to time, holed up in the dark caves, coming out to rob anyone foolish enough to wander into that wild stretch of land, where the normal rules didn't apply. Eynaud thought it a perfect place for a casino, seeing as how Princess Caroline had insisted that her son keep gambling as far from the palace as possible. The SBM bought up land on Les Spélugues belonging to a retired officer. Hearing of these developments, Blanc sent a few of his most trusted croupiers to Monaco—though not before officially firing them, to obscure any links to himself—where they found work with the SBM and began sending reports back to Bad Homburg.

———————

Under Langlois and Aubert, the SBM was to float a capital of 3 million francs, divided into 6,000 shares, each paying 6 percent annual interest. A quarter of the net profits would be deposited into the royal treasury every year. At least those were the terms of the contract establishing the concession, since no outside capital had yet been secured, nor had work begun on any kind of building that might one day generate profit.

The two Parisians pushed ahead with a breathy prospectus to attract investors. It described a casino that was "virtually ready" to open, which was to be run out of "a large and beautiful villa commanding a magnificent view of the harbor, surrounded by a wonderful garden containing 2,500 lemon and 2,000 orange trees, as well as a large olive grove." Langlois and Aubert promised that a town "of small villas in the English style" would soon go up on Les Spélugues, land that could be had "at public auction for about thirty centimes a square meter, while that on the other side of the harbor is already worth more than ten francs the square meter." The prospectus wavered between hyperbole and outright fabrication: "large and beautiful villa" meant a cramped private home, the Villa Bellevue, chosen for its relative distance from the palace, and the land on Les Spélugues was still a craggy mess and worth nowhere near the prices mentioned. The new concessionaires offered no clue as to how they planned to provide regular road, rail, or boat access to Monaco, or about who would pay to build the town of small villas.

Langlois and Aubert did manage to excite a few investors, and 1,000 of the hoped-for 6,000 shares were sold. The act codifying the sale of these shares reads more like an advertisement than a legal document; it is full of hopeful language assuring the reader that more buyers would be found for the remaining shares.

In its original Italian incarnation, casino (from *casa*) described a small house, usually devoted to pleasure. Such was the case with Monaco's first gambling venue, the Villa Bellevue, which opened on December 14, 1856, with little fanfare. A few weeks later Langlois and Aubert opened a second casino at the nearby Hôtel de la Grand Place du Palais, a venue as poorly furnished as it was ambitiously named.

The doors of the two gambling houses opened at nine, though play at the main table games, roulette and trente et un (a counting game, not to be confused with trente et quarante) started around lunchtime. The bank held only 12,000 francs for the roulette tables and 20,000 francs for the trente et un tables. Maximum bets at each game were 3,000 francs, which meant that anyone bold enough to stake the maximum could have wiped out the table's reserves—a happy, if unlikely, feat known as "breaking the bank." The action wound down at eight, unless enough players hung around to justify staying open later. This was rarely the case.

The palace inspector's report on the first month of gambling in Monaco reveals humble beginnings: "On the ground floor of the Villa Bellevue one finds a vestibule, two gaming rooms, one for trente et un and the other for roulette, plus another room destined to become a café. On the floor above we find: a conversation room, reserved for women, and a reading room, a third lounge that will be used for other table games. . . . The garden paths leading to the Casino, as well as the gates, are not yet in a satisfactory state. Difficulties have arisen between the landlord and the Administration that have so far impeded the transformation of this venue into a house of pleasure. Once these difficulties are overcome, the Administration will surely remove from the grounds all that which is offensive to the eyes and nose."

The author of the report, the prince's inspector commissioner, had been hounding Langlois and Aubert to produce a summary of their receipts. He knew only that in the first month of business the two gaming houses had taken in a paltry 33,282 francs. The concessionaires begged off opening their books, claiming the necessary documents were in Paris. "As of now," wrote the inspector commissioner, "it is impossible to verify whether the terms of our agreement are being observed or to determine what the financial situation of the Société des Bains might be."

Had the inspector commissioner been granted access to the books, he wouldn't have been pleased by what he saw. The tables were bringing in nowhere near enough to cover the company's expenses. Since Langlois and Aubert lacked the capital to allow for anything but the lowest table limits, high-stakes players had little incentive to make the rough trip to Monaco. The pair had briefly made good on their promise to establish a daily omnibus service from Nice, but had canceled it after only two weeks, due to lack of interest. They then tried renting a steamship, with equally dismal results. Of the few visitors who did reach the gambling houses, many came to make mischief. Forgers, cardsharps, and petty thieves preyed on the inexperienced concessionaires.

Blanc's croupier-spies would have reported that Bad Homburg was hardly under attack. Between March 15 and March 20, 1857, for instance, the two Monaco gambling houses together welcomed only a single customer, who won two francs. Things got so quiet at the Villa Bellevue that the croupiers spent much of their time out front of the building, lounging in the sun and smoking. Eventually one of them decided to install a telescope in their smoking spot so they could check every so often to see if any player came down the road, which sent them scurrying back to their posts.

Langlois and Aubert never managed to sell any more shares. They did, however, succeed in enlisting the services of an inspector general, a bookkeeper, a *chef de partie* (akin to a modern day pit boss), a lamplighter, ten liveried attendants, and ten croupiers. Their greatest extravagance was a fifteen-piece orchestra, which played every day. On the verge of insolvency, they asked for a loan from the palace. But although Prince Charles wanted badly to avoid the embarrassment of failure, he had no funds to lend. Instead, he and Eynaud pushed the pair to find another buyer, and Langlois and Aubert quietly sold the concession to a man named Froissard de Lilbonne, who in turn immediately sold it to another Frenchman, Pierre Auguste Daval, for 1,208,000 francs.

Daval claimed to be a wealthy rentier from Charente, a prosperous region in southwestern France that produced much of the country's cognac. It was later revealed that he'd subsidized his ill-fated foray into the gaming industry mostly with money borrowed from a wealthy mistress. His cash reserves were no deeper than those of Aubert and Langlois had been. With the Monaco concession, Daval acquired little aside from the right to continue running games out of the Villa Bellevue and the Hôtel de la Grand Place de la Palais, along with the existing tables and betting plaques, a few sticks of furniture, and some uniforms. He tried to run as modest an operation as possible. One cost-saving strategy involved firing off the existing crew of croupiers and replacing them, at a lower pay rate, with some unemployed waiters from Nice.

Within a few months Daval had enough money to start work on the larger casino that Eynaud and Charles had insisted would eventually replace the two existing venues. On a rainy day in May of 1858, the ten-year-old crown prince Albert helped his father, by then nearly blind, to lay the foundation stone for the future casino on Les Spélugues. But cash flow problems plagued the project from the start. The head architect, Gobineau de la Brétonnerie, grumbled about cheap materials, and rightly so; after the casino's foundation gave way one day, he fled to Africa. Laborers complained of irregular pay, as did the prince, who still hadn't seen any dividends. Eynaud wrote Daval: "For three months His Highness has vouched for you while closing his eyes to a host of irregularities and violations. . . . Complete disorder reigns in Monaco under your administration. Your officials are daily embroiled in scandalous conflicts and your employees are unpaid. . . . I remind you that you owe the Treasury a considerable sum."

Then came the rumor, early in 1859, that Prince Charles was broke and desperate, and planned to sell the whole principality to the Romanovs. This set off the locals, already on edge thanks to yet another Sardinian garrison that had docked in the harbor on its way to Turin. An angry mob, including several casino employees, marched on the palace. They were met by the threat of cannon fire and quickly surrendered their cause.

The SBM was more than 2 million francs in debt. Daval reached his breaking point, just as southern Europe exploded into war.

5

WE DO NOT APPROVE OF GAMING HOUSES

THE ARMED CONFLICT PITTING a Franco-Sardinian alliance against the Austrians (later known as the Second Italian War of Independence) broke out in late April 1859, forcing Daval to close the two casinos. Prince Charles offered what faint support he could to the French forces. Meanwhile Daval went to Paris with the hope of raising enough money to see him through this fallow period but couldn't garner any interest. Eynaud was furious that Daval had sought outside investment without first getting palace approval; he'd revealed the SBM's financial insecurity, a deadly blow for any gambling concern. "He is mad," Eynaud told Charles. "I have taken it upon myself to state that, after his repeated failures, his broken promises, and the general nuisance he has been, Your Highness should probably refuse to tolerate him any longer as director of the business. A man like him, who has discredited himself in every way, has become simply impossible." At the end of May, with the two gambling houses still closed, Daval transferred his rights to the SBM to a French nobleman named the duc de Valmy, making no attempt to profit on his original investment.

The duc de Valmy's grandfather Marshal François Kellermann had been a war hero, and it was hoped that associating Monaco with this storied name might bring some much-needed publicity to the SBM. But while Valmy became the public face of the company, he left its day-to-day management to an agent, François Lefèbvre, while he played the gentleman in Paris. This would turn out to be a terrible decision on Valmy's part.

Only with the end of war in July 1859 could Lefèbvre begin his work in Monaco. Instead of reopening the old venues, he focused all gambling into a single large villa, called the Gabarini, while construction on Les Spélugues continued in its fits and starts. There was a quick hint of brightness, as people visited Monaco in unprecedented numbers in the fall and winter of 1859, either because jubilant with victory or upset by the recent destruction, and the Villa Gabarini netted roughly one thousand francs a day in profit. However, Lefèbvre failed to exploit this brief spike in interest; he was too meek to invest in anything more substantial than some new furniture. "The disappointment of those coming to Monaco is so great," wrote a palace official, "that by this time everybody knows there are no comfortable hotels, no bathing facilities, no amusements of any kind." By the end of 1860 the SBM had suffered a net loss of more than eighty thousand francs.

Lefèbvre was about as poorly suited to the job of casino boss as a person could be. The smallest things sent him into a panic. He was "always nervous about the future," as an adviser described him to the prince. The walls of the Villa Gabarini remained whitewashed for weeks because Lefèbvre couldn't settle on a fair price with the painters. He refused to advertise, underpaid his staff, lit the gambling rooms poorly, and skimped on small luxuries such as newspapers in the smoking lounge. And whenever the tables had a particularly bad run, he would take to his bed for days at a time.

Eynaud had to pester Valmy and Lefèbvre for dividend payments just as he had with their predecessors. But political developments outside of Monaco were conspiring in the Grimaldi's favor, and the treasury soon swelled. On March 24, 1860, the French and the Sardinians signed the Treaty of Turin, which saw the Italians cede Nice and Savoy to France as reward for help fighting off their mutual enemies. The former Grimaldi territories of Menton and Roquebrune were incorporated into France a few weeks later, though only after plebiscites had been issued, lest it appear that the people of these lands had been strong-armed into joining the nation. The final step was for Monaco's prince to publicly drop any claims to the territories, which, though they'd shifted their alliance to the Kingdom of Sardinia in 1848, had never properly cut ties with the Grimaldi dynasty, leaving them in a state of political limbo that had lasted more than a decade.

Prince Charles signed an agreement with the French emperor, Napoleon III, in 1861, in which he disavowed all rights to rule Menton and Roquebrune. In return, Charles received 4 million francs and a guarantee of Monaco's continued independence. This French show of protection caused the hated Sardinian troops to quit the principality for good.

For the moment, Charles and Eynaud could afford to be more patient with their concessionaires, though the casino was hardly making anyone wealthy. Lefèbvre meanwhile worried about controlling the hundreds of foreign workers he'd hired to finish the work on Les Spélugues, voicing his concern to the prince about "such a gathering [of foreign workers], often less than peaceful in their natures." Over a few weeks in March 1862, the number of laborers in his pay jumped from 25 to 150, and by the end of the summer the number stood at 500, a substantial figure given that the Monégasque population then numbered roughly 1200. The French minister of the interior also got involved. He feared that undocumented workers, especially Italians, would slip across Monaco's porous border into France. Monaco's governor general promised to increase surveillance and asked the French minister for "a list of the names of Italians that you have deemed dangerous."

It was all becoming too much for Lefèbvre, who suffered a mental collapse and stopped going into the gaming rooms altogether, convinced that he would be hounded by angry clients and employees as soon as he entered. Sensing the director's loss of confidence, several key workers quit. Eynaud counseled his prince to bring matters to a head. Instead of going easier on Lefèbvre, Charles decided to apply even more pressure. He insisted that the new casino on Les Spélugues be completed by the first of January 1863, without exception. The looming deadline broke whatever spirit Lefèbvre had left and he resigned late in 1862, though he hung on to the few SBM shares he'd acquired over the years. Valmy for his part thought it an unwise time to sell, since so much of the company's capital was tied up in construction. He found other managers to replace Lefèbvre in the interim, hoping that the new casino might save him, if he could only manage to hold out long enough to see it finished.

On February 18, 1863, the new casino on Les Spélugues opened its doors for the first time, with little fanfare and to near-universal indifference. It had one room for gambling, one for smoking, and one for concerts, and all of these had been furnished with economy in mind. The few punters that came in those first weeks were hardly the kind of players Valmy had wanted to attract. Many of them started their days by playing cards at a café for a few sous, until one among them won enough to afford the two-franc-minimum stake at the casino. They grumbled about being so far from the main town with nowhere to spend the night, and not even a restaurant or bar nearby. Valmy put his men to work on a hotel directly adjacent to the casino and promised free plots of land on Les Spélugues to anyone who could commit to building a villa there, though he found no takers.

Less than a month after the new casino's opening, Valmy heard reports that the notorious Spanish gambler Thomas Garcia was heading to Monaco bent on wiping out its reserves. He rightly assumed that Garcia had more money on his person than the SBM held in all its accounts. This same Garcia had nearly ruined François Blanc three years earlier, playing the maximums at Bad Homburg and winning huge sums. Blanc, never one to miss a chance for free advertising, had supplied reporters with tales of Garcia's exploits, peppered with details about his thick black beard, his golden rings, his diamond cross, and the beautiful *mascotte* (a woman believed to bring good luck) on his arm.

Valmy doubted he could survive an attack from Garcia. He sent word to Bad Homburg requesting an audience with François Blanc. The possibility of transferring the concession to the man who'd performed such wonders in Bad Homburg thrilled Eynaud. He told Prince Charles: "Monsieur Blanc is enormously rich and very clever; it is very much to be hoped that he will take over the affair. A hundred thousand francs are no more to him than a hundred to other people." Eynaud advised that Valmy set his price low enough to reel Blanc in, though Valmy, by that point nearly bankrupt, didn't need much prodding.

What neither Eynaud, Prince Charles, nor Valmy understood was that for the already wealthy Blanc, Monaco's appeal was more than financial. The real thrill was out there on Les Spélugues, a piece of Europe where the maps were still white. Blanc was tired of the petty politicking in Bad Homburg, and with German unification looming, he knew it was likely that the government of the new German state, whatever shape it might take, would outlaw gambling to keep in line with Europe's prevailing legal and moral codes. Marie Blanc was especially worried about the political climate in Central Europe, and insisted that her husband diversify with the Monaco concession, now a relatively safe play compared to Bad Homburg.

Blanc met with Valmy and Eynaud in Paris. He acted aloof and irritable, blaming his mood on a nagging boil that made it impossible for him to sit, due to its unfortunate placement. Whether true or not, the bit about the boil allowed Blanc to dominate the other two men, who remained seated. Midway through the meeting Blanc abruptly called it to a close, saying he couldn't consider the matter clearly until his "most troublesome disability" had passed, allowing him to "sit down for a few hours on end" to pore over the company's financial records at length.

A few days later Blanc wrote to Prince Charles, the first direct communication between the two men. Blanc promised that if granted the concession he would reinvent Monaco as a modern spa resort. With the proper organization and publicity, he said, Monaco could become "one of the most frequented winter stations in the region." Eynaud could hardly contain himself when he learned how closely Blanc's vision aligned with his own. "It is enormously to Your Highness's interest that Monsieur Blanc should not back out now," he wrote. "He has promised to spend as much as 12,000,000 francs ultimately . . . His plans are on a grand scale . . . I do not think it will be necessary to make detailed stipulations . . . as it would be if we were dealing with one of limited resources, or controlled by a less able man."

Noting Blanc's keen interest in Monaco's spring waters, Eynaud allowed that this was "only a pretext. But in such a business as ours, no pretext should be neglected."

Valmy proposed to sell the concession for 1,860,000 francs. Blanc said he found the number insultingly high, though he could have afforded the amount easily. He broke off all communications, until Eynaud finally managed to bring the two parties back to the bargaining table. In the meantime the gambler Garcia had come to Monaco and lived up to his reputation, winning 45,000 francs, mostly by playing trente et quarante. Valmy was apoplectic. What Valmy didn't know was that just as he grew more desperate to sell, so was Blanc growing more excited about Monaco. While playing cards in a private club in Paris, he'd overheard that a rival, the head of the Wiesbaden casino, had also entered negotiations with the Monaco camp and that he had backing from some powerful Frankfurt bankers. Blanc had also apparently managed to sit down somewhere along the way and had been pleasantly surprised by his study of the SBM's accounts. If the numbers held steady the company would turn a small profit for the year, even if that were only equal to what Bad Homburg might make in a typical week.

Blanc put in an offer for 1,129,000 francs. He wrote to Eynaud saying he wouldn't be privy to any kind of "double negotiation" and that Valmy had two days to accept his offer before it was off the table forever. Eynaud advised the concessionaire to sell, and quickly. There was another meeting and the sale appeared imminent. Then Blanc waffled. The negotiations had taken place in Paris. He wanted to take a closer look at Monaco.

Eynaud coached Charles for his crucial first meeting with the gambling impresario. "Though Blanc may appear rather ponderous he is an extremely clever and intelligent man. Your Highness can do a great deal with him by flattering his vanity and intimating to him that he will have an absolutely free hand, with no Government restrictions or interference other than those laid down in the schedule of conditions." Couching his advice to flatter with some flattery of his own, he closed his letter by remarking on "what great and novel events, both political and financial, have happened during these last three years! Your Government will turn Monaco into a land of real importance, in spite of its small territory."

Blanc came down from Paris in the second week of March. He would have been struck by the relatively balmy weather, the lush vegetation, the expanse of the Mediterranean. The casino, he would have seen plainly, had been shoddily built. But above all he would have recognized that Les Spélugues could be made into whatever he wished it to be, and that there was a hungry workforce and a supplicant local ruler only too happy to help him carry out his vision. In Monaco, he would experience none of the speculative one-upmanship found in other resorts, where competing business owners tried to outdo each other in building the town's most spectacular attraction, collectively driving development in an iterative and uneven fashion.

Eynaud convinced Blanc to up his offer to 1,500,000 francs, in cash. After completing a quick tour of the casino and the grounds, Blanc told Valmy: "Think the matter over. I will return at three o'clock for your final decision. My boat leaves for Nice at four, by which time I must have your answer either way."

———

On All Fools' Day 1863, François Blanc acquired control of the SBM, gaining the exclusive right to offer games of chance in Monaco for the next fifty years. As the new head of the company he pledged, per the original statutes, to supply gas and water to the Monégasques, to ensure regular transportation by land and sea between Monaco and Nice, to complete construction on the hotel, and to host annual benefits for the poor. The company would pay Prince Charles and his descendants a portion of its profits in perpetuity. Eynaud predicted that Monaco would soon be unrecognizable. Merely refurbishing the casino and completing the unfinished hotel wouldn't be enough for a man of Blanc's energies. He would surely build a whole new town to surround the casino "while the old town will remain the traditional business center," a setup that would appease "a population that demands calm and tranquility."

As though a portent of future success, the gambler Garcia's luck at the tables ran out just as the concession was transferred. A casino manager (whether at Blanc's behest or not is unknown) had decided to close all tables offering trente et quarante, the game at which Garcia had been winning so steadily. Garcia moved on to other contests but fared poorly. Though he'd been up as much as seventy thousand francs at one point, he eventually lost that amount, and then a further twenty thousand francs. In the end he had to borrow money from a friend to pay his way home.

———

Prince Charles compounded the physical sequestering of gambling to the edge of the principality with a decree that barred any of his subjects from entering the casino unless for work. Monaco's official palace historian, writing not long after the law took effect, suggested that this had been a necessary protective measure: "We do not approve of gaming houses, and the governments who suppress them act wisely. Established in large centres of the population, they [stimulate] the spirit of cupidity, and bring about . . . demoralization and ruin. . . . But when established far from large cities, and when the distance is such that the cost of the journey can only be met by rich foreigners, one may accord such games the benefit of extenuating circumstances, for they do bring an element of prosperity to the native population, itself severely barred from entering."

The most pressing social issue in Monaco, then, was not vice but poverty. And the solution would come from outside. If everyone involved saw clearly that casino gambling brought about "demoralization and ruin," at least only "rich foreigners" would feel the effects. Or so went the official logic.

6

A WHOLE TOWN REMAINS TO BE BUILT!

And, above all, for the man who has lost all curiosity, all ambition, there is a sort of mysterious and aristocratic pleasure in watching, as he reclines in the belvedere or leans on the mole, all the bustle of people leaving, of people returning, people who still have enough energy to have desires, who still desire to voyage, who still desire to get rich.

—Charles Baudelaire, "Sea-Ports"

FOUR DAYS AFTER BLANC took control of the SBM, the front page of the *Journal de Monaco* heralded a golden age in the principality. "The new management will do great things, and will do them in the grand style. M. Blanc's name and reputation are a guarantee of this. We see what he has done at Homburg, and that is enough for us. The fame enjoyed by that spa justifies our most exalted hopes, we might even say our wildest dreams." That this was hardly an impartial report is unsurprising: Blanc had taken up the paper's editorship three days earlier, yet another privilege that came with acquiring the Monaco concession.

A few weeks later Blanc used the *Journal* to rally the locals to his cause, addressing them directly on the paper's front page: "From an existence of dreaming inaction Monaco must rouse itself to one of courage and activity. A whole town remains to be built! The rich and those with money to spend are only waiting for accommodation to come and enjoy our climate."

There were no specific mentions of the casino or of gambling to sully Blanc's call to arms.

———————

The settlement taking shape on Les Spélugues would function in many ways like a typical nineteenth-century company town. As in a mining or oil town, a single industry dominated, though in this case, instead of, say, an oil baron and a sheriff working sometimes in collusion and sometimes at cross-purposes to impose order, here a casino director and a prince would help each other to profit, while jockeying for control over the locals.

Yet Blanc's gambling resort was something wholly unprecedented in the history of company towns. It was funded almost exclusively by foreign investment, built and staffed mostly with foreign workers, publicized in the foreign press, and, with Monégasques forbidden from gambling, entirely dependent on the spending of outsiders. Blanc encouraged people from around the world to come to Monaco to shirk the laws of their home countries, and more importantly glamorized that escape, making it feel like a daringly modern act of defiance. For a company town, then, Blanc's was one with a decidedly cosmopolitan outlook. Though in Monaco, cosmopolitanism was deployed not in pursuit of any border-transcending humanist or utopian goals, but to achieve local commercial gains and consolidate local power.

———————

In Monaco, Blanc had the money and the freedom to go further than he ever could have dreamed in Bad Homburg. He also had a good reason to outdo his previous efforts. Despite his thriving business and his German wife, the man born in Courthézon would always be odd man out in Bad Homburg, while at the same time, with the French and Prussians circling toward war, those same Germanic associations tainted Blanc's reputation in the country of his birth. Whether in Bad Homburg or Monaco, Blanc knew he'd be forever at the mercy of political forces beyond his control. A piece in the *Journal de Monaco* in June of 1863 spoke of the "growing rumors that Germany, for reasons of what can only be described as hypocritical morality and sham humanitarianism, will shortly abolish gambling. All the worse for Germany then! And all the better for Monaco, which will not be so stupid as to commit financial suicide in order to please a few moralists." The diatribe, likely penned by Blanc himself, smacks of overcompensation. Monaco enjoyed a favorable political situation just then, but no one could say for certain how long it might be until Prince Charles would also be made to bow to the world's moralists. And as people in neighboring towns learned of the profits soon to be reaped in Monaco, they were sure to pressure their own leaders to legalize gambling, or perhaps even call for the use of force to make the Grimaldi toe the antigambling line. Either way, Blanc knew he would ultimately lose his monopoly on gambling in southern Europe.

Blanc's body buckled under the constant stress. He visited a sanatorium in the Swiss town of Loèche-les-Bains for treatment any chance that he could.

As he saw his new town growing up around him, Blanc grew resolved to have it endure after his death. Like any fearful new parent, he went to great lengths to protect his creation against future obstacles. The key lay, as it had in Bad Homburg, in offering more than gambling alone. Where Eynaud had talked about the spa facilities in terms of a "façade" and a "pretense," Blanc had a genuine interest in establishing these nongambling attractions for their own sake. He wanted, above all, to create an emotional bond between visitors and the resort, with the hope of turning casual gamblers into long-term clients more devoted to the idea of his gambling town than simply to its gaming rooms. He wanted people arriving in the resort for the first time to feel that they'd not only left behind the banality of their everyday lives but that they'd arrived among a community of fellow elites who, like themselves, could appreciate the deeper values of its surface comforts. This is why the already wealthy Blanc took such huge financial risks to build an array of facilities in Monaco that had nothing to do with gambling and in many cases lost money. Each new attraction he built complemented the others and performed a symbolic role alongside its primary function, serving as an advertisement not only for a casino-resort but for a whole new way of life.

———————

Among Blanc's most pressing concerns in his first year at the helm of the SBM was the question of where to house the anticipated hordes. He called in his Bad Homburg architect, Jacobi, who took one look at the unfinished hotel next to the casino and declared that every part of it had to be rebuilt or repaired. Jacobi and another architect, Dutrou, altered the original plans and modeled the building on Paris's Grand Hôtel on the Boulevard des Capucines, one of the finest hotels of the age. Blanc drove home the association between Monaco and the City of Light by naming the new building the Hôtel de Paris, the title carved in gold against black marble above its front doors. When a café went up across the way a few years later, it would similarly be called the Café de Paris. The café grounds would eventually house a billiard room, a tobacco shop, a perfumery, and a jewelry store, which, according to hundreds of sensational tales, displayed the pawned fortunes of many a ruined gambler—though in 1863 these additions were still years away.

Marie Blanc was given free rein to outfit the Hôtel de Paris however she saw fit. A palace adviser, noting the vast sums she spent (two hundred thousand francs on silverware alone), assured the prince that such extravagances were all part of François Blanc's plan to have the building "spoken of as a marvel, thus acting as a splendid advertisement." The lobby glittered with fine Louis Quinze furniture. It became unofficial policy to extend credit or waive room charges to big spenders who lost heavily, at least until their luck changed, though in any case the Hôtel was not prohibitively expensive at that time.

With suitable accommodations in place, Blanc hired crews to improve the roads in and around the principality and to refurbish its harbor. He bought four steamers to ferry clients between Nice, Genoa, and Monaco, while a four-horse omnibus took gamblers arriving by boat from the harbor straight to the doors of the casino, free of charge. A wide circular space was cleared in front of the casino's entrance for the parking and display of carriages.

Clients exiting the casino's front entrance would have looked out onto a neatly ordered row of palm-bordered plots, filled with aloe vera and fragrant mimosa, meant to reinforce the idea that the resort functioned as a salubrious space and no mere *enfer*. Blanc had most of the vegetation imported from Africa and the Americas, turning this gambling town at the fringe of Europe away from the continent and toward the Mediterranean and the New World. Years later the American novelist Theodore Dreiser remembered of his Monaco visit how strange it felt to leave the "shaded, artificially lighted rooms with their swarms of well-dressed men and women sitting about or bending over tables, all riveted to one thrilling thing—the drop of the little white ball in a certain pocket—and come out into this glittering white world with its blazing sun, its visible blue sea, its cream-colored buildings and its waving palms." That the resort's varied and imported plants referenced a mix of distant lands and cultures further linked it to a broader Mediterranean syncretism. The idea was simple: the more 'exotic' the resort appeared, the more distant it was from everyday life, and the freer its visitors would feel to spend more extravagantly than they would at home—a strategy repeated again and again in themed gambling spaces, from Las Vegas to Macau. Historians of the Côte d'Azur have noted the irony in the fact that the ultimate icon of Riviera luxury, the palm tree, *Phoenix canariensis*, is not native to the area, but, like the idea of a culturally distinct and coherent Riviera itself, yet one more invention.

While the casino's original architect had built its main entrance facing northwest, looking up toward the green hills, Blanc wanted to capitalize on the building's underused southern, sea-facing side, which offered the most exposure to the sun and sea-breeze, and to the sound of breaking waves. He had an oversized stone stairway built out from the back exit of the gaming rooms and onto a terrace. This served as an impromptu outdoor catwalk, ideal for displaying the latest fashions, with the bright sun necessitating the carrying and display of fine hats and parasols. The terrace was made narrow enough to encourage men and women to throng thrillingly close together, bringing all the flirtations of the metropolitan boulevard to the ocean's edge. On a clear day you could see the island of Corsica. Blanc also installed outdoor gas lighting and hired guards to patrol the terrace well into the night, at considerable expense.

On a second level down from the terrace were a shooting grounds and a clubhouse, built on a semicircle of manicured grass. Here marksmen tested their aims against live pigeons. (Women could watch, but were not invited to shoot, though this policy changed after the First World War). Monaco's *Tir aux Pigeons*, or pigeon shoot, was an ersatz version of something already fake to begin with: rich men pretending they had to hunt for their dinners. The birds were kept in collapsible metal cages and their tail feathers had been clipped to make them fly erratically. At the appointed time someone called "Pull!" and the cage fell open. A few dozen feet back, a shooter with his rifle loaded with buckshot had one chance to peg the scrambling target. If he hit the bird he kept shooting for another round; otherwise he handed the gun to the next competitor. Dead pigeons fell into the bay below where locals waited in rowboats. Those that hit solid ground were given to casino employees. During the high season the *Tir aux Pigeons* went through roughly five hundred birds a day. No fee was charged for the shoot, and the SBM consistently lost money running it, though that was beside the point. As one casino manager put it, the *Tir aux Pigeons* was "never regarded as a rival of the Casino; on the contrary, it was started by Blanc himself to attract the right kind of people." The shoot also fostered a cottage industry, as bookmakers offered odds on a given marksman's accuracy. Surely it also helped convince more than one member of the shooting set to forego a few weeks at the family manor for a quick jaunt to Monaco. While pegging pigeons on a patch of grass outside a casino hardly equaled deer-stalking in the rolling hills, neither could the English countryside boast roulette wheels and French courtesans.

The main nongambling attraction in Monaco, as Blanc had promised in his original intimations to the prince, would be its state-of-the art spa facility. Construction began on a modern bathing establishment, which occupied a spot at the edge of the harbor in the Condamine district, where once there had been only been sheds manned by workers cleaning and packing lemons for shipment on the three-masted ships that came to trade in the port. The SBM hired an esteemed spa doctor to oversee the facility and lend it the gravitas of the relatively new science of hydrotherapy.

———

As in Bad Homburg, Blanc wanted to attract a broad audience while maintaining an illusion of exclusivity. And so, although the town going up on Les Spélugues welcomed all comers, its casino was run like a heavily guarded palace. Before entering, one's outfit first had to pass inspection by the large unsmiling men dressed in blue-and-red uniforms, capped in gold braid, who flanked the building's heavy doors, and came to be known as the "dress police." Inside, gamblers paid a small fee, meant to scare off those more interested in watching than playing, and they also filled out entry cards listing place of birth and current address, so that credentials could be checked. Stacks of folders rested behind the counter, thick with lists of those refused entry or ejected from the floor for bad behavior. Readmission proved nearly impossible once one's name found its way into one of those folders. As clients passed from the front doors to the gaming rooms, guards sometimes asked them to take off their hats, bare heads making it easier for them to recognize anyone they had previously barred.

Officially, if not always in practice, entry was forbidden to:

Priests

French and Italian officers (in or out of uniform)

Anyone suspected of having "insufficient means"

Convicted criminals

Men identified as "commercial travelers" (who might gamble with company funds)

Women identified as *femmes galantes* (women of easy virtue)

Some of the SBM's clients admitted that they enjoyed being subjected to this kind of scrutiny. One French gambler said that being admitted to Blanc's casino felt akin to being received by "society" upon arrival at the finest thermal resorts in previous centuries.

Passing from the main foyer into the gaming rooms would have felt like traveling between worlds. There were Italian oil paintings in one room, French tableaux in another, and another was decorated in Moorish Revival style, like an opium den in some lush orientalist fantasy. There were columns of marble and onyx, parquet floors, paintings on the ceiling, and crystal chandeliers concealing gaslights. The decorators left no surface unadorned. Gold leaf trimmed most of the fixtures, while silk curtains framed the windows and overstuffed couches lined the walls; there were mirrors everywhere.

A twenty-four-piece band played in the ballroom. And each room had its own spittoon, made of pure marble.

The opulent decor hinted at the kind of freedom that could be bought with the wealth that waited at the tables: the freedom to go anywhere and to take the best of any culture, the freedom to master the whole world and its products. Even the basic rhythms of nature had been reordered to suit players' needs. During the day an air ventilation system (at that time a novelty) kept patrons cool, while bright lighting from the chandeliers and other sources allowed for the betting to go on deep into the night.

Employees called the main gaming rooms "the kitchen." And as in the back of a busy restaurant, an assembly-line mentality prevailed, along with its attendant obsessions with speed and precision. The company bestowed kitchen-like job titles, which let employees know exactly where they stood within the rigid chain of command. Croupiers answered to *sous-chefs*, who oversaw several tables; *sous-chefs* answered to the *chef de partie* (literally, line cook) who took in the action from his high chair; the *chef de partie* answered to the *inspecteur des tables*, who in turn answered to the *inspecteur de la chambre*; and everyone answered to the *directeur des jeux,* chief overseer of the casino floor, who answered only to François Blanc.

One rarely saw the *directeur des jeux,* who was headquartered in a tiny unmarked office just behind the anteroom where people filled out their entry cards. From time to time some small scene might force him to make an appearance: an unruly drunk started yelling about not being admitted; a ruined gambler threatened suicide; one punter accused another of palming his chips. Then, quietly, and with the help of a few guards, the *directeur* would shuffle the aggrieved parties offstage. "A Mlle. Pichon . . . caused a terrible scene in the gaming rooms," wrote one *directeur* in his weekly security report, "screaming that she'd lost her fortune and that she had no other choice but to kill herself, and to make good on this threat, quickly produced a revolver out of a pocket in her dress and was about to turn it against herself, but the guards . . . managed to disarm her easily. I took her to my office without her resisting, and she soon calmed down." A patron who became overly irate might be led into a surgery on the second floor, where a doctor waited on hand to help calm the offending party. Casino guards had little patience for these dramas. Known as *commissaires*, they had the right to arrest any unruly customers, who were then handed over to the Monégasque authorities. A former Monaco croupier claimed that if any "lowlife" seemed to be bothering other customers he or she would be immediately ejected, often on trumped-up charges, such as suspicion of theft.

An unwritten rule held that gamblers who lost all their money could apply to have the casino cover the cost of a trip home. An SBM security report tells of an elderly woman, claiming to be "completely deaf" and having lost "all of her fortune," being given three hundred francs and a ticket back to Paris. The practice was known as receiving the *viatique*, translatable as "pocket money for the trip," but carrying a darker connotation as well, as it could also refer to the final Eucharist administered to the dying. The recipient of the *viatique* was to leave town as quickly and quietly as possible, and everyone understood that the money was technically being loaned rather than given, and that those who'd begged for it wouldn't be readmitted until their debts were paid. As one SBM manager put it, "the casino never forgets."

Blanc watched his workers as closely as his clients. His stable initially comprised thirty croupiers, who wore natty suits devoid of pockets and with sleeves cut far shorter than normal, for the sake of security. The croupiers were rotated regularly among the tables, which limited the opportunities for any one of them to collude with a client. It was forbidden to tip a croupier directly. Instead, gamblers were encouraged to put coins or bills into "number-thirty-seven" a thin slot between the betting area and the wheel. Employees divvied up these tips, but only after management had taken its half off the top.

Blanc made sure to conduct these kinds of internal surveillance in a very public manner. While some people may have taken pleasure in "slumming" at clandestine clubs, Blanc wanted his customers to know that they'd always find a square game in his house, which was far from the case in most other gambling environments, as he knew well from his time as a professional gambler. All of those security workers watching and being watched added to the casino's sense of extravagance. As with diners in a restaurant deliberately overstaffed with genuflecting setters, waiters, and busboys, Blanc's guests could appreciate how many people had been dispatched to attend to their needs. A single roulette table, for instance, took five croupiers to run. One handled the chips, while the other four, seated in pairs on either side of the table, took turns spinning the wheel. Given that a table stayed in operation so long as a single client looked interested, and factoring in the managers, security workers, and service staff on hand, a lone gambler might attract the attention of more than a dozen SBM employees.

While aristocratic gamblers had thought of spa casino wagering as a kind of performance, theirs were intimate dramas, unfolding in sequestered environments and among social equals who were usually already familiar with one another. Gambling in the main rooms of Les Spélugues, by contrast, was an intensely public affair. With the tables placed in the center of large and wide-open spaces, all attention focused on the bettors. A room that in today's Las Vegas might hold twelve tables squeezed in tightly to maximize profits per square foot would in Monaco have only held one or two. The glittering chandeliers and candelabras, as well as the natural light pouring in from the oversized oculi of iron and glass that ringed the building, heightened the sense of theatricality.

In Monaco gamblers learned to become what were known as *beaux joueurs*, beautiful players, who pandered to the assembled gallery, sparking gossip about how much this one bet or how stoically that one bore her losses. Sidling up to the rich green felt, they were made to feel like stars in some impossibly glamorous performance. They handled finely crafted betting plaques that were like little works of art, inlaid with mother-of-pearl. As in department stores and exhibition halls, the casino put clients on display as much as the things they consumed. And Blanc's customers were imbued with the same sense of power they felt in those other nineteenth-century temples of commerce: the power of choice. Where a typical spa casino might have offered one or two roulette wheels, these being expensive to build and maintain, Monaco's gaming rooms had as many as eight running concurrently, different brands of the same product.

Blanc could whet the appetites of even the most hardened gamblers. One stunt involved "retiring" a roulette wheel that had supposedly paid out enough in a single spin to exhaust the day's reserves. A croupier would drape a shroud of black crepe over the wheel while workers were sent to collect more gold coins, a sort of mock mourning to show that the casino, too, suffered by the whims of the goddess Fortuna. Rather than undermining public confidence in the SBM's solvency, tales of "breaking the bank" only served to tempt gamblers further.

Middle-class clients, who aspired to mimic aristocratic modes of privilege but were less interested in repeating their excesses, wanted to believe that their conspicuous consumption also held the potential for the conspicuous acquisition of wealth. And yet, with its relatively high table limits, plenty of opportunities remained at Blanc's casino for members of the aristocracy to maintain the lie that they disdained money. The former croupier Paul de Ketchiva claimed that no one could lose "so gracefully as the old *noblesse*— who shrugged their shoulders and ordered another bottle of champagne when they lost a mere fifty thousand francs, and at once took solace in the arms of one of the beautiful *demimondaines* who lined the walls of all the *salles*."

By the *salles*, Ketchiva meant the *salles privées*, smaller rooms on the second floor, safely out of sight, and open only to clients of sufficient means. Here the action tended not to get going until the small hours, after the closing of the main rooms. It felt more like a gentleman's club than a modern casino. The Prince of Wales, who also frequented Bad Homburg, was sometimes spotted in the *salles privées*, but only after having enjoyed the charade of entering the casino under an assumed name. The *salles privées* attracted many of the finest professional gamblers of the era. They cut romantic figures. The English poet John Addington Symonds imagined them spending their off-hours "lounging and smoking in the gardens, listening to Verdi in the music hall, gormandizing in the *salle à manger*, and enjoying every beauty of southern spring, together with the fiery pleasure of that hazard." Of one particularly dashing professional, he wrote: "Perfect coolness and concentration of fever producing calm, marked this man. His whole soul was in the play."

In Blanc's first year heading the SBM, Monaco welcomed almost thirty thousand visitors. Many were regulars from Bad Homburg who'd come to see how Monaco would compare. Gross receipts from the tables totaled a respectable 640,000 francs. Blanc, however, spent several times that amount on construction. He was disappointed with the numbers. For the new town to flourish, one final piece had to fall into place. Or rather, he would have to force it to fall into place.

7

THIS LITTLE PARADISE

I am convinced that it is not gold that brings the rich, and artists, to Monte Carlo, but rather the desire to free themselves from everything, to tempt chance, to bet against fate, and this is why we must give them dreams, pleasure, and beauty.

—François Blanc, SBM Shareholders' Meeting, 1875

THE PARIS-LYON-MÉDITERRANÉE RAIL COMPANY (PLM) extended its line to Cannes in 1863 and to Nice the following year. The rail company directors initially had no specific plans to connect the line with Monaco, but this changed in 1865, when Blanc began privately transferring SBM-owned land around the casino to the PLM, at no cost, for the laying of rail and building of stations. A few years later, a French muckraker suggested that Blanc had provided the PLM with additional financial incentives and that he'd promised to cover the costs of any unsold tickets if sales fell short of a certain minimum.

The expansion of the European rail network in the 1860s went hand in hand with another dramatic change from which Blanc would benefit: the spread of the mass press. His timing in Monaco could hardly have been better; he was building Europe's grandest gambling resort in one of its most scenic regions just as the cost of illustrated newspapers was falling and readership growing dramatically. Blanc spent prodigiously on print advertising. With rare exception, people first experienced his gambling resort from a distance, as an abstract idea rather than as reality.

Early publicity materials focused on the region's curative potentials, even while Monaco's spa facilities were still in the blueprint stages. Mentions of the casino, if included at all, appeared in only the most general of terms, and usually in passing. A typical ad, which ran regularly on the back page of the *Journal de Nice* in the early 1860s:

MONACO SEA BATHING. Under new management. Large bathing facilities—hot and cold bath—complete hydrotherapeutic services—sea bathing facilities open from 1 April to 1 December—the recently built magnificent casino, open year round, offers visitors all manners of entertainments found in German spas.

The idea was for people to learn about the gambling through news items, rather than paid advertisements. Monaco, as officially publicized, meant health, fashion, bright sunny days, and a casino offering entertainments of all kinds. Leave it to the reporters to describe the piles of gold on the tables, the courtesans and "shylocks," and audacious gamblers determined to break the bank.

In truth, as Blanc knew well, the press of that era did not function objectively. People regularly paid newspapers to present whatever they wanted publicized within the guise of a regular article. The skill with which the charade was carried out increased with the amounts spent. Blanc rewarded cooperative papers through the promise of regular advertising. The SBM took out large ads on the back page of the *Journal de Nice*, for instance, but not before specifying that there be "no direct or indirect attacks against the Prince of Monaco or its government." In a single fiscal year the SBM spent more than half a million francs on newspaper advertising alone, or roughly one franc on publicity for every two francs spent on wages.

Blanc used bolder tactics as well. He sold a prime plot of land for well under market value to Hippolyte de Villemessant, the founder of the influential Paris daily *Le Figaro.* In turn Villemessant dedicated the first four pages of an issue of *Le Figaro* to a Monaco travelogue. "Monaco is an earthly paradise, a fairytale land," Villemessant gushed; "It is impossible to spend more than a week there without desiring to stay for one's entire life . . . Anyone buying two or three million francs' worth of land here would prove that he knows a good thing when sees it, for it will probably be worth at least four times as much in two or three years' time. M. Blanc has transformed this region, once pleasing rather than rich, into a veritable California; only he does not discover gold mines, he creates them." Villemessant closed by advising "young intelligent men, who wished to better themselves but have not yet found the means to do so" to set off in haste for the principality.

For her part, Marie Blanc loathed having Villemessant as a neighbor. She deemed the newspaperman coarse.

Setting off the long and mutually profitable relationship between Monaco and the tabloid press, SBM managers had all the latest society news from the resort circulated to a coterie of friendly journalists; anything concerning the gambling exploits of members of the Romanov dynasty or British peers garnered ample column space. Big city writers who came to report on Monaco were put up in the finest suites at Hôtel de Paris and parties were thrown in their honor.

SBM managers learned to couple such largesse with intimidation, sometimes with the help of the local authorities. When the editor of *Le Petit Niçois,* Alziary de Roquefort, ran a serialized feature that promised to reveal the secret workings of the casino and the palace, Monaco's chief of police paid him an unpleasant visit. Roquefort refused to reveal his source, to which the chief responded by banning the paper from the principality. Monaco's governor general, M. de Ste. Suzanne, warned Roquefort that the SBM was thinking of revoking the four-hundred-franc monthly fee paid to the paper. Complaining of such treatment in a letter to the SBM, Roquefort asked: "What does M. de Ste. Suzanne have to do with the business dealings of your enterprise?"

In 1866, a petition originating in Nice called for the French government to shut down Blanc's casino—with force, if necessary. It carried seven hundred signatures. Blanc believed that influential figures in Nice were also trying to block Monaco's bid for connection to the railway. Meanwhile Blanc, the prince, top SBM managers, and even specific croupiers were receiving death threats. Ultimately, the Niçoise petition failed. Blanc founded an annual horse race in Nice as an act of goodwill, personally putting up the substantial prize money.

For a place so dependent on projecting a certain image of glamour, Blanc's gambling resort had a terrible name. Les Spélugues carried with it associations of caverns and disrepute. After much pestering from Blanc, the prince considered other options, including Charlesville, and Albertville, in honor of the crown prince Albert. Finally, on July 1, 1866, Prince Charles declared that all land in Monaco east of the valley of Sainte-Dévote would thereafter be known as the *quartier de Monte-Carlo,* named for himself. The rechristening of the area reinforced the sense that the resort existed on a plane removed from Monaco's everyday life and even its own history. Visitors to Monte Carlo could imagine they were taking part in creating something novel just by having come there.

In the spring of 1868 the Prussian government voted to suppress public gambling in all its territories, with the law to take effect five years later. Blanc would continue to squeeze what he could out of the fading Homburg concession, but he now turned most of his attentions to Monte Carlo. Advertisements recommended a diet of "Bad Homburg in Summer, Monaco in Winter." With books such as James H. Bennett's surprise bestseller, *Winter and Spring on the Shores of the Mediterranean* touting the health benefits of the Southern climate, Blanc redoubled his efforts to promote Monte Carlo's spa facilities.

The year ended happily, as Monaco was finally connected to the PLM line on October 25, 1868. This coincided neatly with the French rail network's expansion to another southern pilgrimage site: Lourdes, the small town in the foothills of the Pyrenees, where a young girl's Marian visions ten years earlier had inspired the construction of a basilica in honor of the Virgin.

Where in the early years of rail development a town typically built its first train station at the edge of the urban center, Blanc insisted that Monaco have two train stations, one serving the residential quarter in Monaco proper and the other in the very heart of its new economic core. Wedged between the casino's southern terrace and the *Tir aux Pigeons*, the Monte Carlo station stood as a testament to Blanc's international influence, a more grandiose version of the mentions of "Under New Management" he put in his early advertisements.

Social reformers were quick to paint train travel and resort gambling as twin evils of the industrial age, with the two said to work symbiotically, each driving greater need for the other. A British writer, seeing dejected gamblers heading from the casino to the Monte Carlo station with their heads hung low, had "the sad reflection that a fresh batch would soon arrive in time for the evening concert; it is not desirable that the half-frenzied losers should remain in these peaceful elysiums; a fresh and continuous stream of victims is much preferred." Trains brought people intent on victimizing as well. As with any frontier town, many came to Monte Carlo to escape troubles at home. Petty theft was rampant. When Countess Kisselev alighted at the Monte Carlo station just days after it opened she was immediately robbed of a pocketbook containing twenty-six thousand francs. Blanc personally reimbursed his old Bad Homburg favorite.

Nearly two hundred thousand visitors traveled to Monaco in the year after the connection to the railway. The Hôtel de Paris started booking out months in advance and Blanc added a wing to the building. The Monégasques, then numbering a few thousand, grew uneasy amid the rush of alien bodies. The influx of workers and tourists put strain on the water supply.

New arrivals seeking work struggled to find their places among families that had been intimately entwined for centuries. Monégasques watched with disgust as the largest public works went to foreign firms, better organized and financed than were local contractors. Especially offensive to the Monégasques were the dandyish construction workers from the Piedmont region, who paraded around in bold checkered shirts and wore red geraniums in the bands of their straw hats. The bullying tactics of a Captain Doineau, Blanc's chief foreman, who favored hiring Italian laborers over the locals, led to a fierce protest outside the palace gates. Blanc was out of Monaco at the time, and Prince Charles, seeing a chance to show strength, expelled Doineau from the principality. Blanc fought for his foreman but couldn't make Charles yield. Eynaud, as always, worked furiously to reestablish good terms between casino boss and prince.

Despite repeated pressure from the palace to give preferential treatment to Monégasques, Blanc hired a workforce as international as his clientele, being far more interested in individual skill than national origin. He relied heavily on personal recommendations from existing employees, so that one hard worker might catch his eye and soon the man's brothers and cousins and friends were on the payroll as well. French and Italians made up the bulk of the workforce, far outnumbering the Monégasques, and many of the top management positions went to Germans transplanted from Bad Homburg. A list of casino supervisors contains names as diverse as Lavitonnière, Zwerner, Kohl, Chomprek, and—appropriately—Babel. The eighty-four-member chorus of the Opéra de Monte Carlo comprised men and women of French, Italian, Russian, Belgian, German, English, American, and Spanish origins, along with a lone Monégasque member.

Blanc antagonized the more xenophobic locals by encouraging foreigners to build villas and open businesses in Monaco. At first there were only a few pioneers, but eventually, by parceling off small sections of SBM-owned land and selling them for next to nothing, Blanc set off a real estate boom. Within months, land values in Monte Carlo went from twenty centimes to twenty-five francs a square meter. The ever-friendly *Le Figaro* suggested that it was a "veritable Californian Gold Rush."

Property holders with an interest in the resort's future spent their own money improving the gardens and roads. Shops went up. Rows of little houses. A few independently owned hotels. A laundry. Some Bavarians opened a brewery in the neighborhood of Fontvieille, which also housed a plant for making pasta. Gasworks went in, bringing light to recently paved roads, and a new main artery, the Boulevard des Moulins, connected Monte Carlo in the east to Monaco-Ville in the west. One nostalgic guidebook writer would describe how the Condamine neighborhood by the harbor had been transformed from a "bower of oranges, lemons and violets [into] a thriving suburb. A pretty tree-lined avenue is now a road of 20 houses . . . The delightful rococo fountain has been replaced by a pharmacy."

With Monaco's long-term independence seemingly assured, and its economy growing steadily, Prince Charles rewarded his subjects by abolishing all income taxes, on February 8, 1869. One historian claims that he did so only after prompting from Blanc, who believed (incorrectly, it turned out) that this would put an end to unrest over jobs going to foreigners. Whatever his motivations, Charles unknowingly set Monaco on the course to becoming the world's first modern tax haven.

Eynaud wrote to the prince that any Monégasque who might previously have hoped for the fall of the Grimaldi dynasty or for Monaco's annexation into France would now recoil at the thought, if for no other reason than financial self-interest. It was "as though a fairy wand had called forth all these improvements, these buildings and the incredible prosperity and animation of this little paradise, which for so long was sad and deserted." Not only the former Spélugues but also other areas people had been too fearful to settle because of their distance from the palace were now teeming with commercial activity. Just over 215,000 rail passengers booked trips to Monte Carlo in 1875 alone. Those few Monégasques who could remember the upheaval of 1848 were outnumbered by newcomers bound by self-interest as much to Blanc as they were to the prince. The writer Guy de Maupassant skewered the close collusion of politics and industry he detected in the principality. "Opposite to the palace, rises the rival establishment, the Roulette," he wrote; "There is, however, no hatred, no hostility between them; for the one supports the other, which in turn protects the first."

Blanc's visits to the sanatorium in Loèche-les-Bains grew more frequent. He complained of struggling to catch a deep breath. He did hang on long enough to see his and Marie's daughter Louise wed Prince Constantin Radziwill, scion of one of Europe's most prominent families, at the Parisian church of Saint-Roch in the summer of 1876. Louise, as with her sister Marie-Félix, had received the finest education and was seen frequently in the city's most exclusive salons. That his daughter married into the esteemed Radziwill dynasty must have been especially pleasant for the man born poor and obscure in Courthézon.

Guests at the wedding had noticed the father of the bride looking pale and speaking with difficulty. A few months later, Blanc delivered what would be his final address to SBM shareholders. "Nobody loses in Monte Carlo," he beamed; "Everyone who comes here has hope." He died on July 27, 1877, at the age of seventy-one, in Loèche-les-Bains, leaving behind a fortune estimated at 88 million francs (or $17.5 million in 1877 dollars). He'd overseen the construction of nine separate nongambling amenities in Monaco, while under his watch others had built an additional 35 hotels, 433 furnished apartments, and 116 villas.

François Blanc, Eynaud, (who had become one of Blanc's few real friends and had died just a few weeks before him), and Prince Charles had ushered in changes in Monaco that ran deeper than new roads, fine food, good music, electricity, and growing numbers. They'd unleashed an unprecedented sense of optimism—a shared belief in the resort as a force unto itself that would carry them all forward together. Monte Carlo seemed to promise infinite possibility and perpetual boom. The question remained, however, as to who would rise to take the place of its late founder.

8

KARL MARX'S COUGH

THE BULK OF THE Blanc estate went to Marie and to her three children: Louise, Marie-Félix, and Edmond. François had left only tiny allotments for his two eldest children, Camille and Charles. His reasons for doing so are unknown, though if the boys were indeed born out of wedlock, their illegitimacy could have been a factor. As thanks for his loyalty, a small parcel of shares went to Blanc's personal secretary, Count Antoine Nicolas Bertora. While serving the husband, Bertora had apparently charmed the wife. In a letter to Prince Charles, Eynaud remarked on this secretary's "great influence over Blanc, and especially over Madame Blanc." Bertora would go on to run the SBM in all but name for nearly two decades.

Bertora hailed from an old Corsican family that had been friendly with the Bonapartes, and before working for the Blancs, he had served as one of Napoleon III's chamberlains. He split his time between his Monaco villa and his townhome at 3 Rue d'Antin, a pricy Paris address close to where the Opéra Garnier now stands. He said that his title of Count had been bestowed by the pope himself. One historian suggests that Bertora proposed to Marie Blanc, without success, just a few months after her husband's death. Regardless of the romantic arrangements, Marie made Bertora the representative of her shareholding interests, and he also voted on behalf of Louise Blanc and Prince Radziwill at shareholders' meetings. Bertora worked mostly in the shadows, while nominal control of the casino fell to a brother-in-law of Marie's (on her side) named Henri Wagatha, one of several relations François Blanc had posted in prime managerial positions over the years.

Marie Blanc maintained her interest in Monte Carlo's gardens and she had hothouses built, equipped with rare breeds procured from an expert in Florence. She made sure the *plongeurs* of the Hôtel de Paris stopped their practice of dumping out food scraps in the terrace garden, as this killed off some of her best flowers. But she mostly avoided the resort, preferring her villa in Moûtiers, as well as the Parisian town home she shared with Louise and Prince Radziwill on Rue de Rivoli, overlooking the Tuileries garden. She spent freely. Much went toward jewelry, a lifelong passion, and much toward philanthropic causes. Confidence men preyed on her hospitality. Less than three years after her husband's death, Marie had to take a 1,500,000-franc loan from the SBM to see her through a dry patch, putting up four thousand shares as security.

———————

The *veuve* Blanc would occasionally be summoned to represent the SBM at galas and other social events. In this official capacity she attended a command performance by Sarah Bernhardt on January 25, 1879. Adopting the persona of a young nymph, Bernhardt read some saccharine words penned by a Marseillaise poet: "Artists, I have gathered palms to crown your heads. Blessed be you all! You who have awakened the Gods." The words met with wild applause, not only for Bernhardt but also for the target of her blessing, Charles

Garnier, as close to a Bernhardt-like celebrity as could be found among the architects of his time. Garnier took a quick bow, capping a night of festivities held to inaugurate his new opera house.

The celebration did not take place in Paris. By then, Garnier's masterpiece, the nearly two-thousand-seat Opéra de Paris, had already been open to the public for four years. Rather, the night marked the debut of another, and far smaller, Garnier creation. This concert hall didn't tower over the intersection of several major thoroughfares in one of the busiest metropolises in Europe—it was attached to the Monte Carlo casino.

Such public association with the greatest living actress and architect of the age marked Monte Carlo's arrival as a legitimate cultural hub. The seeds of the project can be traced back to 1874, when Blanc put nearly 5 million francs at the disposal of the French minister of Public Works to help fund the construction of Garnier's Opéra de Paris. Not coincidentally, the French government improved railway service to Monaco the same year. In angling to someday commission the mastermind of the Opéra de Paris for a job in Monte Carlo, Blanc hoped to link the two cities in the minds of his clients. Garnier's addition to the Monte Carlo casino offered a small taste of Paris without the costly trip to the City of Light itself, a strategy gaudily repeated in Las Vegas more than a century later. Garnier dutifully borrowed from the tropes and styles of his Paris building nearly verbatim for his project in Monaco.

The concert hall's ornate twin towers were made tall enough to be seen from miles away by land and sea, giant beacons boasting of the wealth waiting to be won inside. As one guidebook writer noted, even "blasé Parisians" were struck by the building's beauty. Here was a replica of one of the great icons of Haussmannized Paris, reduced to a less daunting scale and standing astride the Mediterranean rather than dirty city streets, its sun-facing façade framed by pleasant palms. Though he didn't live to see it, here was François Blanc's founding vision for Monte Carlo encapsulated in a single structure: gambling, culture, and luxury to be enjoyed not only in one town but under one roof.

The opera hall was annexed onto the casino's southwestern wing, meaning that people could only gain entrance to its spectacles after they'd passed through the gaming rooms. Concertgoers were exposed to the exciting sights and sounds of the casino, and they were also forced to fill out entry cards, a relatively time-consuming step and the last barrier keeping them from the tables. This also allowed the SBM to gather biographical data about its clientele.

As with the gaming rooms, the décor of the theater evoked the interior of a palace or finely furnished estate house. Garnier mixed national and historical styles—from Louis XIV to Italian Baroque—and accented the room with paintings of ancient bacchanals and mythical scenes. On the terrace outside, visitors strolled by two Garnier-commissioned sculptures: "Dance," by Gustave Doré, and the more clumsily rendered "Song," by Bernhardt. Both artists had hurried to complete their works in time for opening night and so molded the sculptures in clay and cast them in plaster rather than in marble or bronze. Bernhardt, a Monte Carlo regular, would have seen her work aging terribly in the sun. (She allegedly lost one hundred thousand francs at the casino in one night, after which she tried to kill herself with sedatives at the Hôtel de Paris, though a friend saved her at the last moment.)

For all its gilded surfaces, the Salle Garnier's purpose was to welcome rather than intimidate. The SBM typically patronized works that were already well established and had the broadest international appeal. The 1881 season, for instance, featured *La Traviata, Rigoletto*, and *The Barber of Seville*. Advertisements announced performances of "Comedy, Vaudeville, and Operetta," all safe middle-class fare. These were given twice a day and free of charge. Concertgoers chose from among the roughly 650 hand-carved seats, upholstered in red velvet and rising in uniform rows at a slight angle to the back wall, on a first-come-first-served basis. Little difference existed in the quality of seats and, unlike in Paris, Garnier devoted the venue's walls to decoration rather than box seating. Only the prince commanded a private box, at the very back of the hall, while top SBM brass could reserve the adjacent loggias.

Such seemingly populist strategies actually lent the performances an air of exclusivity. No money changed hands, freeing some people to believe they'd come to the casino only out of a genuine love of music, and that by doing so they'd been accepted as equals among fellow amateurs of culture. As in the brightly lit casino, the large windows and gas lamps allowed audience members to regard one another as easily as they could the people on stage. (The darkening of theaters during performances is a relatively recent phenomenon.) Shortly after the venue opened, the London *Times* suggested that the gambling resort offered the greatest quality and selection of musical performances in the world, and thus "when decent sort of people confess to having paid a visit to Monte Carlo, it is the music which has been their inducement."

———————

On the night of April 24, 1880, an enterprising thief tried to capitalize on the popularity of the Salle Garnier to pull off a daring robbery. A show had let out just before ten and the audience was crowding into the gaming rooms. Then an explosion rocked the Moorish Room. People rushed madly for the exits, some escaping through the blown out windows. In the end only minor injuries and a few ripped gowns were reported.

Over the following days the SBM's inspectors deduced that someone had smuggled in a homemade bomb: a small cartridge packed with gunpowder and wrapped in rubber, with a wick popping out the end. Likely smuggled in under a hat or in the pocket of an overcoat, it had been planted under a clock. The assailant (or assailants) had apparently planned to throw the casino into darkness and rob the tables in the ensuing panic. But though a few gaslights did burn out, oil lamps were quickly lit and not a single croupier left his post. The floors were covered in broken glass, since several chandeliers had come crashing down, and some shards of wood from the tables had been strewn about, but workers made repairs through the night and play resumed the next morning.

The SBM suffered no great losses, even while reimbursing everyone who made claims on bets supposedly left on the tables during the fracas, so long as these requests were "justified or seemed sincere." The prince's representative at the casino noted that just a few hours after the explosion the bookkeepers still did their regular count and the day's take was healthy. Despite some nervous chatter among the resort community, 1,554 new entry cards were issued for gaming rooms in the week after the bombing, a slightly lower figure than the previous week's, but a drop that had more to do to with the winding down of the winter season than anything else. The prince's representative added that the SBM could always depend on its core of serious players—no mere bomb could break their habit. Receipts came to 330,000 francs, beating the total for the same week in the previous year. The bombing's only significant effects were that it led security workers to more carefully scrutinize entry cards, and thereafter no one was allowed to enter with an umbrella or cane, or to leave hats, coats, or luggage unattended on any tables or couches.

Monte Carlo's founding family aligned itself with another storied dynasty in November 1880, when the youngest Blanc daughter, Marie-Félix, married Prince Roland Bonaparte, grandson of Napoleon's brother, Lucien Bonaparte. The *New York Times* report on the ceremony called Prince Roland the handsomest man in the French army, while noting that his branch of the Bonaparte family had fallen into poverty, which, as the *Times* writer put it democratically, "enabled him to appreciate his wife's generosity." Bertora, who may have arranged the union, served as an official witness. The wedding took place in the same Saint-Roch church in Paris that had hosted the marriage of Marie-Félix's sister to Prince Radziwill. It was in front of this church on 13 *Vendémiaire* Year IV (October 5, 1795, by the French Revolutionary Calendar) that Roland Bonaparte's great-uncle used the famous "whiff of grapeshot" to quell an insurrection of roughly thirty thousand Parisians, seen as a pivotal moment in the career of the ambitious general and, by some, as a symbolic end to the French Revolution.

The young Marie-Félix had a rebellious streak. While Bertora represented her mother, brother, sister, and brother-in-law at shareholders meetings, Marie-Félix named a different representative and voted against Bertora on key decisions, siding instead with her half brothers, Camille and Charles. But whatever check she might have offered against Bertora's influence didn't last long. She died at twenty-two, less than two years after her wedding day. (Her infant daughter, Marie, would inherit a substantial chunk of the Blanc fortune when Roland Bonaparte died in 1924. She grew up to be a student of Freud's and a distinguished psychoanalyst in her own right; she married Prince George of Greece and later used her position to help many Jews escape the Nazis.)

———

The elder Blanc had been spared the death of Marie-Félix. She died not long after her daughter's wedding, at age forty-seven, succumbing to chronic respiratory ailments. In the reports filed by the palace representative at the SBM in the weeks following Marie Blanc's death, there was much talk of arrangements between Bertora and the Blanc children, who'd come from Paris to sort out the inheritance and organize the sale of her many possessions. Her jewels went on the block at the Hôtel Drouot auction house, an event that brought out the crème of Parisian society. Her brother-in-law Henri Wagatha held on for a few more months as the casino's deputy administrator but was voted out by the board, likely with prompting from Bertora, who would have seen little value in keeping on Marie's relation now that she was out of the picture. The SBM granted Wagatha a pension, though not before collecting on the large debts he and his wife had run up at the Hôtel de Paris.

In company reports following Marie's death the principal shareholders were listed as Prince Charles; the families of the two Blanc daughters; Edmond Blanc; and Bertora, who despite officially holding only a few shares would remain the key decision-maker at the casino for more than a decade. Missing from this list is the Blanc family member who would eventually succeed Bertora and steer the company through its Belle Époque heyday.

The Marie Blanc–Count Bertora years were good ones for the casino, with annual receipts numbering in the tens of millions of francs by the time of Marie's death. SBM memos from this era speak to how well the Blancs and Bertora had done in attracting a socially mixed and truly global clientele. Company managers made sure to list the arrivals of notable foreigners in their weekly reports, placing emphasis on visitors who'd traveled from far abroad. An 1879 report noted the presence of "the Chinese Minister from Paris, accompanied by an interpreter in national garb, who regarded the roulette with great curiosity." A year later a report listed the following "notable arrivals":

M. D'ubexi, Judge from Épinal; M. de la Chavanne, Magistrate from Briançon; M. Castremont, Naval Officer; M. le Comte de Cournemine; M. Malafert, Regional Councilor; M. Halanzier, former Director of the Opéra de Paris; M. Malachie, Judge from Tarascon; M. Fleutet, Deputy; M. le Comte Carrado, Major General; the Marquis Birago, Italian; Prince Grégoire; the Baron Nolcken, General Major, Russian; M. de

Moreau, Chamberlain to the King of Bavaria; M. Paz, Foreign
Minister of the Dominican Republic in Holland.

A client list so diverse in political, judicial, military, and cultural
backgrounds would no doubt have pleased Monte Carlo's founder.

An especially unlikely visitor arrived in the spring of 1882. Suffering from respiratory ailments that would soon claim his life, Karl
Marx spent a few weeks in Monte Carlo on the orders of his physi-
cian Dr. Kunemann, who, as with many medical professionals of his
generation, had recently become a devotee of heliotherapy, which
preached the curative potential of prolonged exposure to the sun.
Writing to his daughter Jenny, Marx conceded that the place was
pretty enough, with its "magical gardens on barren rocks that slope
from steep heights all the way down to the blue sea, like the hanging
terraces of Babylonian gardens." But, Marx being Marx, he couldn't
help but add some choice words about the harsh economic realities
that so clearly paid for all those surface niceties, dismissing Monaco
with a biting reference to the fictional comic-opera principality of
"Gerolstein," from an Offenbach operetta that would have been familiar to his daughter. "The economic basis of Monaco-Gerolstein
is the gambling Casino; if it should close up tomorrow, Monaco-
Gerolstein would go into the grave—all of it!" He assured Jenny: "I
do not like to visit the gambling hall." Still, he had come there to
take the cure, and so didn't expect to leave "this robber's nest" before
early June, telling his daughter that it was up to Dr. Kunemann to
decide how long he would stay.

That the good doctor Kunemann should prescribe a visit to
Monte Carlo to someone as ill disposed to gambling as Karl Marx
offers strong evidence of how effectively François Blanc had spun
his Monte Carlo story. The former Les Spélugues now functioned as

a full-scale spa resort, a place that seduced avid gamblers as much as it did those who came to enjoy the nongambling facilities the casino had funded. Future generations of travelers proved something Blanc had known from the start: that these two types of clients need not be mutually exclusive.

———

Prince Charles III died on September 10, 1889, the last living link to the François Blanc era. Charles was succeeded by his forty-year-old son, who took the title of Albert I, and inaugurated his reign by reviving an ancient custom. The head of every Monégasque family was invited to a grand banquet at the palace and Albert personally asked each patriarch in turn if he consented to his rule.

Albert's aides brought him up to speed with the situation at the SBM, which was far from stable. In the wake of Marie's death, the Blanc children had been selling off their shares in a flurry. Advisors warned the new prince about the perils of so many shares falling into unknown and foreign hands. The new "holders of these shares, so recently and expensively acquired, will misinterpret the founding views that led to the granting of the concession they now hope to exploit, as well as those of our country, where they do not reside." Of the shares in circulation "Mme. la princesse Radziwill still has seven thousand and Edmond Blanc four thousand; but for how much longer?"

The prince and his advisers need not have worried—at least, not just then. The SBM remained in the control of the Blanc dynasty for many more years, though it was to be headed by one of the least likely candidates for the job.

9

PRODIGAL SONS AND WAYWARD DAUGHTERS

CAMILLE BLANC INHERITED HIS father's sad watery eyes, his short stature, his slow metabolism, and his ambitious nature. What he failed to inherit was a large enough piece of the SBM to let him act on this ambition. François left him only 100 of the company's original 30,000 shares. While she was still alive, Camille had pressed his stepmother, only fourteen years older than he was, to let him play a more active role, but she rebuffed him, as did Count Bertora after her death. And so Camille spent the 1880s in limbo. He ate well and often, played the horses alongside his half brother, Edmond, kept an expensive mistress (a former acrobat), and founded a stud farm and racing track in Nice. His name appeared more often in the decade's sporting pages than in any SBM documents.

Then, in 1894, Bertora's name faded abruptly from the SBM's records, replaced by that of Camille Blanc. There's no record explaining how exactly Blanc wrested power from the man who by that point had run the company for seventeen years. A likely scenario is that at some point Bertora committed a gaffe big enough to alienate him from the Blanc children and then Camille convinced his siblings and half siblings to shift their allegiances his way. All Blancs voting in unison would have defeated any other power bloc.

Still, it's odd that it should have been Camille, and not Edmond Blanc who took control, given that Edmond was the majority male shareholder. But Edmond loved the horses and exotic women even more than Camille did, and the latter may have encouraged his half brother's playboy lifestyle to keep him distracted from company affairs. Edmond also harbored political ambitions and might have wanted to distance himself from the family business. He served for two stretches as mayor of the Parisian suburb of Saint-Cloud, where he built his own racetrack, on which jockeys still compete for the Prix Edmond Blanc. He also won election as deputy for the commune of Bagnères-de-Bigorre, though rival politician and socialist hero Jean Jaurès convinced the Chamber of Deputies that Blanc had used his wealth to commit electoral fraud and Edmond was stripped of his seat, though he managed to be re-elected to the same post a few years later.

It would seem the Blanc siblings recognized that Camille—outwardly gregarious and affable, but inwardly shrewd and calculating—was the best suited among them to head the casino. And indeed he relished the job of impresario, chatting breezily with customers and flirting with the dancers in his pay. In photographs of visits from foreign dignitaries, Camille Blanc can always be seen front and center, often more conspicuously positioned than the somewhat shy Prince Albert. The younger Blanc continued his father's strategy of running Monte Carlo as an aristocratic resort packaged for bourgeois consumption, while trying to outdo him in the scale at which he did so. Everything in Monte Carlo grew bigger and bolder under his watch. As Camille told his shareholders, "the more spectacular the sports events, the more extravagant the dinners, the readier the guests will be to plunge at the tables."

By the time Camille Blanc began his tenure, the SBM was

already issuing hundreds of thousands of entry cards a year. The Compagnie Internationale de Wagon-Lits started offering a regular Calais–Mediterranean Express rail service, which ran three times a week during the winter months. The trains came equipped with sleeping cars and were overseen by white-gloved attendants. A British writer called a sleeper on the express "the dearest bed of its size in the world." Camille had an elevator installed at the Monte Carlo train station to take alighting passengers straight up to the casino terrace, while inside an electric escalator conducted gamblers from the ground floor to the *salles privées* on the second story. The SBM promoted the thrills of these novelties as part of the overall Monte Carlo experience. While across the ocean Coney Island operators charged admission for rides on elevators and moving sidewalks, the SBM's promotional materials announced that such bodily excitements were provided free of charge.

Another sign of the resort's spectacular growth came in 1898, with the completion of the grand Hermitage Hôtel, just a few feet away from the Hôtel de Paris. Its circular lobby was capped by a giant dome of iron and stained glass, an engineering marvel crafted by students of Gustave Eiffel. The hotel's name nodded to the resort's popularity among well-heeled Russians, who came each winter aboard the Saint Petersburg–Vienna-Nice-Cannes Express (another service of the Compagnie Internationale de Wagon-Lits), with their servants sometimes sleeping on the floor outside their private cars. The Romanovs and their entourage booked out dozens of the Hermitage's rooms, for months at a time. People joked that Monte Carlo should be renamed Saint Petersburg by the Mediterranean.

The Russians loved the lavish restaurant that served both the Hermitage and the Hôtel de Paris. It was stocked with Limoges porcelain and Baccarat crystal, and housed one of the finest cellars in Europe, built underneath the casino gardens with enough room for 350,000 bottles. One night at the restaurant, Grand Duke Dmitri and friends, after growing bored with their caviar tasting, made a game of smashing champagne bottles against the room's marble columns, destroying forty until they tired of that as well.

The restaurant's director and maître d'hôtel, Georges Fleury, was said to draw the highest salary of any hotel staffer in the world. Fleury and company for a time had competition from the nearby Grand Hotel, headed by César Ritz and Auguste Escoffier, before the duo went on to fame in Paris and London. Escoffier created a few dishes especially for the resort crowd; there was Poularde Monte-Carlo (a young hen spayed for fattening, stuffed with crayfish, truffles, and rice) and a delicious Mousse Monte-Carlo as well. A British travelogue writer, Victor Bethell, recalled a pleasant night at the restaurant of the Hôtel de Paris in the late 1890s. He saw orchids, Venetian crystal, and fine white linens decorating every table. Most dazzling of all were the female diners, "displaying the smartest frocks and the latest hats, provided by their long-suffering husbands—or somebody else's husbands . . . The actresses and *demi-monde* here reign supreme, and are arrayed in all their war-paint." Bethell's evening ended with *Tannhäuser* at the Salle Garnier; it was "simply perfect."

If the Hôtel de Paris was Monte Carlo's favored dinner spot, then Ciro's was the place for lunch. A former bartender from Naples, Ciro had apprenticed for a time at Delmonico's in New York and American diners enjoyed his broken English. Bethell described a typical menu:

Hors d'Oeuvres variés
Oeufs pochés Grand Duc
Mostèle à l'Anglaise (a local fish, split open, stuffed with bread-crumbs, and fried)
Volaille en Casserole à la Fermière
Pâtisserie
Fromage
Café

Vins et Liqueurs
Château Carbonnieux, 1891
Fine Champagne, 1846

Following the meal Bethell and his tablemates went back to business. "After a cigar, we paid a visit to Smith's Bank next door, drew out our capital of £600, then strolled across to the concert at the Casino. This lasted till 4.15, and at 5.p.m we made our first onslaught on the Bank."

———————

By the time Bethell and his mates were preparing to launch their onslaught, the SBM had survived many such attacks. The Monte Carlo of Blanc *fils* thrived on efficiency, routine, and control. In keeping with the era's trend toward greater bureaucratization, Camille had parceled the SBM's operation into three interconnected branches: the Games department handled the running of the tables and surveillance; the Interior department handled maintenance, hiring, and purchasing; and the Exterior handled legal matters, accounting, advertising, and entertainments, maintained the casino gardens and provided utilities to the people of Monaco.

Each day at the casino began precisely at 9:30 a.m. with the gaming inspector shining his lantern under the tables to check for any wear or imperfections. He was allowed to help himself to whatever bits of currency had been dropped the night before by careless players. After the inspector removed the coverings from the tables, workmen brought in the full cash boxes, two men to a box. The inspector also had to confirm the perfect balance of each roulette wheel with a custom-built spirit level.

The typical roulette wheel came from one of the small French workshops that specialized in the product, its edges done in polished mahogany and a dome of bronze at its center. The wheel sat within a gunmetal casing, fitted through a hole carved into a wooden table. A metal tube ran through the wheel into the casing. Rivets kept the table pinned to the floor, while the base of the casing reached the ground independently of the table, meaning that no amount of shaking could influence the wheel's motion, though people tried anyway. The wheel was buttressed on all sides by the metal cash boxes, which were more than an arm's length from the edge of the table. Even if a gambler had managed to manually alter the wheel's spin, he would have still been unable to make his number come up with any accuracy, as the hard edges of the wheel's slots knocked the ball around after gravity had pulled it down to the center, just as in a carnival game where the ring you've just thrown so deftly inevitably bounces off the tops of bottles a few times before landing somewhere far from your target. The prevailing logic had it that the balls had absolutely to be made of ivory, regardless of costs, since ivory wouldn't conduct electricity or respond to magnetic pulls and was thus impervious to manipulation by the scientifically astute.

Camille Blanc trained his croupiers far more rigorously than his father had. Only rarely did one start out at the casino holding that coveted post. Most had come up from the company's lower ranks and only after finishing the six-month program at the SBM's in-house night school. Learning to sort and pay out bets was the hardest skill to acquire. Where a bank teller documented each one of his transactions, a croupier did everything in his head and on the fly. At that time Monte Carlo didn't use the colored chips typically found in today's casinos; instead virtually any kind of legal tender was accepted. Keeping track of everything—coins mixed with paper, francs and rubles mixed with dollars and drachmas—could be maddening.

The British journalist Adolphe Smith put the top salary of a Monte Carlo croupier in that era at £17 a year. A croupier told Smith, "It seems as if money had lost its value at the casino. We see what to us represents a year's salary lost and won with the levity we might ourselves display over penny stakes should we have a game of cards at home." Smith wrote that the SBM spied on croupiers in their off-hours to see if they lived beyond their means. Company reports confirm such claims of internal surveillance. One describes how "Charles Bauscher, croupier of German origin, naturalized as a Monégasque in 1888, who we had been watching for some time, was caught paying out to players sums greater than what they were due. When he was not manning the tables, his confederates did not appear in the Rooms. He was fired the day before yesterday." These kinds of infractions were often handled by a fraternity the croupiers had formed to self-regulate, and which meted out punishment, swiftly and harshly. Terminations could be coupled by police charges and even lifetime bans from the principality.

———————

Just as the SBM moved toward greater efficiency in its operations, so did some of its patrons start to approach gambling as a kind of scientific and rational pursuit. Croupiers privately mocked the heavy thinkers they called *licencés en roulette* (akin to saying someone had graduated with a BA in roulette), those gamblers who believed past outcomes of a game could somehow influence future ones. System players recorded the results of each spin, looking to reveal some inner logic only waiting to be divined by the properly attuned mind. Karl Marx had noted such delusions during his Monaco convalescence. "In reality, the great majority of gamblers, male and female, believe in the science of this pure game of hazard," Marx wrote his daughter. "Gentleman and ladies sit in front of this Café de Paris or on benches in the wonderful garden which belongs to the Casino, hold little tablets (printed) in their hands, head bent, scratching and calculating, or one explains importantly to the other 'which system' he prefers, whether one is to play in 'series' etc., etc." On seeing gamblers filing into the casino clutching their mathematical guidebooks full of complicated charts, Marx related having "the impression of seeing inmates of a lunatic asylum."

The popularity of guides such as *Insurance Against all Losses at Monte Carlo* and *Mathematical Observances Relating to The Game of Roulette* offers indication of just how many lunatics were willing to enter the asylum. These books tended to outline some variation of a progressive betting strategy known as a "martingale," which counseled gamblers on how to bet greater and greater amounts until they won their desired initial wager. Someone wanting to win 50 francs, for example, might stake 50 on red and then, if they lost, staked 100, then 200, if that bet lost as well, and so on. Guides described another "infallible" betting system, a reverse martingale, where gamblers increased bets twofold after a loss and decreased it the same amount after a win.

The problem with these systems was that someone experiencing a bad run of luck might end up having to bet thousands of francs just to win back an initial fifty-franc stake. And even if a system worked in the short-term, the average player was rarely satisfied with winning double his initial bet, which might have happened on the first spin, and tended to linger at the tables until the odds eventually caught up with him. There was and remains no way to undo the house's mathematical advantage. The roulette table, as they say, has no memory.

Still, people loved hearing stories of gamblers who'd hit on some new system to defeat the casino, no matter how far-fetched the scenario might be. In the 1890s a song about one such gambler, called "The Man Who Broke The Bank at Monte Carlo," became so popular that by one account it could be "heard wherever the English language was spoken." As with any good gambling tale it offered a kind of capitalist wish fulfillment: a middle-class nobody heads to Monte Carlo hoping to raise enough money to cover his rent and, after "Dame fortune" smiles on him, he parades around Paris, now a true "gent," attracting lusty looks from previously unattainable women.

The model for the song was an English confidence man named Charles Devine Wells, who'd already gained a reputation in the scandal rags as a swindler by the time he arrived in Monte Carlo in 1891. His main racket was to patent inventions and sell the rights at inflated rates, even though only one of the 192 patents he took out ever went into production (a skipping rope that played a tune while it was being spun, which for a time sold briskly). Over the course of three days at Monte Carlo, Wells turned a £400 stake into £40,000, and purportedly managed to "break the bank" at roulette on six separate occasions. But the term "break" is misleading here. That any gambler could even temporarily hinder the Monte Carlo casino's ability to run smoothly was, by that point in the SBM's history, pure fantasy. There was ample cash in the coffers waiting close by, if out of sight.

Wells told reporters that he'd devised a secret mathematical system while working on one of his mechanical inventions. But this was a lie. Wells did occasionally use a betting system, known as the *coup de trois,* in which he allowed his stake to ride for three successive wins and then withdrew the entire amount and started over again. Yet this was already a popular strategy and offered no real mathematical advantage. In truth, Wells just bet more daringly than did the average player, while a run of extremely good luck took care of the rest. He burned through his winnings soon enough, buying an enormous yacht, christened the *Palais-Royal,* and throwing over-the-top parties. He once hosted a dinner for thirty-five guests, one for each number of the roulette table, and seated himself at a chair marked 5 in reference to a spin on which he'd won his largest amount at Monte Carlo. Red being his lucky color, there were red carpets, walls, and ceilings, servers in red livery, red flowers, and red foods—lobster, prawn, cabbage, and strawberries.

He was back in Monte Carlo less than four months after his first adventure and had another impressive run, winning roughly £10,000. He came back two months later, and now Camille Blanc insisted on personally acting as *chef de partie* at his table. This time none of his numbers came up and he started betting desperately. That his luck ran out only after Blanc was overseeing things is intriguing, but there's no other evidence to show that his defeat was due to anything but chance. After losing all his money, Wells wired a friend in London for more, under the ruse that he needed funds to fix his yacht (he said that it employed a special fuel-saving device of his own invention that required constant tinkering). He lost that amount as well.

In the winter of 1892, a joint team of French and British police arrested Wells aboard the *Palais-Royal,* for selling coal on the black market. The complaints from investors in his patent schemes had been mounting for years and he was charged with fraud. He served eight years hard labor and declared bankruptcy from prison; the so-called Man Who Broke The Bank at Monte Carlo died without a cent to his name.

If the turn of the twentieth century witnessed the paradoxical embrace of rationalism on one hand and a growing fascination with mysticism, the occult, and pseudoscience on the other, one saw this same binary playing out at the Monte Carlo casino. For every gambler who put his faith in mathematical systems, another believed the tables could be bested through magic. To these players, hidden forces influenced the fall of the cards, dice, and wheels, and these forces could be swayed in one's favor if the right talisman was presented or the proper prayer incanted.

Some believed in sympathetic magic, transferred by the power of touch, which is why the bronze equestrian statue of Louis XIV that graces the lobby of the Hôtel de Paris has been rubbed bare, but only in one section, Louis's knee, which legend holds to be especially lucky. Adolphe Smith told of a woman who'd managed to trick the pope into blessing a lucky five-franc piece she'd hidden among her rosaries; it served her well until a tablemate, unaware of its sacred status, bet and lost the coin. Other gamblers preferred more vital material. Smith recounted meeting a woman in Monte Carlo who, after he congratulated her on a winning streak, let him peek inside her purse, where he saw a little gray lump resting on some silver coins. It was a bat's heart. She'd asked a railway porter to catch her one of the bats she'd seen hanging from the eaves of a food storage warehouse near the station and had cut out the heart herself. Believing that the moon governed both bats and silver, she said the organ's magic could only be worked on that particular element. Bats weren't the only animals thought to bring good fortune. One gambler brought a concealed pig into the casino; more practically minded believers claimed that a pork chop in your pocket did just as well. Others swore by the powers of live turtles, to be kept in one's coat. Locks of hair, skins of venomous snakes, rats' tails, and hangman's' nooses were also popular. Monte Carlo wisdom also preached the benefits of rubbing the swollen parts of a hunchback's body.

Everyone had a lucky number. Chaplains at the principality's Saint Paul's Anglican Church had learned to only deliver hymns numbering thirty-seven or higher, since giving any hymn between one and thirty-six sent half the congregants out the door to bet the number at roulette. Then there were the signs and objects to be avoided, lest they carry a *malfaisance*, or jinx. The Hôtel de Paris never displayed carnations, an especially unlucky breed, and neither it nor the Hermitage had rooms ending in 13. Some players, believing gambling to be the devil's purview, rested their hands on the tables while surreptitiously curling their fingers into diabolical horns in silent homage to the dark arts. People swore that Fridays were the slowest days in Monaco—*vendredi* being the day of Venus, and Venus being a woman, and women, as the guardians of the domestic sphere, being naturally ill-disposed to the family-rending pull of gambling. With such forces at play, only a fool would head to Monte Carlo before Friday had passed.

Superstitious gamblers had much to discuss after an earthquake struck the Côte d'Azur on February 23, 1887. A story circulated about how during the quake the wife of a French banker dropped to her knees, pledging to donate all her gambling winnings to the church and to devote herself to religious service if God spared her— this right out front of the Monte Carlo casino. After surviving the ordeal, she figured lighting half a dozen candles to the Virgin in a local church would suffice. Another favorite tale was that of Sir Arthur Sullivan calmly surveying the bedlam from the steps of the Hôtel de Paris, coolly lighting a cigar as a woman in her nightgown ran screaming out of the building. The quake hit on Ash Wednesday, which the religiously inclined interpreted as an act of divine retribution. Yet while three hundred people died in a San Remo church and buildings fell in Nice and Menton, the gambling resort suffered no casualties and little damage. A reporter for the *Times* remarked: "We can imagine the sensation that would have been caused throughout the world had the casino fallen a victim to the shock. What so appropriate as that on the first morning of Lent that home of wickedness should have been suddenly destroyed by the forces of outraged nature, [but] the course of roulette ball is unaltered by seismic disturbances."

————

Casino profits remained strong under Camille Blanc, and Monte Carlo's train station was welcoming more than a half-million passengers a year through the 1890s and early 1900s. Even as the numbers swelled, Blanc made sure not to lose sight of the needs of his wealthier clients, several of whom voiced displeasure at having to mix with the hoi polloi that had managed to infiltrate even the *salles privées*. In 1902 Blanc opened the International Sporting Club, down the hill from the main casino. This gambling venue would function like a private club, rather than just pretending to do so. Only "members of Royal families and of the Diplomatic Corps, active Officers, and Members of approved foreign Clubs" could be admitted to the gaming rooms. Given its international and influential clientele, the club's official statues formally prohibited "all discussion of a political or religious nature."

The Sporting helped bring some of the era's wealthiest gamblers to Monaco. Aside from the Romanovs, there was King Leopold II of Belgium, who supposedly began each day of his southern visits by having gallons of warm water from the Mediterranean dumped on his head. His Cap Ferrat villa sat on the largest estate in the area; Leopold later gifted it to his lover Caroline Lacroix, whom he'd met in Paris when she was a teenage prostitute and he an unhappy tyrant in his sixties. Perhaps at the Sporting, Leopold had the chance to exchange notes on statesmanship, mistresses, and roulette with the emperor Franz Josef, another Monte Carlo regular, who wintered in Cap Martin with his wife, ducking out whenever he could for a night of fun in Monte Carlo.

Wealthy Americans were also contributing to the casino's reserves in greater numbers, as the resort's reputation grew stateside. James Gordon Bennett Jr., who in 1887 launched the Paris edition of his father's *New York Herald*, visited often and boosted sales of his paper with glamorous items about the Riviera exploits of countrymen such as William C. Vanderbilt and J. P. Morgan, who reached Monaco aboard their luxury yachts.

Charles M. Schwab, then president of United States Steel, caused a flurry in January 1901, when he happened to be in the gaming rooms on the day that the earl of Rosslyn came armed with a supposedly unbeatable system for besting the roulette tables, with members of the British press in tow. The earl promptly lost everything he had. One reporter covering the debacle happened to know his steel magnates and spotted Schwab playing quietly at a nearby table. A passing mention of this sighting led to a series of false items about Schwab wandering around Monte Carlo in a state of delirium, playing the maximums at roulette with company money, to the delight of a "frenzied audience." "Schwab Breaks the Bank," ran the headline in the *New York Sun*. An infuriated Andrew Carnegie cabled Schwab: "Public sentiment shocked. Times demands statement [that] gambling [is] false. Probably have [to] resign. Serves you right." Carnegie then wrote to J. P. Morgan, demanding that Schwab be removed from his post: "Never did he show any tendency to gambling when under me, or I should not have recommended him you may be sure." A recalcitrant Schwab cabled Morgan's public relations aide: "Realize now it was a mistake to go there at all but never expected publication." Morgan in the end didn't ask for Schwab's resignation, though Schwab left United States Steel less than two years later.

———

Stories told about Belle Époque Monte Carlo grew alongside the resort in scale and boldness. By the 1880s SBM managers found they could no longer count on the newspapers on their payroll to produce entirely measured accounts. With readerships and advertising revenues on the rise, there was too much to be gained from printing salacious stories about "Wicked Monty."

As with any place more often talked of than seen up close, polemicists found value in offering Monte Carlo as the most shining example of whatever it was they wished to praise or denounce about the modern world. While some championed the resort for its unabashed celebration of personal freedom and upward mobility, others decried it for so staunchly rejecting the ties of family, community, and country. Incorrectly understood as an overnight success, Monte Carlo was either representative of all that was vanguard and progressive, or, with its opulent décor and quasi-aristocratic lifestyle, as reactionary and outdated. It was said that the gaming rooms caused people to become obsessed with risk and the pursuit of financial gain above all else; on the other hand, weren't the embrace of risk and the desire for personal wealth fundamental to a successful market economy? Some argued that the resort crowd practiced an enlightened internationalism, while others dismissed it as a motley crew of self-absorbed parvenus and "rootless cosmopolitans" with loyalty to no one but themselves. The willingness of local boosters to promote and fund opera, ballet, and car races in equal measure either offered an inspiring example of the kind of open-mindedness that could revitalize a stagnant European culture, or was a worrisome indication that traditional divisions between high and low culture had been damaged beyond all repair.

The Monte Carlo suicide story was a favored trope in the popular press and in sensational fiction. Tales of people killing themselves after having lost everything at the casino were legion. French readers learned in the pages of *Le Petit Journal* about a Russian who shot himself at the edge of one of the casino's roulette tables, while *La Stampa* carried an item about two young women, one British and the other German, driven to self-murder by their passion for gambling. *Guardian* readers encountered "a Spaniard, recently arrived from New York," who committed suicide after having been undone by "the seductive tables of M. Blanc," while across the Atlantic the *New York Times* reported on a young Frenchman who'd hanged himself in a seedy Riviera hotel after losing his life savings at Monte Carlo.

Death in Monte Carlo was shown as the logical punishment for leaving home, for succumbing to Mammon, for living life at too fast a pace. Not just death, but the most shameful and selfish kind of death, the final proof of how absolutely gamblers in Monte Carlo had disavowed the idea that a person owed duty to anyone but to himself.

Names, nationalities, and methods of crime varied from paper to paper and decade to decade, but the stories tended toward the same basic structure: An innocent young man or woman came to the resort in search of adventure; having momentarily escaped the watch of family and community, he or she succumbed to a "passion" (the word appeared again and again) for play, and after losing a final desperate bet, paid the ultimate price for having stepped out of line and out of place. Suicide stories featuring lowlifes or drifters failed to pique the public interest and were given only slim column space. To work its unsettling magic a Monte Carlo morality tale required the ruin of the beautiful young bourgeoise, or the seemingly contented patriarch, or the promising and dutiful officer. What made Monte Carlo so terrifying was that the place itself could turn normally good people bad, as if by osmosis.

A sign posted by the train station in Nice warning of the evils that would befall tourists if they wandered over to the competing resort featured a list of recent suicides caused by gambling losses. So did this anti–Monte Carlo pamphlet, printed in Nice in 1876:

1. April 8, 1873. Mr. Michel D . . . student of medicine at Bucharest, was found dead, with a pistol bullet in his heart, on the beach near the Italian Theatre at Nice. He had lost all at Monaco the same day.

2. May 12, 1873. Mr. G . . . committed suicide by causing his head to be severed from the trunk by the train, between the two tunnels at Monaco. He had been wandering about for the two preceding days, having lost all at the gambling tables.

3. In the night of the 16th to 17th May 1873 a young Russian, Mr. Pierre F . . . committed suicide by pistol at Nice, after having lost all he possessed at Monaco.

4. On the night of 13 September 1873, a stranger, well dressed, was found on the shore, near the Lazaretto at Nice. On the corpse was found a pocket book, of which all the leaves except one had been torn out. On the remaining one was written the following: "Monaco will be the destruction of many others." Before death he had destroyed every clue to his identity.

5. Oct 8, 1873. Mr. Hans L . . . a young Bavarian, fired two pistol shots into his chest at the Hôtel Suisse at Monaco. On his table was found a note with these words: "Pay yourselves with what I have left."

People whispered about casino security guards colluding with local authorities to dump dead bodies into the ocean, cash stuffed into jacket pockets to discredit any theories about deaths caused by gambling losses. Soon characters in Monte Carlo novels were asking to be sat at the notorious "suicide's chair" in the casino, or paid visits to the "suicide section" of the local cemetery, though in reality no such places existed. By the 1890s reporters covering Monte Carlo found it newsworthy just to note the number of suicides seemed to be "falling off," or that there were "only five suicides this year."

While there is no evidence suggesting that suicides were more frequent in Monaco than they were anywhere else, the SBM's archives reveal that the company did sometimes deal with suicides, both attempted and successful, and that managers tried to handle these matters as discreetly as possible. There is a whole folder in the SBM archives dedicated to one such suicide, dubbed the Testa Affair.

In the spring of 1901, Enrico Testa, of the small Italian town of Avellino, penned several letters to Camille Blanc, whom he held responsible for the recent death of his son Eugenio. Before shooting himself, Eugenio Testa had written his father from a Monte Carlo hotel room, detailing his despondency over some recent gambling losses. The senior Testa wanted the SBM to pay for his son's burial cost and to arrange for him to come to collect his effects. There is no record of Blanc's ever acknowledging these requests, though without doubt he was aware of the case.

A confidential report from the casino inspector surmised that "Eugenio Testa, an Italian officer, committed suicide in March 1901 at The Hôtel Bristol" and that "Dr. Collignon, called in to file the report, attributed the cause of death to a cerebral congestion [today known as an ischemic stroke]." The same report noted that the dead man "had in his possession jewels of some value that disappeared and which were later seen worn by members of the Monégasque Public Safety force." Monaco's head of security, a man named Delalonde, corroborated Dr. Collignon's diagnosis of cerebral congestion and claimed that any talk of suicide was the result of those conspiring to blackmail the SBM. Yet the guilty parties privately worried that the truth would eventually out. The SBM's report detailed how the dead man's brother, a police commissioner based near Florence, had been discussing the case with an Italian diplomat in Nice, and had filed a complaint with his minister of foreign affairs.

In the end the family's efforts came to nothing, and Camille Blanc, Dr. Collignon, and Delalonde never wavered from the official story. In a relatively small town such as Avellino, a son dead by suicide would have meant something altogether more difficult for the elder Testa to bear than a son dead of stroke. But still he refused to accept the official report. He knew enough about what happened to prodigal sons in Monte Carlo. There had been three decades worth of *La Stampa* headlines telling him as much.

———————

The free mixing of sexes in the gaming rooms was another frequent point of discussion in Monte Carlo news items. A reporter for the *New York Times* lamented how "husbands thoughtlessly encourage their wives or daughters to risk a few five-franc pieces, or napoleons, on the table, and thus inoculate them with the gambling frenzy." One French writer decreed that all women who entered the Monte Carlo casino should automatically be considered "*femmes publiques*," while a British novelist described the resort itself as possessing "the fatal beauty of a glorious courtesan."

Many men did visit the casino looking for a different kind of action than that overseen by the croupiers. Contemporary observers suggested that prostitutes plied their trade openly in Monte Carlo with the winking approval of the casino inspectors, who received bribes (sexual and monetary) from *les horizontales*. One British writer remarked on the variety of young women with immaculate hairdos and jaunty porkpie hats, who paraded between the gaming rooms in their high-heeled shoes and gaudy dresses, smoking cigarettes and chatting freely with their tablemates and the croupiers. "Who they are, how they love, or what they are doing at Monaco," he wrote, "Charles III and M. Blanc alone can tell." Theodore Dreiser regarded the women he saw at the casino as "evil, rather glorious and showy spiders spinning nets for none too satisfactory men . . . Interesting as spectacle, but worthless; weeds masquerading as true social flowers." A recently published official history of the SBM includes colorful vignettes of famed *femmes galantes* in Monte Carlo, such as the dark-eyed Spanish dancer and courtesan Caroline Otéro, known in her day as La Belle Otéro, who supposedly ruined herself at the casino. As Otéro herself wrote: "What does one come to Monte Carlo for, if not to lose?" According to the SBM account, the company rescued Otéro from complete destitution as reward for her long loyalty, covering the costs of her tiny hotel room in Nice for many years. In happier times, a local restaurant served Suprèmes de Sole Otéro in her honor.

The archives show that, at the very least, Monaco's officials weren't overly concerned with policing prostitution. In a 1903 French police register listing the hundreds of foreigners expelled from the principality over nearly four decades, the number of women expelled for prostitution, suspected or otherwise, makes up only a tiny fraction of the total number of expellees; men charged with stealing or committing fraud make up the vast majority of the list.

At a time when many Europeans worried about increasingly fluid gender roles, stories about strong women (whether courtesans, mistresses, wives, or none of the above) who managed to separate men from their money gave voice to concerns about how women were gaining more exposure to the public sphere, more participation in the marketplace, and the potential for outright economic and sexual independence. The figure of the woman for hire—supposedly wasteful, idle, transitory, and decadent—represented so much of what upset contemporary observers about Monte Carlo. Prostitutes were regarded as the ultimate arrivistes, callous social climbers. Perhaps it was the fear that both gambling and prostitution could potentially allow women to navigate their own lives outside of the realm of the domestic home that so tightly bound these two practices together in the minds of so many observers. Casino gambling laid bare the practices of economic exchange; the gold was there on the table to be seen by all. So too did associating the resort with venal sex reflect a broader use of the figure of the prostitute as the most blatant example of modern capitalism's complete domination of all facets of life. Prostitution transforms pleasure into a financial transaction, while the SBM promised that gambling would transform a financial transaction into an act of pleasure.

———

Anti-Semitic elements on the French right latched onto the idea of Monaco as a place more concerned with money gained though unproductive means than with morality, and suggested that the SBM and the Grimaldi dynasty were being guided by the unseen influence of Jews. They spoke of Monaco's decadence to frighten readers with a harbinger of what their own nation risked becoming if the socialists and parliamentarians had their way. Monaco, they warned, had been corrupted by foreign elements who fed like parasites on the territory in which they made their home. Prince Albert was attacked for his second marriage to the American and Jewish Alice Heine and for his public support of the falsely accused Jewish officer Alfred Dreyfus. Such rhetoric wasn't restricted to France. A pamphlet published in London suggested that it was obvious that Monte Carlo should be run by Jews, since "plundering one's neighbors naturally attracts the children of Israel; besides is there a place in the world more favourable for the exercise of their trade—lending upon usury?" Novelists spun pathetic scenes of ruined gamblers pawning beloved family heirlooms to the nefarious "Shylocks" who held court at the Café de Paris.

———————

Much of the language describing Monte Carlo personified the casino as a diabolical being (usually female) bent on destroying the weak, lulling unsuspecting victims into "the unwholesome lethargic fantasy of an opium-dream," as one writer put it in 1890. John Addington Symonds likened the place to "the habitation of some romantic witch," while French novelist Paul Bourget dubbed it a "cosmopolitan pandemonium." A London reporter counseled that evening was the most dangerous time to arrive, as the uninitiated would be made dizzy by the sight of the casino and its terrace, eerily lit by a thousand globes of fire. At night one felt as though one had abandoned the "countries of reality to enter into that brilliant region where all passions combine to obliterate the mind and obscure the reason." With Monte Carlo seen as such a powerful adversary, reformers and religious figures were often sympathetic to the plight of gamblers, and spoke of those poor sheep who'd been "ruined," or "fallen prey" to the casino. People spoke of prodigal sons and daughters who had (as Enrico Testa believed of his own son) been undone by squandering their wealth in wild living in this foreign land. "Honest families . . . no longer wish to be exposed to losing their fortune and sometimes their honor due to the acts of prodigal sons," suggested the author of an anti–Monte Carlo broadsheet in the 1890s. Novelists and playwrights picked up the thread: there was Hall Caine's *The Prodigal Son*, and E. Phillips Oppenheim's *Prodigals of Monte Carlo*.

The Norwegian painter Edvard Munch certainly thought of his own relation to Monte Carlo as that of victim and victimizer. He first came to the resort while based in Nice for the winter of 1891, ostensibly for health reasons, but was soon spending little of his time taking the cure and far more of it at the casino. Even as his dissipation grew, Munch wrote gleefully to his hometown newspaper about the region's natural wonders. In January 1891 he told readers back in Oslo that while they were suffering through a "Siberian cold," he was living it up on Europe's southern coast. "Listen to these names—Menton, Nice, Villefranche, Monte Carlo," he wrote; "isn't there joy in the very words?"

But all was not sunshine and joy for Munch. Like Alexis in Dostoyevsky's "Roulettenburg," a character with whom he'd recently grown fascinated, Munch became so obsessed with roulette that even his painting couldn't keep him away from the tables for any long stretch of time. "Once you've penetrated the enchanted castle of Monte Carlo you're already bewitched—and you'll return—you have to," he wrote in his journal; "The same thing happened every day—Every morning I swore not to go back there—and then the afternoon comes—I have everything ready to get back to work— I'm about to begin—then the idea that I could go back despite everything hits me like a thunderclap—it's no longer a question of reflection—it's only a question of finding out what times the train leaves—I'm suddenly seized by the fever—the minutes are hours—the trip from Nice to Monte Carlo is an eternity—finally I am mounting the steps that lead to the casino."

Munch feared the fate that was said to have befallen so many of those who shared his compulsion. Walking along the dark paths of the gardens near the casino he was seized by the thought that the fields were "fertilized with the blood of thousands. . . . This is where they commit suicide—all those we have read about—Precisely here—I had just read in the newspapers about two suicides—an English lady and a French officer—Yes—I had to look at the earth—behind the bush as though I would still be able to see blood." He found even less respite inside the casino. The crowds and the cavernous high-ceilinged rooms overwhelmed him. He saw women with a strange flush in their faces, as though they were wearing too much rouge, and men as pallid as the women were reddened, droplets of sweat running from their noses. He thought the gaming rooms strangely quiet, aside from the noises of the wheels spinning, and the nervous tapping of hands. People hunched quietly over the tables, hypnotized, their faces lit spookily by lamps. The scene, he wrote, was like that of "an enchanted castle—where the demons are having a gathering." Most unnerving of all was the fat croupier who with his black rake collected "the fat shiny yellow serpent" of coins, representing hundreds and hundreds of hours of labor.

Munch recalled escaping for a moment on a bench at the edge of one of the rooms, only to be further disturbed by the sight of a young man across from him, kneading his black hat incessantly. He couldn't look away and had to get up so as not to upset the man with his staring. His attentions then turned to another man lying prone on a bench, smiling up at the ceiling and mumbling to himself, and then to another man whizzing by and suddenly throwing his hat up into the air. Munch fled the madhouse, but not before suffering the embarrassment of slipping on the polished tile floor. Outside at the train station, he saw a woman coming toward him. As with the man he'd spied on the bench she was "staring into space—absent-mindedly—Her pale lips are moving—she is counting—calculating—Un, deux—trois—She is at the roulette table." He longed for the solace of his room in Nice.

Despite his disgust with the place and with himself, Munch returned to the coast in late 1891 for another winter stay. The trip was ill timed. Just as Munch was settling into Nice again, a journalist was gaining acclaim back in Oslo for his exposé, "On the Misuse of State Bourses"—the subject of which was the young painter Edvard Munch, who'd apparently funded his Riviera jaunts from a government scholarship that he had requested to cover the costs of some art classes in Paris.

Munch did have something to show for his troubles. He painted what is arguably (there is competition from Max Beckmann's *Dream of Monte Carlo*) the most beautiful and unsettling tableau of Monte Carlo ever produced: *At the Roulette Table in Monte Carlo*. Rendered in an unearthly glow, it shows a crowd of ghostly gamblers, a group portrait of victimhood. The viewer is made to look down at these poor souls watching as the thickset croupier rakes in another pile of winnings. It is a scene of pure horror—though here Munch's subjects endure their private nightmares in somewhat more subdued fashion than that of the painting he finished not long after his Riviera misadventure, *The Scream*. Two figures haunt the left of the frame in Munch's Monte Carlo painting; each one appears to be writing in a notebook, presumably recording the results of the latest spin. Munch himself seems to have been a "system player," and the figure dominating the image (whose features are not dissimilar from Munch's) may have been meant as a stand-in for himself. "This table is like a living thing," Munch wrote in his journal, "whose brain would be the roulette wheel—which has its own way of doing things—lucky man who would know how to analyze this brain."

Oscar Wilde and Lord Alfred Douglas spent a few days in Monte Carlo in mid-March of 1895, a brief escape from their legal woes. The *Observer* reported that the pair was ejected from their hotel following complaints by other guests, which, if true, complicates the image of Monte Carlo as a place where the limits of polite society did not obtain. Wilde had unpleasant memories of the trip; in his prison letter, *De Profundis,* he wrote to Douglas: "At a time when I should have been in London taking wise counsel . . . you insisted on my taking you to Monte Carlo, of all revolting places on God's earth, that all day, and all night as well, you might gamble as long as the Casino remained open. As for me—baccarat having no charms for me—I was left alone outside to myself." Douglas, in *Oscar Wilde and Myself,* wrote that he hadn't forced Wilde to travel to Monte Carlo nor did Wilde cover any of his expenses or losses; he'd only wanted to distract his friend with a trip to a place he'd never seen before—but Wilde failed to appreciate the resort because he "never had the pluck to put a Louis on the table because . . . he always felt that a gold piece was a good deal of money."

What one writer found revolting, another found enchanting. "All my life before going abroad I had been filled with a curiosity as to the character of the Riviera and Monte Carlo," remarked Theodore Dreiser in his travelogue, *A Traveler at Forty.* He finally reached the resort a few years before the First World War, head full of fantasies about the pleasures to be found there. Though the era's great chronicler of ambition and its fraught relationship with morality ceded that the place fueled "truly sinful" desires that "ignore the care of the home, the well-being of children, the conventions and delights of the monogamous state," he discerned a kind of artistry in the fast life that Monte Carlo promoted, since these same sinful desires also fueled the discovery of new excitements. For Dreiser, Monte Carlo was a Versailles for the twentieth century—an excessive and gaudy folly to be sure, but one made beautiful by the shamelessness of its embrace of hedonism. "Nothing under the sun is as dull as the conventional home," he wrote, "and if life were made for that, let me die right now. Monte Carlo is immoral, but it is a spectacle, a glittering variation from the norm of humdrum existence, and, as such, it is worth almost any price to attain."

———————

On the morning of August 6, 1907, two travelers deposited a trunk in the cloakroom of Marseille's Gare Saint-Charles, with instructions to ship it to London. A few hours later, a rail porter noticed dark reddish stains gathering in one corner of the trunk. The police were called. Opening the luggage, they discovered the dismembered body of a woman. Her head and legs were missing. The authorities traced the trunk back to a married team of con artists who'd been working Monte Carlo: Vere Goold, an Irishman, and his French wife, Marie Violette Goold (née Girodin). The couple was tracked to Marseille, where they'd checked into a hotel under the names of Mr. and Mrs. Jervis. Under questioning, Goold claimed to hail from a titled family from County Cork, and referred to himself as Sir Goold, though he eventually dropped this pretense to nobility. In the Goolds' hotel room police discovered a valise containing a woman's head and two legs. The victim was Emma Lévin, a well-to-do Danish widow and Monte Carlo regular, known to flaunt her wealth. She had last been seen at the Hôtel de Paris.

The Goolds said that they'd been renting a villa in Monaco. Madame Lévin had paid Madame Goold a social call one afternoon when a man burst in, yelling that Lévin had ruined him, and stabbed her in the heart. Madame Goold had fainted and could recall no other details. When her husband came home, the frantic couple had cut up the body and hidden it in their luggage, worried that they'd be blamed for the crime. After further interrogation Madame Goold changed her story. Now it was her husband who'd gotten drunk and stabbed Lévin, and he'd cut up and stored the body himself. She said she played no part in the crime, and had no idea what had motivated her husband's violence. Confronted with this version, Goold corroborated his wife's statement. He said that Lévin had been trying to extort money from him and that he'd killed her in a fit of rage.

But the French police still wouldn't accept this version, as the evidence pointed to premeditated murder. Finally, after the Goolds were brought back together to witness a reconstruction of the crime, and confronted with all the holes in their various statements, Vere Goold confessed that his wife had befriended Lévin with the express purpose of inviting her to the villa, so they could steal the jewels they'd seen her wearing around the resort. Madame Goold had smacked the victim with a mallet and her husband had stabbed her. Together, they cut up the body. The Goolds were both found guilty of murder and exiled to Devil's Island.

———

In the same year the Goold crime was making front-page news in Europe, the SBM suffered another major blow, when French officials, responding to decades of complaints from competing resort speculators, overturned the country's prohibition on gambling. More than a hundred gaming houses opened on French soil in the next five years. The new laws still restricted legal gambling to private clubs and to casinos housed in thermal resorts. Most importantly for Monte Carlo, France also forbade its gambling operators from providing any form of roulette, a game deemed especially addictive.

The French casino owners found ways to make the most out of

what they'd been given. While Monte Carlo offered free entertainment and inexpensive food to help bring people to the tables, the French casinos worked the opposite way, charging large markups on drinks, food, cigarettes, and entertainment. French speculators focused their attentions on an attraction not offered in Monte Carlo. Baccarat, a counting game, had once been a mainstay of the Palais-Royal clubs, but it had failed to catch on in the Rhine casinos or in Monte Carlo. François Blanc had never put stock into the game since it offered only slim margins for the casino. It became the specialty of Monte Carlo's French competitors. Along the coast they played the game two ways: the first version, known as chemin de fer (railroad), pitted gamblers against one another directly, with players bidding for the right to act as banker for a given round. In the second version, usually known simply as baccarat (also as *banque à deux tableaux* and *baccarat en banque*), gamblers played against the house. No-limits chemin de fer, in particular, attracted big spenders with the wherewithal to bid for the right to bank, and potentially win large amounts. So despite being heavily taxed—with 60 percent of gross profits going to the French government and roughly 20 percent on top of that amount paid to local authorities—the French casinos gained steadily on the SBM, though everyone knew that true parity with Monte Carlo could only be achieved once the French government allowed roulette.

With baccarat in fashion along the coast, the SBM adjusted its own policies of not offering banking games, though as an olive branch to his new competitors, Camille Blanc confined the game to the International Sporting Club and to the main casino's *salles privées*. He refused to allow the kinds of no-limit versions that were the specialties of the competing resorts, likely supposing that if the French casinos became known for high-stakes baccarat, their owners might be pleased enough with that corner of the market to leave roulette to him, at least in the short term.

Monaco's population at this time stood at roughly twenty thousand, though that figure emphasized the largely transient expatriate community, while the native Monégasques numbered only a few thousand. Many of the SBM employees had made their homes outside the principality. These started where the spectacle ended, on the hillside just above the casino in the French town of Beausoleil, which had grown alongside Monte Carlo, and had first been known as Monte-Carlo-Supérieur. Land was slightly cheaper there than in Monaco, which is perhaps why the hotel branch of the Wagon-Lits train company elected in 1899 to open its flagship Monte Carlo hotel, the Riviera Palace, in Beausoleil rather than in Monte Carlo proper. The fate of Beausoleil was so deeply entwined with that of the SBM that no one thought it odd that the town's first official mayor, elected in 1904, was Camille Blanc.

Sharing the same worries that had plagued his father, Camille kept watch for any kind of nongambling attractions that might help keep people loyal to Monte Carlo after the inevitable loss of its monopoly on roulette. In 1910 he played to the growing public fascination with aeronautics by arranging for a daring display by the French aviator Henri Rougier, who skimmed his small biplane six hundred feet above the Tête de Chien (Dog's Head), the rocky promontory overlooking the principality. Rougier made news in Monaco the following year as the winner of the first inaugural Monte Carlo Auto Rally, another SBM-funded sporting event. The Monégasque tobacco wholesaler Alexandre Noghès, president of the principality's Cycling Club, which had morphed into the Automobile Club of Monaco (ACM), had conceived of the rally, inspired by the Convegni Cyclisti, which saw cyclers departing from various towns around Italy to converge on a single destination. Drivers in their gleaming machines descended on the principality from

Paris, Brussels, Geneva, Vienna, and Berlin. Each competing car had been festooned with a sign reading MONTE-CARLO RALLY, helping to strengthen the association of the resort with modern luxury in the minds of the thousands across Europe who gathered to watch the cars pass by. Rougier arrived from Paris in under twenty-eight hours, though he won the 10,000-franc prize not because he had made it in the fastest time but because the judges felt his automobile arrived in the finest condition. This seemingly arbitrary decision angered many of his competitors.

The Monte Carlo Auto Rally proved so popular that Blanc dreamt up another version of the event a few years later, now with entrants piloting airplanes rather than cars. Over the first two weeks of April 1914 the SBM hosted what was meant to be the first annual Monaco Air Rally. The legendary aviator Roland Garros was among the men who took off in staggered intervals from London, Vienna, Madrid, Turin, and other cities bound for Monaco. After several stops to refuel and a final one to switch out to water-landing gear, the planes glided into Port Hercules while crowds cheered from the hills. Garros won the 25,000-franc first prize in his custom Morane-Saulnier Type N.

The sight of machines flying overhead soon took on more ominous meaning. Prince Albert learned of the outbreak of war while sailing through the Azores. He hurried back to Monaco in early August 1914, while Camille Blanc came down from Paris. The Monte Carlo casino and the International Sporting Club were closed immediately. But not for very long.

10

MONACO AT WAR

PRINCE ALBERT DECLARED MONACO'S official neutrality, while securing assurance of shadow protection from France. Openly picking sides would have denied Monte Carlo's pleasures to half the gamblers of Europe.

Albert had seen enough of war to know he had no taste for it. Unable to hop aboard a sea-bound whaler like other restless men of his generation looking to escape stifling home lives, he had hit on a military career as a way to get a stay on his royal duties while still playing the dutiful son. At twenty-two he fought for France in their disastrous campaign against Prussia and later served as a vice admiral in the Spanish navy. He found he preferred studying the seas to patrolling them, and devoted most of his adult life to the relatively new science of oceanography. As he told reporters, "The scientist builds up; the militarist tears down." His first ship, the *Hirondelle*, boasted an onboard laboratory, operating theater, darkroom, and a fifteen-man crew that included a sketch artist who documented their deep-sea discoveries. When forced to be on land

Albert mostly avoided his palace, preferring the family château in Marchais, which, with its 1,250 hectares, far outsized the principality. Whether in Marchais or Monaco, official guests were more likely to find Albert in some version of his naval gear—rumpled sailor's hat, tweeds, boots without sheen, heavy black peacoat—than in any kind of royal regalia.

––––––––––

Prince Albert and Camille Blanc agreed that it was poor form to keep Monaco's casinos open, at least in those first heady months of war, when people were still singing patriotic songs in the streets. But the wheels were spinning again by the end of 1914. The SBM operated with a skeleton staff. While Albert's subjects were exempted from duty (one of the perks they enjoyed in exchange for remaining under dynastic rule while democracy took hold all around them), more than one thousand SBM employees had been mobilized to serve the Allied forces. Blanc suspended the policy of charging admission at the Monte Carlo casino, and the once-exclusive Sporting now opened its doors to anyone wishing to play. The mood in the gaming rooms was subdued. Clients were encouraged to wear somber colors and avoid ostentatious displays. War bulletins were posted each night in the halls. Prices dropped at the Hôtel de Paris, while other hotels shuttered altogether, and the once bustling Ciro's thinned out.

Despite the cutbacks and attempts to keep a low profile, reporters speculated gleefully about the millions of francs said to be pouring into the principality. A writer for the *New York Times* headlined a 1915 piece: "The Oasis of Europe—Monte Carlo: Where Royalty Goes to Forget the War by Gambling Away Small Fortunes Daily and Where Opera and Pleasure Rule." Chiding the Monégasques for their business-as-usual attitude in the face of war, he asked: "What matters the fate of nations or the world, while the little ivory ball spins about the revolving wheel?" The French press meanwhile dubbed Albert "le prince Roulette" and "Albert le Croupier." Writers were quick to imagine wartime Monaco as the secret backroom of Europe, where an international cast of profiteers and double agents struck their treasonous deals. The former Monte Carlo croupier Paul de Ketchiva helped feed this kind of thinking by describing the casino as "the meeting place for some of the arch-plotters of Europe . . . German and Austrian Secret Service had secret coups of agents there and . . . royal plotters met to discuss high and warlike politics."

Accusations that the SBM profited from international espionage dated back to well before the First World War. An 1884 exposé alleged that top managers were running a German spy ring out of the casino, and in the 1890s SBM brass worried about accusations in the Niçoise papers that the principality was the center of operations for Italian spies. Muckrakers made much of Monaco's links to Germany through François Blanc and the workers he'd brought over from Bad Homburg, whose sons and daughters were now said to number among the principality's most notable families. In 1916 a Monégasque publishing house produced a detailed pamphlet refuting such claims, stating, for example, that only eight of the company's three thousand employees were of German origin.

Novelists joined the fray. In E. Phillips Oppenheim's 1915 *Mr. Grex of Monaco*, a cabal of profiteers, drawn equally from Allied, Central, and neutral states, meets at the casino to redraw the map of Europe, all within spitting distance of an equally international clientele too obsessed with sex and money to notice. "If you only knew the underground workings of this place, the mentality, the way in which everything is run," a Monte Carlo insider warns a friend in Robert Service's 1922 novel *The Poisoned Paradise*. "Why, here you're not living in the Twentieth Century at all. It's medieval." Readers wanting to believe that they'd been dragged unknowingly into pointless destruction no doubt took pleasure in stories concerning villainous politicians and plutocrats safely waiting out the war among the fleshpots of the Riviera. Many who consumed these stories likely believed that the central architects of this global conflict were the same cosmopolitan statesmen and industrialists whose escapades at places like Monte Carlo they'd so long read about in the popular press.

The potential for sworn enemies to sit across from one another at Monte Carlo's tables was real enough. Any officer, regardless of nation, could play at the casino, so long as he was not in military uniform. The writer Charles Graves (brother of Robert) suggested that the English army was so convinced by stories of intrigue at the casino that they dispatched an officer with special training in counterespionage to watch over things in Monaco, which might have sounded like the war's luckiest assignment—at least until 1918, when the officer was poisoned by an unknown assassin.

Prince Albert allowed the Allies to set up military hospitals in the principality, and soldiers convalescing in that dream-space must have felt a strange kind of distance from the realities of the trenches, whether they entered the casino or did not. A fortunate few civilians also found respite from the fighting along the coast. The Bloomsbury painter Roger Fry spent the bloody spring of 1915 relaxing in a Roquebrune villa belonging to a friend, and there produced a pleasant pastoral, *Roquebrune and Monte Carlo from Palm Beach*. Other than the date of its production, the painting offers no evidence of any kind of strife taking place nearby.

———————

Just before the war, Albert had enjoyed a hunting trip in Wyoming, where he shot bears with no less able a guide than Buffalo Bill Cody. But by the fall of 1918 Monaco's prince was closing in on seventy and just standing upright sent him into shooting pain. His mustaches had gone wintry white and he found he'd lost his usual appetites. Prohibited from traveling, Albert passed much of the war alone aboard his yacht, stuck like a fish under glass in the bay of Monaco. His only child, the crown prince Louis Grimaldi—from his first marriage, an unfortunate alliance to the daughter of a Scottish nobleman—was meanwhile off playing hero somewhere in France.

As eager to escape home and his official duties as Albert had been, Louis joined the French Foreign Legion as soon as he graduated from military school. Now in his late forties and gone round in the middle, the crown prince was no longer the young legionnaire. At the outset of war, Albert had asked French officials to keep his son as far away from any real action as they could. Louis was given the rank of staff officer and almost immediately promoted to lieutenant colonel. He did participate in at least one key mission: taking back the family estate in Marchais, which the Germans had claimed in the summer of 1914 and had planned to blow up, before being thwarted by French forces. Prince Albert later had a display case built to house one of the mines discovered at the château. It was "a reminder," he said, "of the German mentality."

The problem was that Louis was unmarried and a cousin, Wilhelm, second duke of Urach, stood next in line for the throne. (Louis's great-aunt, the princess Florestine, had married well, into German nobility). The Allies worried that if Prince Albert died and a stray bullet should find Louis's head, Monaco would pass into German hands. There was talk that France planned to annex the principality just to make sure that never happened, a prospect that would have terrified the Monégasques. Folded into France, Monaco would not only lose its legal autonomy and monopoly on roulette but the Monégasques would have to pay taxes, and would be called on to serve in battle.

But the French weren't especially keen to take over the principality just then. Though they'd recently relaxed the country's gambling laws, French officials recognized the value in keeping an official border between France and the pleasure center at its southeastern edge. An independent Monaco free to bring in the roulette-hungry hordes made good business sense for the other resort towns on the Côte d'Azur, while also giving French lawmakers a weapon to be deployed against the more ferocious antigambling reformers: at least, they could answer to those who complained about the spread of gambling in France, they'd kept the country free of that infernal game.

To the French president, Raymond Poincaré, the solution to the matter of Grimaldi succession was clear. He knew—as everyone knew—that the crown prince Louis had fathered an illegitimate daughter, Charlotte Louise Juliette. She was born in 1898, the result of an entanglement in Constantine with a laundress named Marie Juliette Louvet, while Louis was serving in Algeria with the Foreign Legion. As a child, Charlotte had been kept mostly out of sight. (We know little about her relationship with her mother.) While Louis remained stationed in North Africa he'd sent Charlotte to a French convent school. As she grew into a young woman she was seen more regularly at the palace, though not in any official capacity. She spent the war years with the French Red Cross, reading to the injured and helping them write letters home.

Putting Charlotte in line for the throne was a thorny issue. Members of the Grimaldi dynasty had ruled Monaco (aside from the moments of revolutionary upheaval) for more than six hundred years because their blood was noble, and their subjects had submitted to this rule because theirs was not. This was the logical order of things. But the whole system relied on the idea that noble birth was made legitimate by the sacred bonds of marriage. A child born to a laundress out of wedlock was no kind of heir.

French officials had no time for this kind of antiquarianism. That same legitimist thinking had supported the whole edifice of archdukes and kings and emperors that had helped bring Europe to war in the first place. President Poincaré pressed for resolution.

July 17, 1918, is remembered as the bloody day on which Lenin's men set about assassinating much of the Romanov clan, severing ties with the dynastic past of what would become (for a time) the world's largest nation. The same day, French and Monégasque officials ensured the continuation of one of the longest-reigning dynastic lines in Europe, in the world's second-smallest sovereign country. The treaty was made public the following year, during the Paris Peace Conference. France pledged to recognize and defend the perpetual right of the Grimaldi to rule an independent Monaco, so long as the family acted "in complete conformity with the political, military, naval, and economic interests of France." The document specified that if the throne of Monaco fell vacant "for lack of a direct or adoptive heir," the principality would become a protectorate of France. This detail would seem to have threatened the continuation of Grimaldi reign: no heir, no independence. But President Poincaré himself had insisted on the exact wording: for lack of a direct or adoptive heir.

On October 31, 1918, Albert, acting on his princely privilege to introduce or veto any new law as he saw fit, amended the law of succession that his father had codified a few decades earlier. Now it included the following caveat: "In the absence of a direct heir, the reigning or hereditary Prince may adopt a child who shall be legally entitled to succeed him." Later, in a solemn ceremony, witnessed by Prince Albert, and, reportedly, President Poincaré and the French minister of foreign affairs, Louis Grimaldi officially adopted Charlotte Louise Juliette as his daughter. It is strange to think that the president of France and his minister of foreign affairs should have tended to this family drama, and so close to the signing of the Armistice that ended the greatest war the world had ever known. Strange also that Charlotte Louise Juliette, now Charlotte Louise Grimaldi, was twenty years old at the time, and had technically been adopted by a fellow adult—a detail apparently of small concern to the parties involved.

———————

With the matter of succession sewn up, Prince Albert turned to his other pressing concern. He was short of ready money. The Grimaldi family had long been rich in land and titles, but cash had always been a more complicated matter. Few pastimes are more expensive than amateur oceanography, and there were other costly adventures. Albert had sponsored a massive archaeological dig and built an oceanography museum (which Theodore Dreiser found "amazingly dull" and precisely "the sort of thing a prince making his money out of gambling would endow"). He also supported several charities, styling himself a European Carnegie or Rockefeller, men he lauded for how they'd put their money to public use. The considerable fortune of Albert's second wife, Alice Heine, the New Orleans–born daughter of a prosperous German banking family, had helped to support these projects for a time. When the prince was still in her graces she'd paid for two enormous ships, which he dutifully named *Princesse Alice* and *Princesse Alice II.* But that source of funding had mostly evaporated, along with any love between the couple; they separated in 1902.

Albert relied mostly on the stipend he received as a shareholder in the SBM. The exact amounts of his annual payments from the casino are unclear, but journalists of the time claimed it reached totals that today would number in the millions of dollars. The historical record offers no explanation as to why Albert's stipend for 1918 proved insufficient. Perhaps faced with his impending mortality he wanted to pour as much into his research and philanthropy as he could, or maybe he was just tired of the deprivations and confinement of the war years and had an urge to spend wildly. In any case, he approached Camille Blanc for an advance on his next year's stipend. The request flummoxed the casino director, who'd suggested many times without success that Albert might ease the casino's own cash flow problems by taking a cut in his stipend. Blanc of course had his own free-spending streak. Stories circulated about his long-time mistress, Madame Chinon, dubbed the "Madame Pompadour of Monte Carlo," whose losses at the tables were always forgiven by the house.

The SBM had little to spare at that moment. Although the company stayed profitable throughout the war, profits had fallen to a third of what they had been in 1914. Blanc was also dealing with the workers who had gone off to serve their home countries and were now trickling back into the principality, expecting steady jobs alongside their hero's welcome. Three days after the signing of the Armistice, Blanc got a letter from a group of SBM employees recently demobbed from the French army: it said that while Monégasques with centuries-long ties to the principality certainly deserved respect, they had not been called upon to make the same sacrifices as those French citizens who had fought for "the continued existence of all civilized Peoples" and were thus entitled to "priority in the distribution of jobs." Blanc rehired as many of these workers as he could. He meanwhile refused the prince's request for an advance on his stipend.

Albert's humiliation was compounded by an exposé on the principality that ran that year in one of the Parisian papers. Its author said that "In Monaco, only two men matter: Camille Blanc and the Prince." The writer had come up with a very short list for a very small place, and had placed Albert last. It was a deliberate move, meant to suggest that true power in Monaco dwelt not in the House of Grimaldi but in the House of Blanc.

Less than five years later, only one house was left standing. A saying from the era held that at Monte Carlo, "*Rouge* wins sometimes; *Noir* often; but *Blanc* always." But any Monte Carlo regular could have spotted the fault in such logic: no matter how long or lucky, all streaks must end.

11

THE MERCHANT OF DEATH

The destinies of nations are his sport, the movements of armies and affairs of Governments his special delight. In the wake of the war, this mysterious figure moves over tortured Europe.

—Max Aitken, Lord Beaverbrook, as quoted in "Zaharoff Still a Mystery Man," *New York Times*, March 7, 1926

WHEN NOT IN MONTE CARLO, holed up in the Hôtel de Paris with his Spanish mistress, the munitions dealer Sir Basil Zaharoff based himself chiefly out of a five-story *hôtel particulier* at N° 53, Avenue Hoche, in the eighth arrondissement of Paris. There was a certain symmetry in his choice of address. The avenue's namesake, Louis Lazare Hoche, had, like Zaharoff, risen from obscurity to military prominence (in Hoche's case as a general of the Revolutionary army), and it was one of twelve thoroughfares shooting out like the points of a star from Bonaparte's monument to his own martial prowess, the Arc de Triomphe. The windows at N° 53, said to have been made of bulletproof glass, were always shuttered, and the blinds always drawn. They were adorned with pretty flower boxes, a decorative touch seen more often in London than in Paris; reporters offered this last detail as evidence of Sir Basil's laughable pretensions to play the English gentleman and escape his "true" roots.

According to several Zaharoff biographers and historians of Monaco, Prince Albert dined with Zaharoff at N° 53 several times over the autumn of 1918. The arms dealer had been apprised of the prince's difficult financial situation via a secret rendezvous in Paris at the Ritz with Monaco's foreign minister. Zaharoff also discussed Monaco's political future with the French prime minister Clemenceau and learned of the secret treaty guaranteeing Monaco's continued independence. At some point toward the end of 1918 Albert asked Zaharoff for the loan he had failed to secure from Camille Blanc, coupling his request with a vague promise to help Zaharoff take control of the SBM when the opportunity presented itself, and Zaharoff gave Albert a large sum of money.

———————

Zaharoff drew more media attention than any other munitions baron of the 1920s. Perhaps this was because his name could have sprung from the mind of the laziest pulp fiction novelist. Or it might have been because he looked the part, with his tall, thuggish frame, his full-length trench coat and rattan cane, his top hat for town and pith helmet for more exotic climes, and his Van Dyck beard carefully waxed into fine points, as though he were making an extra effort to resemble the devil so many wished him to be. The press of his time created such a cartoonish persona for Zaharoff that when the artist Hergé needed an arms dealer to stoke conflict between two banana republics in one of his *Tintin* adventures, he could draw nearly verbatim from the headlines, changing a few letters to produce the villainous "Basil Basarov."

One story affixed itself to so-called "Merchant of Death" in the spring of 1923 and has stayed there for good; it held that between 1923 and 1926 Zaharoff was the secret owner of the SBM.

To untangle Zaharoff's connections to Monte Carlo one must wind through tales of intrigue and treason, superstitions and curses, corruption and lust and madness, and in the end, the picture remains unclear. Zaharoff guarded his privacy closely, which only led to wilder speculation about his origins. Some contemporaries claimed he was an exiled White Russian waiting out the Bolshevik Revolution in Paris; others, that he was an agitator from Athens who'd faked his own death and assumed a new identity; still others suggested that Zaharoff himself encouraged these conflicting accounts to cultivate an air of mystery while obscuring his pedestrian English origins. That he must be hiding Jewish ancestry seemed obvious to many. As one Monaco paper put it, he was a "vampire . . . born in Bulgaria under the name of Zacharie Zacharias (Jewish, of course)."

Drawing from the most rigorous sources, we can trace the following short biography, however impressionistic it might be:

Basileios and Helene Zacharias were Greeks who lived in Constantinople before fleeing sometime in the first half of the nineteenth century to escape mounting ethnic violence. Settling in Odessa and seeking assimilation, the family Russified its name to Zacharov, rendered in the French style as Zaharoff. Returning to Turkey in the 1840s, they set up in the trading town of Mugla, thirty miles from the Aegean coast, and here Zacharias Basileios Zaharoff was born on October 6, 1849. The senior Zaharoff failed to establish himself in business and the family moved back to Constantinople, to the Greek quarter of Tatlava. Basil attended one of the city's best English schools, likely with the help of a wealthy relation. While anyone with business aspirations in polyglot Constantinople would have learned to strike a bargain in more than one tongue, Zaharoff mastered a huge repertory: Greek, Turkish, French, English, Spanish, Italian, and Russian. He spent the warm evenings after school working as a hotel guide, exchanging currency for tourists at wildly inflated rates and making underworld contacts in the process. By some accounts he supplemented his income as an amateur boxer and petty thug.

An uncle, Sevastopoulos, took the adolescent Zaharoff into his textile business and when the firm grew, named him partner. It was a promotion in title only, since Sevastopoulos refused to pay his nephew proper commissions or share any of the profits. After three years of labor unrewarded, Zaharoff took the amount he felt was owed to him from the company safe and fled to London, where with his fair complexion and ear for accents he passed as a British merchant, until Sevastopoulos caught up with him and had Zaharoff charged with embezzlement. According to one of Zaharoff's few intimates, who claimed to have heard the story of the trial from the defendant himself, just as Sevastopoulos prepared to deliver his damning testimony to the crowded London courtroom Zaharoff leapt up and presented the original signed contract detailing the terms of their partnership. (Presumably the prisoner had been left unshackled and had also succeeded in hiding the document in his prison garb.) Sevastopoulos promptly broke down in tears and demanded the immediate release of his beloved nephew.

Zaharoff, who by then had shortened and anglicized his first name to Basil, found his reputation tainted by the scandal and so made his way to Athens, where he caught the attention of an agent for Nordenfelt, the Swedish armaments firm. He quickly rose from clerk to agent for all of the Balkans, and eventually to major shareholder, along the way helping to bring Hiram Maxim's machine gun to Europe. Eventually Zaharoff switched alliances to the Vickers munitions company and profited from every one of the era's major conflicts, whispering in the ears of statesmen from rival nations who queued up to buy his guns, cannons, and submarines.

The Great War made his fortune. Zaharoff pledged himself to the Allied cause (though many said he traded with both sides and had an active interest in seeing the war drag on for as long as it did) and received decorations, including a knighthood, for his service. In 1923 the *Wall Street Journal* placed him fourth on a list of the richest people on earth: not quite Henry Ford but well ahead of the Mellons and the Vanderbilts.

A man with enemies in so many places and with no real home would logically only be able to unwind in a place like Monaco, far from the world's political stages. Zaharoff had been wintering in the resort since the 1880s with his lover, Doña Maria, the duchess of Marchena y Villafranca de los Caballeros. In her youth she had been known as one of the greatest beauties in Spain. At seventeen, Maria (her full name was Maria del Pilar Antonia Angela Patrocinio Simona de Muguiro y Beruete) married Prince Francis of Bourbon, a cousin of King Alfonso. The prince turned out to be mentally ill and had to be institutionalized, though divorce was impossible. Zaharoff met Doña Maria shortly after her wedding and they enjoyed a decades-long affair, which they managed to keep out of the press. Profiles of Zaharoff were peppered with winking asides about his more than fifty years of bachelorhood. A writer for the *New York Times* accused the "eccentric" Zaharoff, of being "a woman hater." Noting how consciously Zaharoff had cultivated his mysterious persona, the writer asked if there was something Zaharoff "so wishes to keep hidden that he thinks safety lies in hiding much more?"

The mere pursuit of profit rarely figures into theories about why the already wealthy Zaharoff should have wanted to involve himself in the affairs of the SBM through his alleged loan to Prince Albert. Some biographers and journalists have suggested that Zaharoff planned to take over Monaco so he could install Doña Maria as princess; his idea being to bankrupt the casino and freeze out Albert by drying up his sole source of income. Whatever his motivation, Zaharoff reportedly bought up shares in the SBM through various straw men, until finally making his play in the spring of 1923. In some accounts, while Camille Blanc was conveniently out of the principality on business, Zaharoff burst into the SBM offices at the

Hôtel de Paris flanked by henchmen and claimed control of the building and everything else the company owned. In other versions the arms dealer simply revealed to the shocked board of directors that through various third parties he now held a majority share in the SBM.

Camille Blanc did indeed resign in the spring of 1923, officially for reasons of health. Camille's nephew Léon Radziwill remained as a large shareholder in the SBM, but was said to have shifted his alliance easily to Zaharoff. According to an April 1923 piece in the *Los Angeles Times,* Zaharoff was by then turning "the famous casino upside down, shaking out the non-essential employees;" thousands of SBM workers feared for their jobs under the new regime. Zaharoff named a figurehead as the SBM's new president, Alfred Delpierre, who had overseen some of the purchasing and logistical responsibilities for the French forces during the war. Zaharoff also wisely tapped Léon Barthou, brother of Louis Barthou, who briefly served as prime minister of France, for another top position.

Daily operation of the casino fell to another supposed wartime crony of Zaharoff's, René Léon. The local papers regularly launched combined attacks against Léon and the arms dealer who supposedly backed his every decision. The editor of the Monégasque paper, *Tout Va,* wrote that the principality "knows only one head: His Most Serene Highness, Prince Louis II, and the others, whether they call themselves Zaharoff or René Léon, are nothing but casino creatures."

In all his years in Monte Carlo, Zaharoff never displayed any interest in the actual operation of its famous casino. He reportedly hated gambling and never once set foot in the building. One anecdote repeated across various sources describes a woman disturbing Zaharoff as he held court on the sun-dappled terrace of the Hôtel de Paris to ask if, "since everything here belongs to you," he might give her some advice on how to win at the tables, to which he answered: "Don't play."

The Grimaldi dynasty experienced its own period of transition in tandem with the upheaval at the SBM. In early June of 1922 the already frail Prince Albert took a hunting trip in the Pyrenees and caught cold. He died a few weeks later of pneumonia. Crown Prince Louis, then serving as part of the French military presence in Upper Silesia, was called to Monaco. New York's *Evening World* congratulated Louis on having "inherited the softest job on earth." The succession was not without controversy. A London butcher calling himself "The Most Noble Marquis George Frederick Grimaldi" claimed to be heir to the throne as a descendant of an eighteenth-century prince of Monaco. He said that Louis had no legitimate right to rule since he had been born of Albert's first marriage, which had ended in divorce. There were reports of the London pretender visiting Monaco, posting public notices and demanding that his claim be heard, but these came to nothing.

At fifty-two, Prince Louis II struggled to adjust to life outside the military. He hadn't spent much time in the principality and would never feel at ease among his subjects. Six feet tall and burly, he tended to intimidate people on first meeting them. He had little practice speaking in public and in private said very little. The locals called him "The Bear." In his official royal portrait, Louis posed as a stern military general, his breast festooned with medals and covered with a large sash, and his head topped by a severe flattop, a cockaded helmet in his right hand. He kept full-length versions of this portrait in all his residences. Even after taking the throne, Louis still spent nine months of the year at the estate in Marchais, where he had a telegraph put in to keep him up to speed. When he did come to Monaco he often dined alone at the Hôtel de Paris, where the house orchestra knew to greet his entrance with "The March of the Foreign Legion."

His official title read as follows:

LOUIS II, HONORÉ-CHARLES-ANTOINE, Prince Sou-
verain de Monaco, Duc de Valentinois, Marquis des Baux,
Comte de Carladès, Baron de Buis, Seigneur de Saint-Remy,
Sire de Matignon, Comte de Torigni, Baron de Saint-Lô, Baron
de la Luthumière, Baron de Hambye, Duc de Mazarin, Duc
de Mayenne, Prince de Château-Porcien, Comte de Ferrette,
de Belfort de Thann et de Rosemont, Baron d'Alktrich, Seigneur d'Isenheim, Marquis de Chilly, Comte de Longjumeau,
Baron de Massy, Marquis de Guiscard, Brigadier General of
the French Army, winner of the Grand-Croix de la Légion
d'Honneur, the Médaille Coloniale, and the Croix de Guerre.

When Louis ascended to the throne, his daughter, Charlotte,
and her new husband, Pierre de Polignac, also took more prominent
positions in Monaco's tight-knit social world. Pierre had courted
Charlotte early in 1920. That the dashing French aristocrat had, unlike many of his peers, seen action in the war may have added to his
appeal for the service-minded Charlotte. Pierre was a cosmopolitan
man-about-town, with pomaded hair, full, arched eyebrows, and
long eyelashes; he counted Jean Cocteau and Marcel Proust among
his closest friends. News items on the wedding of Pierre and Charlotte in the summer of 1922 reported that Monte Carlo's croupiers
had served as ushers for the ceremony, though such a detail sounds
too good to be true.

De Polignac took the title Prince Pierre Grimaldi and transi-
tioned far more smoothly than his father-in-law had into his regal
role. When one of Pierre's cousins spoke of accompanying the young
couple on the train from Nice to Monaco on the morning of their
wedding, he said that as they passed through the tunnel just before
Monaco's main station they heard cannon shots announcing their
arrival, and that "once we'd passed through the tunnel, a new Pierre
was born, and the old Pierre lost forever." The fractious marriage
ended in divorce in 1933, but in the 1920s Charlotte and Pierre

were briefly and brilliantly united in their modern sense of style and their shared love for the arts. An American society columnist described them as very much "of their day and generation, fond of sports and amusements."

The future prince of Monaco, Rainier Grimaldi, was born to Pierre and Charlotte in the summer of 1923. Zaharoff attended the baptism and presented the family with a fine gray pearl. A report in the *Washington Post* noted that French politicians in attendance were worried by the gesture, as they suspected Zaharoff—whom "no one doubts as being the true power behind Monte Carlo"—of being an agent for the British. The pearl had apparently belonged to a wealthy gambler who had pawned it, then killed himself after losing the money he received in exchange, and the *Post* piece closed with an eerie premonition: "The superstitious are suggesting that the Zaharoff pearl may prove an emblem of ill luck" for the Grimaldi line.

In the fall of 1924 Doña Maria's husband died, freeing her to wed Zaharoff. He was seventy-eight and she, fifty-six. A photograph snapped shortly afterward shows the pair in a Monte Carlo garden. Although it is a posed portrait of the newlyweds, Zaharoff, seated on a bench, looks as though he might have sprung up at any moment to rip the teeth out of the photographer's face. His enormous hands, gloved snugly in black leather, lent credence to his reputation as a former boxer and underworld thug. Well into its eighth decade, his body remained imposing, if softened by layers of thick tweed and the smallest of paunches. Even in that year of nuptial happiness Zaharoff in the photo has the unyielding stare of an assassin, meeting the camera's gaze on equal terms; his unsmiling face is a collection of straight lines gathering round an aquiline nose. There is little in the photograph to contradict the image of the black-hearted "Merchant of Death."

After so many years of bachelorhood, Zaharoff's wedded life lasted only seventeen months. Lady Zaharoff died of pneumonia in the winter of 1926 at the Hôtel de Paris. On the day of her funeral, a crowd gathered outside the Church of Saint Charles, a modest structure just a few hundred feet from the casino, to glimpse the grieving widower. Zaharoff's driver had taken a winding route to shake any reporters. He slipped in through a side door unnoticed. Looking uncharacteristically feeble in a heavy fur coat and slippers, he could only walk supported by his valet. There were few other mourners. Maria's body was transported to the Zaharoff estate in France, the Château de Balincourt, to be buried in the family crypt that Basil had recently built for the both of them. Riding in one of the cars making up the cortège, Zaharoff told a friend that he would never return to Monaco. There is no record that he ever did.

Days after the funeral, Zaharoff sold all his shares in the SBM to the French banking firm of Daniel Dreyfus, earning roughly three times his original investment. Some writers have interpreted the sale to the Jewish-owned Dreyfus bank as a deliberate act of defiance, revenge for the allegations in the Monaco papers that Zaharoff had been hiding Jewish ancestry. Zaharoff's right-hand man, René Léon, also Jewish, oversaw the transaction of shares to the new firm and survived the regime change. He soon heard the same cries of "wog" and "shylock" that had been hurled at Zaharoff.

The arms dealer retired from public life, spending his last years confined to a wheelchair, cared for by "six Hindoo [sic] attendants and a British secretary." The glee in news items such as "Mighty Man Of Mystery, Zaharoff Now A Cripple" is clear. "Once, kings, Prime Ministers, and statesmen were but puppets to this man, now he is as helpless as any kitten that might cross his path as he is being wheeled around his estate." Zaharoff died of a heart attack in 1936 at the Hôtel de Paris, falling into the arms of a "dry-eyed" valet who had been helping him dress. His body was taken to Balincourt to be laid next to that of his wife. The *New York Times* reported that only seven people attended his funeral. A year later, tomb raiders tunneled into the Zaharoff crypt looking for jewels. They managed to pry open Maria's casket, but Basil's was impregnable. They emerged empty-handed.

———

The SBM archives do little to confirm or deny the myriad reports of Zaharoff's supposed links to the casino. The only physical trace of Zaharoff is in a thin folder of clippings and memos from 1918. It is a typed copy of a letter presumably written by Zaharoff. At the top of the document someone—likely an SBM archivist—has marked: "Letter from Sir Basil Zaharoff, important shareholder in the SBM." In the margins the same pen has written that this is a letter from Zaharoff to a "Bethell," which may refer to Victor Bethell, a British peer and author of a book of Monte Carlo remembrances, though his memoir contains no mention of Zaharoff. The letter seems to have been penned in reply to this Bethell's application to become a member of the board of directors of the SBM. It is dated April 26, 1918, and has been sent from 53 Avenue Hoche. Zaharoff thanks Bethell for his "congratulations," though there is no clue as to what Zaharoff was being congratulated for. Zaharoff has written: "I had strongly recommended you to Monsieur Blanc right after you and I first spoke about this subject, and since my opinion has not changed at all, I'll reopen the matter with him."

The document would appear to make Zaharoff and Blanc intimates rather than enemies, at least in 1918. And here Zaharoff comes across as someone with the power to advise about candidates for the SBM's board of directors, a full five years before his supposed hostile takeover of the company. One wonders how the SBM archive—filled mostly with memos from managers and reports from the prince's representative at the casino—came to house this bit of private correspondence between Zaharoff and Bethell.

There are loose indications to corroborate the suggestions of the banking firm of Daniel Dreyfus's involvement in casino affairs. Jean-Louis de Faucigny-Lucinge, who briefly helmed the SBM after the Second World War, mentions in his memoir that he was one of four associates of Daniel Dreyfus to have joined the board of the SBM. But he says that this happened in 1932, and not in 1926, when most sources claim the bank acquired its stake in the SBM. There is no mention of Zaharoff in Faucigny-Lucinge's memoir. Matters are further complicated by a recent history of Monte Carlo published by the SBM itself, which includes the claims that Zaharoff "made the Hôtel de Paris his headquarters during the First World War" and "became for a time the second largest shareholder of the Société des Bains de Mer." Most perplexing of all is the fact this official company account maintains that "to impress his beautiful duchess, [Zaharoff] schemed the resignation of Camille Blanc. Camille however managed to unite all the small shareholders and so remained in charge of the company." This last claim is refuted by the SBM's own archives.

Whether or not Zaharoff in fact had anything to do with it, we cannot deny that Camille Blanc somehow lost control of the SBM in the spring of 1923. A company memo from that year, penned by the board of the SBM and addressed to Camille Blanc, explains the decision. There is talk of "this moment when we pass through a crisis of regime change in our management personnel," and of "the bloated spending of the recent years," and of the fact that "the men who have accepted the heavy burden of succeeding [Blanc] will perhaps bring their own new ideas and methods;" there is also discussion of "a pension of 150,000 to M. Blanc, given in the spirit of generosity." But there is no mention of Zaharoff.

One of the oddest pieces of archival evidence is a communiqué purportedly written by Zaharoff himself and published in the "Letters" section of the London *Times*. It is dated less than a week after the burial of Doña Maria and reads:

> Sir, You conclude the obituary notice of my wife, the Duchess of Villafranca, with the statement that I am the largest shareholder in the Casino of Monte Carlo, whereas during the 40 winters I have spent here I have never entered the Casino, which in no way interests me. I am, Sir, truly yours, BASIL ZAHAROFF. Monte Carlo."

By most accounts Zaharoff avoided all contact with the press.

One fact is indisputable: by 1923, René Léon—whether in any way associated with the Merchant of Death or not—was managing the casino's daily operation. One of Léon's earliest appearances in the SBM archives comes in the summer of 1923, where we find him responding tersely to some local shopkeepers who'd asked that the company purchase more goods and services from local purveyors, rather than going to French competitors. Léon, with his trademark haughtiness, answered that the SBM always put local commerce first—despite, he added, the obvious insanity in doing so, given the wildly inflated prices of Monaco's merchants. Léon also mentioned, in a postscript, that he planned to pass along copies of this exchange (including all the names of the indigent businessmen involved) to Prince Louis, for his personal records.

Léon would direct the SBM for more than a decade. With origins no less murky than Zaharoff's, he would transform the landscape of Monaco and its gambling resort more drastically than any single figure since the time of François Blanc.

12

SALVATION BY EXILE

*One could get away with more on the summer Riviera, and what-
ever happened seemed to have something to do with art.*

—F. Scott Fitzgerald, "Echoes of the Jazz Age"

FRANÇOIS BLANC HELMED THE SBM from his late fifties into his
seventies. When his son Camille lost control of the company he
was seventy-five and his alleged usurper, Basil Zaharoff, was sev-
enty-three. When René Léon started out in Monte Carlo he was a
bachelor in his thirties.

Some historians posit that Léon served as Zaharoff's right-hand
man during the First World War and that, after being planted at
the SBM, Léon won over enough board members to survive the
regime change when Zaharoff sold out. Those less convinced by
speculation about Zaharoff's ownership of the company suggest instead that René Léon came to the SBM through Léon Radziwill,
son of Louise Blanc and Prince Constantine Radziwill. This theory
holds that the two young men had served together in the war, and
that when Léon Radziwill became the nominal head of the SBM in
1923 (after his step-uncle Camille retired for legitimate reasons of
health, rather than because of a Zaharoff-led coup) he handed the
operation over to his more business-minded friend. Whatever the

succession story, to understand how and why René Léon reinvented Monte Carlo in the wake of the First World War, we must first travel back to the summer before he began his tenure at the SBM.

———————

In July 1922, the Cunard liner *Cameronia,* origin New York harbor, cut into Monaco's Port Hercules, shaded by the high rocks that seal the principality in on three sides. Eight hundred sweating passengers disembarked, determined to see the sights promised to them by dime-store novels, the society pages, and Thomas Cook. They left disillusioned. The Grimaldi castle was more flea market than fairy tale, most hotels were shuttered, and the streets deserted. No piles of gold spilled from the roulette tables, no glamorous courtesans whispered to confederate croupiers. There were no monocled counts in mufti, nor any ruined gamblers threatening spectacular suicide. The Monte Carlo casino was a hollow shell, empty save for a few small-stakes regulars.

Postwar inflation, austerity measures, travel restrictions, and the influenza pandemic conspired to all but ruin Monaco's tourist trade. The crumbling of the German, Austro-Hungarian, and Ottoman empires also spelled the end of several noble houses and with them many of the casino's best clients. Worst of all, from the SBM's perspective, was the Bolshevik Revolution. Camille Blanc would scan the papers daily, for whatever news he could get out of the east, reading stories of soldiers killing officers, of political executions, of villas burned, of lands seized. He would cross-check the company's prewar list of regular clients against another list to which he'd been adding names with alarming frequency, until the picture came into focus: for every three of his regular Russian clients, two had been killed off by war or revolution.

If the people who organized the *Cameronia's* stop in Monaco thought the place still exuded sufficient glamour to make it worth a visit, planning it for the height of summer was pure folly. Even during its prewar heyday, Monte Carlo, like the other Riviera playgrounds, had never had much traffic between May and September. To most Europeans of that era, a hot July day spent lying out half-naked on the sand, getting up from time to time to throw one's body under crashing waves, would have sounded like an exquisitely cruel form of torture.

But fashion is a fickle thing. Even as Monte Carlo foundered, scattered settlements just west of the resort teemed with new life, like the little rock pools dotting the shoreline.

In the same July that left *Cameronia*'s passengers so underwhelmed by Monte Carlo, the American painter Gerald Murphy and his wife, Sara, spent two weeks in Antibes with Gerald's friend from Yale, Cole Porter, and Cole's wife, Linda. Antibes at the time was a place where they turned off the phone service for two hours at noon so the operator could take her lunch, and then altogether after seven at night. The local movie house opened only once a week. Cap d'Antibes, the peninsula south of the main town, was more rustic still, undeveloped except for a few villas built on the leafy hills. The big attraction was the Hôtel du Cap, run by an Italian named Antoine Sella, though it closed each year for most of the spring and summer. This had been the arrangement for the more than thirty years that Sella had run the place.

Some travelers go out of their way to visit sites in their off-seasons, as it allows them to get away from the kinds of people who would presume to tell them exactly where to be and when to be there. The Murphys were such travelers, as were the Porters. Gerald said of Cole that he "always had great originality about finding new places." That summer the Porters had rented a vine-covered villa not far from the shuttered Hôtel du Cap, even though, as Cole Porter put it, they were "considered crazy" for doing so.

From the villa a gravel road led down to a beach the locals called la Garoupe, after their name for the breed of olive shrub found in the area. A thick tangle of seaweed covered the beach, but underneath the Murphys and Porters saw sand, light brown and fine, a welcome relief from the pebbly shores usually found along the coast. They shared the beach only with a few fishermen tending their skiffs. For Americans used to seasides built up with boardwalks, hot dog stands, and rigged carnival games, a stretch of sand devoid of tourists would have been a thrilling sight. Gerald said he and Sara and the children "dug out a corner of the beach and bathed there and sat in the sun, and we decided this was where we wanted to be."

———————

The search for some seemingly unsullied place like la Garoupe had been a large part of what had brought the Murphys to Europe the previous year. They crossed the Atlantic in June 1921 with their three young children for what became a more than decade-long sojourn on the continent. They left much behind, including a brownstone on West 11th in the Village and a solid wholesaling career for Gerald, had he wanted one. After graduating from Yale he'd taken up studies in landscape architecture at Harvard and had worked at the Mark Cross leather goods company, founded by his father, whom he was being groomed to replace.

But the setting had felt wrong. America, after having emerged as the world's superpower, was touted as big, open, and modern, but the Murphys found it small, provincial, and stagnant. Much of their dissatisfaction stemmed from the introduction of the Volstead Act in 1919. It was less about the hassle of having to sneak around to get a drink and more about what the Prohibition laws said about where the country seemed to be heading. "You had the feeling that the bluenoses were in the saddle," Gerald told his biographer Calvin Tomkins, "and that a government that could pass the Eighteenth

Amendment [prohibiting the manufacture, sale, or transportation of alcohol] could, and probably would, do a lot of other things to make life in the States as stuffy and bigoted as possible."

Many Americans shared the Murphys' disillusionment with the country in the wake of the war. Critics of the American cultural landscape felt that as the nation grew into an industrial giant it somehow lost its way. According to such thinking, Americans made great machines but lacked emotional depth; an assembly-line mentality prevailed. Gerald Murphy, who aspired to be a painter and proved himself a good one, worried that his peers cared more for their petty vanities than for art or beauty, for what Sara called "the simplest, bottomest things—the earth and all the elements and our friends." He complained of struggling to sustain conversations with men for more than five minutes without great effort, with such chit-chat inevitably turning to political platitudes or, as he put it, "the 1914 Cadillac vs. the 1914 Ford," and other matters that "smacked of the pavement."

Gerald had other reasons for feeling stifled. He struggled with his attraction to other men, which he called, in a letter to his friend Archibald MacLeish, "a defect over which I have only had enough control to scotch it from time to time;" one that made life "a process of concealment of the personal realities." He once wrote Sara, "I wonder if I shall ever recover from the feeling of being 'inspected' when with a group of men? I supposed the fact that I'm not the most comprehensible type to the average male mind accounts for a lot." A lapsed Irish Catholic, he was also overwhelmed by his mother's devout religiosity, and ashamed of his lack of excitement for his bright future in the family business.

For the restless couple the solution to their problems lay in a turn toward stranger skies. They weren't the only ones fantasizing about escaping across the Atlantic. Malcolm Cowley, a focal figure in 1920s expat Paris, wrote that for Americans "feeling like aliens in the commercial world" there was great relief in "the idea of salvation by exile. They do things better in Europe: let's go there." Despite the industrial violence of the war, many Americans still believed in a Europe somehow untouched by modernity, where life passed at a leisurely pace and all the pressures and conflicts of work and commerce melted into air. Edmund Wilson's explanation of why Edna St. Vincent Millay spent time abroad in the 1920s is telling: "Europe frightened her less than New York."

Yet those Americans traveling to Europe to flee what they perceived as the crushing burden of economic prosperity were able to do so because of these same financial advantages. Given the postwar inflation and favorable rates of exchange, American incomes went much further in Europe than they did at home, and the dollar held strong against the franc throughout much of the twenties. People who lived off trusts, such as the Murphys, found this an especially lucrative setup. Americans were also helped by the steady fall in the price of ocean travel that came with victory and the surplus of warships needing to be refitted for civilian purposes.

If Europe was the target, then Paris, historical epicenter of the great cultural soul, was the bull's eye. Self-imposed exiles came to the City of Light to be aligned with the rich legacy of French artistic production, seeking inspiration in the same environs that had fostered Baudelaire, Hugo, and Manet. Paris, at least according to romanticized American notions, was the kind of place where one could claim "artist" as a profession without eliciting a condescending smirk, the city that had attracted outsiders of all sorts, looking to work in peace and be surrounded by beauty. As Gertrude Stein wrote (in her jerky, elliptical style) in *Paris, France*: "Foreigners were not romantic to [the French], they were just facts, nothing was sentimental they were just there."

In Paris the Murphys befriended artists such as Fernand Léger and Pablo Picasso and became satellite members of Serge Diaghilev's Ballets Russes company. They helped out by painting sets and hosting parties to mark the debut of a new piece. Gerald recalled how

"Every day was different. There was a tension and an excitement in the air that was almost physical. Always a new exhibition, or a recital of the new music of *Les Six*, or a Dadaist manifestation, or a costume ball in Montparnasse, or a premiere of a new play or ballet . . . There was such a passionate interest in everything that was going on, and it seemed to engender activity." The couple floated money to several soon-to-be-illustrious friends. Igor Stravinsky remarked that Gerald and Sara "were among the first Americans I ever met, and they gave me the most agreeable impression of the United States."

Paris marked the beginning of a longer journey. Only when they reached the Côte d'Azur did the Murphys find what they'd been searching for. In Antibes they could imagine living the kind of life they wanted, and carved out a space there to suit their needs. They had stumbled upon what to their eyes was *terra incognita*. Though John Dos Passos, who spent much time in the South of France with the Murphys, described Antibes as "the sort of little virgin port we dreamed of discovering," for Gerald la Garoupe was as much about creation as it was about conquest. Every yard of beach he cleared of seaweed and driftwood and raked into orderliness was another yard he alone had brought into being. Though driven more by generosity than rapaciousness, he in many ways followed the longstanding tradition of explorers seeking to remake lands left 'wild' by a more 'primitive' local population to suit their own visions. Hiram Bingham had Machu Picchu and Howard Carter would have the Valley of the Kings; Gerald Murphy had his stretch of southern beach 3,500 miles from America.

Near the end of their two-week stay in 1922, the Murphys asked Antoine Sella if he might change his policy of closing the Hôtel du Cap through the summer, as they wanted to come back the following July. Devoting so many resources to so few guests was no doubt excessive, but the Murphys had money and style and they came from America, and the hotelier saw that if they wanted to be in Antibes in July and August, others would soon follow their lead.

Among those who came to see the Murphys in Antibes was F. Scott Fitzgerald, who based his novel *Tender Is the Night* largely on the time he and Zelda spent along the coast with Gerald and Sara. Early in the book a young actress named Rosemary Hoyt meets a glamorous expat American couple, the Divers, on "a short, dazzling beach" not unlike la Garoupe. "Do you like it here—this place?" Rosemary asks the Divers. Another character answers on their behalf: "They have to like it. They invented it."

———————

While René Léon was ensconcing himself as head of the SBM, the Murphys returned to Cap d'Antibes on July 3, 1923, with their three young children and a French nanny in tow. They were given free run of the Hôtel du Cap and its seafront restaurant Eden-Roc, with a cook, waiter, and chambermaid attending to their needs. They shared the place with a shy Chinese diplomat and his wife, who decided to stay on when they learned Sella planned to remain open through the season.

Sella was far from the only person charmed by the Murphys in those easy years, when they shone at their brightest, before everything went so terribly wrong for them. Gerald and Sara and their children had such vitality about them that people wanted to give them whatever they asked, just to play some small part in their golden story. Archibald MacLeish recalled how "Person after person—English, French, American, everybody—met them and came away saying that these people really are masters in the art of living." As John O'Hara wrote to Gerald many years later: "All your friends wanted to capture Gerald and Sara and their life—the life, the way of life."

The Murphys invited Picasso, his wife, Olga (a former dancer for Serge Diaghilev's Ballets Russes), their son, Paolo, and Picasso's mother to come visit them at the hotel. Gerald said that while together on the coast he and Picasso never talked about art, which pleased Gerald immensely. But Picasso clearly appreciated the region's mythic qualities; he drew neoclassical bathers on the Hôtel du Cap's stationery. Some years later, while living in Cannes, he remarked "It's strange, in Paris I never draw fauns, centaurs or mythical heroes . . . They always seem to live in these parts." Picasso was taken with the way Sara wore her string of pearls to la Garoupe, slung backward down her brown back (she liked to joke that it was "good for them to get the sun") and produced a few paintings and illustrations of statuesque women that look much like Sara, rendered with pearl necklaces slung over their backs. In *Tender Is the Night*, Fitzgerald also played on Sara's trademark accessory when describing Nicole Diver: "A young woman lay under a roof of umbrellas making out a list of things from a book open on the sand. Her bathing suit was pulled off her shoulders and her back, a ruddy orange brown set off by a string of creamy pearls, shone in the sun."

The Murphys came to call Antibes home—their "real home," as Honoria Murphy recalled her father saying of the town, and especially of the house they built there, which they dubbed the Villa America. Many American friends came to visit, including Ernest Hemingway. Those who could afford to rent villas provided for those who couldn't, so long as guests proved entertaining. "Even when you were broke," Fitzgerald recalled, "you didn't worry about money, because it was in such profusion around you." Hollywood arrived, at home under the imported palms. "It wasn't parties that made it such a gay time," Sara recalled. "There was such affection between everybody. You loved your friends and wanted to see them every day, and usually you did see them every day. It was like a great fair, and everybody was so young."

The Americans brought to the coast a relaxed sense of style and a flair for entertaining. The Murphys in their small way also helped to popularize sporting life along the Riviera; Gerald swam miles in the Mediterranean and practiced gymnastics and yoga on the beach.

And though they didn't dress fashionably for the times, others soon turned their look into high fashion. To describe the couple's way of dressing, an Italian such as Antoine Sella might have used the word *sprezzatura,* coined by a Renaissance diplomat in a guide advising courtiers that they might disarm their rivals by making "whatever is said and done appear to be without effort and almost without any thought about it." Still, if the Murphys' understated elegance was in fact highly calculated, no courtly cunning lay behind their breezy manner of dress. Sara would set up picnics on the beach, hair wrapped in a kerchief, a light backless dress, barefoot or in simple shoes; Gerald took to the striped cotton shirts favored by French seamen, complemented by linen pants or short swimming trunks and by the espadrilles he'd spotted in a boating store in Marseille.

Blue, white, and gold were the colors of the day. Ocean, sand, and sun.

———

The Murphys and their friends were not alone in "colonizing" the coast in 1923. That same summer Coco Chanel sailed along the Mediterranean with the Duke of Westminster, who liked to watch her lay out on the prow of his yacht, the *Flying Cloud.* Darker than any of the duke's deckhands, she helped start the vogue for tanning. "I think she [Chanel] may have invented sunbathing," said the European playboy Jean-Louis de Faucigny-Lucinge; "at that time she invented everything." Europeans woke up to the summertime charms of their own backyard and the coast became a "suburb" of Montparnasse, as Malcolm Cowley put it—the southern version of that hub of postwar Parisian artistic and intellectual life. The renaissance of the Victorine studios in Nice also added to the region's allure, as stars like Rudolph Valentino and Mistinguett came for work and the films shot there revealed the region's beauty to global audiences.

In similar fashion to the mixing of social classes of many nations at the Rhine casinos in the mid-nineteenth century, so along the Riviera were the gates of high society opening to anyone charming enough to get invited to the party. A letter Fitzgerald sent to a friend in 1926 reveals the incongruous mix of personalities and backgrounds: "There was no one at Antibes this summer, except me, Zelda, the Valentinos, the Murphys, Mistinguet [sic], Rex Ingram, Dos Passos, Alice Terry, the MacLeishes, Charlie Brackett, Mause Kahn, Lester Murphy, Marguerite Namara, E. Oppenheimer, Mannes the violinist, Floyd Dell, Max and Crystal Eastman . . ."

The region had been attracting writers for centuries. Homer's "wine dark sea," site of so many storm-tossed adventures, called out for new myths to be written. These were, after all, the hallowed lands of Nikaïa (Nice) and Antípolis (Antibes), where the Greeks planted olives, Phoenicians sought safe harbor, and the Romans built their great highway. Each villa seemed to have at least one writer in residence. Of the Fitzgeralds' Villa Paquita he briefly occupied in Juan-les-Pins, Hemingway said it had "everything that a man needed to write except to be alone." Virginia Woolf visited her painter sister, Vanessa, at her studio in Cassis and fantasized about buying a Riviera room of her own. "This island," as she dubbed Cassis in her journal, "means heat, silence, complete aloofness from London; the sea; eating cakes in the new hotel in La Ciotat; driving off to Aix; sitting on the harbor dining; seeing the seaside sardine boats come in. . . . Leonard in his shirt-sleeves; an Eastern private life for us both; and Indian summer running in & out of the light of common day; a great deal of cheap wine and cigars."

———————

The key to understanding this particular moment and its appeal to René Léon in Monaco lies in the loosely defined and largely unspoken ethos that emerged as this informal community of privileged summer revelers began to congregate in the established resorts and once-sleepy fishing villages along the coast. It was an ethos that championed anything fast, fleeting, and thrilling. Its proponents believed that time and talent should be spent in much the same way as money: on things of no lasting importance. "I am not a bucket but a sieve," the photographer and Côte d'Azur gadabout Jacques-Henri Lartigue said of his southern spending habits during those years. Too much brilliance, youth, and wealth had been wasted on war. To drink, dance, curse, swim, shout, and drive—these were the only goals. With the concept of duty to one's larger community badly compromised by the years of destruction, the Murphys and their entourage turned inward, devoting their energies to the cultivation of the self. They didn't assign a great deal of value on fixed allegiances or traditions. They preferred movement to stasis, superficiality over depth, and fleeting excitements over lasting relationships. By trying to experience time and space as intensely as possible, to burn their brightest, they sought to expand the limits of their personal boundaries and to mark their places in a disordered world. "The era stands alone," wrote Sarah Murphy, "but we did nothing notable except enjoy ourselves." The so-called "Lost Generation" haunted many corners of the globe, but amid the smell of eucalyptus and mimosa their gin-soaked nihilism took on a light-hearted playfulness.

The new tempos of the machine age drummed out on the serpentine roads, in the silvery waters, and in the skies above the mountains. The overriding sense of acceleration in the pace of life was reflected in the Villa America crowd's taste for, as Mary Blume has written, "cocktails that hit fast and hard, clipped speech, short nicknames, clothes that were thrown easily on, and off, and above all swift motor cars." With the automobile, no coastal sight felt too remote, nor any adventure beyond reach. Lartigue noted in his diary in 1921: "It's like magic, having an automobile down here, All you need to say is 'I feel like being in Cannes, I feel like being in Monaco,' and you're off, and you're there." An unsigned postcard sent from Nice to Bandol sometime in the 1920s reads as speed incarnate—no opening salutations, only: "Is the engine working? What a beautiful road! I'm leaving for Cagnes."

Previous generations had regarded those who practiced nomadic lifestyles—gypsies, tramps, runaways—with fear and loathing, but on the Côte d'Azur that same peripatetic existence became a form of celebration. The Murphys and their entourage did not see themselves as mere vagabonds. They were adventurers.

The importance of this distinction was not lost on the young Frenchman charged with revitalizing the fading resort twenty-five miles to the east of Antibes. He would be one of the few people to distill anything lasting and profitable from that fleeting moment marked by excess.

13

THE BLUE TRAIN

The great and beautiful Blue Train arrived, fully conscious of its superiority.

—*Menton and Monte Carlo News*, December 19, 1925

IF BY THE MIDTWENTIES the Côte d'Azur was booming once more, reinvigorated by the arrival of people like the Murphys, the problem for René Léon remained that people like the Murphys did not much care for places like Monte Carlo. They might come see a performance at the Salle Garnier or for the occasional cocktail at Ciro's, but mostly they avoided the place, deeming it a stuffy Victorian relic. When they wanted to gamble the Murphys preferred their local casino in Juan-les-Pins, and beach lovers like themselves would have been left cold by Monaco's rocky shoreline.

Léon recognized how badly Monte Carlo was failing this lucrative client base. Though not much of a drinker, he could have fit in comfortably among the revelers in Antibes. He was a keen sportsman and by all accounts a charming conversationalist. In photographs from the time, he looks every bit the Jazz Age boulevardier, with his homburg pulled down low almost to his eyebrows, which seem to have been heavily plucked, perhaps drawn on. Léon also possessed a desert dry sense of humor, ironic and detached, and could have traded barbs with a Dorothy Parker or Robert Benchley with ease. Responding to an engineer from Nice who claimed the ability to create artificial rain at any time of day and who wanted the SBM to hire him to install a rainmaking contraption in Monte Carlo, Léon wrote only five words in red ink: "Myself, I prefer the sun."

With this same lack of sentimentality Léon declared that the resort, barely six decades old, was already badly outdated and in need of rejuvenation. He wanted above all to attract the restless new breed of resort-hoppers who came to the coast armed with their Baedeker guides and, increasingly, their own automobiles, and who preferred exploring places that were still "undiscovered"—smaller towns such as Saint-Raphaël and Monaco's former territory, Menton. If the Murphys and their circle had unintentionally turned the idea of Riviera life into a kind of performance, Léon wanted to make Monte Carlo their preferred stage.

———————

Léon was no less able an impresario than Camille Blanc before him. He could be seen smiling broadly as he sauntered through the gaming rooms, joshing with the croupiers, putting his clients at ease. He spoke gently, with a habit of dropping his heavy-lidded eyes and then peeking up bashfully at his interlocutor. Some deemed this an affectation meant to disarm rivals and charm underlings into a false sense of camaraderie, but quite likely it stemmed from a genuine shyness, for though Léon could be found most evenings holding court at one party or another, he seems to have taken little pleasure from the high life. He ate spare and simple meals, smoked rarely, and though cocktails were often seen in his hands, drank very little. He began each day promptly at eight with a debriefing from Pierre Polovtsoff, son of a minor (and financially ruined) Russian noble, whom Léon had named president of the Sporting Club, quipping, "It's high time we had a gentleman in the administration." Their meetings took place in a small room on the Sporting's second floor, which Léon had converted into a makeshift living quarters. His days filled quickly: interviews with the press; matters of hiring and firing; financial forecasting sessions. As with Monte Carlo's founder, Léon had a brilliant mind for numbers, having been a math major at university before the war. Weekends he spent alone in his villa in Mont-Agel, which he named the Sanctuary.

Like his predecessors at the SBM, Léon wanted to strike an ideal balance between exclusivity and accessibility; he wanted Monte Carlo to be easily reached, yet not open to absolutely anyone. A steady stream was preferable to a flood. Léon was helped in this capacity by a new collaboration between the Wagon-Lits rail company and the PLM: the famed Blue Train service from Calais to the Côte d'Azur, which debuted with a limited run in December 1922, and was providing regular year-round service by the end of 1923.

As with Monte Carlo, the Blue Train was equal parts access and intimidation. It was an exclusively first-class service, though even if you could afford the tickets, you weren't guaranteed a seat. Places sold out months in advance and many riders procured theirs from well-connected friends rather than vendors. The service took train travel from technological reality to social idea—the idea being that either you were a Blue Train person or you were not. A Blue Train person did not simply reach his destination—he *arrived, fully conscious of his superiority.*

A well-worn piece of Blue Train wit held that the Riviera never quite equaled the excitement of the trip down. First were the tube-like carriages, painted bright blue with gold lining to distinguish them from the square brown cars found on standard commuters, promises of the sea and sun to come. Cars that normally seated fourteen in other services, on the Blue Train seated ten. The cars were upholstered in blue velvet and trimmed in mahogany. In the dining car (fresh-cut flowers, monogrammed plates, obsequious staff) they served five-course meals rivaling anything out of Paris. There was a live-eel tank and an onboard barbershop. Passengers remarked on the quiet and the stillness. Everything that rattled and squealed on other cars had been made fast and buffed into shining submission by workmen in Leeds. *The millionaire's train,* people called it. *The train of paradise.* "Happiness untrammeled," said the British travel writer Robert Byron of his time aboard.

Officially, it was called the Calais-Méditerranée Express. Although the route began at the northern tip of France, in the popular imagination it included London, since the bulk of the Calais passengers arrived there from the morning boat train from Victoria Station to Dover. After ferrying across the Channel and alighting at the Gare Maritime, the London passengers first glimpsed the shining cars whose regal color had inspired the train's nickname. Leaving Calais just before three, the train reached the Gare du Nord by dusk, and then headed across to the Gare de Lyon to hook onto additional carriages before a nonstop bolt overnight to the coast. Posters advertising the service encouraged travelers to "sleep [their] way from the City's fogs to the Riviera sunshine," but rest was surely far from many minds. The sleeping cars, until then usually kept a prim distance from one another, were on the Blue Train closely connected by way of concertina-like platforms, steps from where they served the cocktails. Sigmund Freud, who suggested a "compulsive link" between rail travel and sex, "clearly derived from the pleasurable character of the sensations of movement," would no doubt have understood the appeals of such a setup.

Passengers may have noted an unusual concentration of lovely young women on board, unaccompanied, flirting with equal skill in English and French. Charles Graves maintained that the SBM hired women to ride the trains and seduce riders to make sure they wouldn't disembark at any earlier resort stops before Monte Carlo. The casino supposedly covered the women's passages and hotel bills (though they were forbidden from staying at the Hôtel de Paris), and gave them some money for play. Graves claimed to be on a first-name basis with the five women first hired for the task. They were: Irene ("Titian hair, with languorous brown eyes. She was tall, and wore black and green mostly"), Jacqueline, Trixey, Pat, and Kathleen, whose favorite ruse was to pose as an American film star on holiday, incognito. She told her prey "that it would be her luck at the tables that would determine her length of stay there."

The train reached Marseille by breakfast. Passengers remarked on the pleasantly jarring experience of falling asleep to the sights of rain-darkened concrete and black countryside and then waking to sunrise over crystalline water. The scene was rendered all the more dazzling by coming in teasing glimpses as the machine passed through long stretches of blasted rock. Heading east, the service called at towns that were either already renowned resort destinations or became increasingly so thanks to their being part of this fortuitous route: Hyères, Saint-Raphaël, Cannes, Antibes, Juan-les-Pins, Nice, Beaulieu, Cap-d'Ail. The great panorama of the coast rolled by: commercial ports, naval ports, fishing villages, towns large and small, some past their primes, some just coming to life. Cutting through the landscape at such unprecedented speed, passengers were, like Gerald Murphy, made to feel their role in 'civilizing' a place that had long been considered wild. Above, the Massif des Maures gave way to the red Esterel mountains and finally to the Alpes-Maritimes. The train passed big green palms, olives, eucalyptus, all kinds of citrus, wide-canopied Aleppo pines. The greatest spectacle of all was the glistening Mediterranean, a sea, as Fitzgerald rhapsodized in *Tender is the Night,* "as mysteriously colored as the agates and cornelians of childhood, green as green milk, blue as laundry water, wine dark."

Paused at one of the stations, passengers would have smelled oleander, heliotrope, and mimosa, whipped up by the mistral winds. The trade in fragrance was big business here; up in his lab in the hills of Grasse a Russian perfumer named Ernest Beaux had been experimenting with enhancing the scents of local flowers with synthetic materials; in 1921, when he presented Coco Chanel with nine new fragrances, numbered in sequence, she chose No. 5, the key ingredient of which remains the jasmine of Grasse. These floral smells mingled with homier stuff: the waft of tomatoes frying in olive oil and garlic, of lambs on the spit, the chickpea musk of just-baked *socca,* thin as pancakes, wheeled down to the market stalls in warm drums on the backs of bicycles. Londoners, especially, in their tweeds and starch, must have marveled at the sight of wide-brimmed sun hats, parasols, patio chairs on red-bricked terraces, of men in their shirt sleeves laughing over a game of *pétanque,* of fruits and herbs and fragrance piled high to be sold, of tanned waiters squinting up from their work, trying to mask their obvious delight as another fresh batch rolled in.

The train reached Monaco in time for lunch, stopping first at the station near the palace and then at Monte Carlo proper, look-ing out at the *Tir aux Pigeons* that had lately opened its shooting competitions to women. Porters and drivers jostled to serve, flur-rying around the mountains of luggage. And while the train had come to a halt, one's own movement did not, since everything had been arranged to keep arriving passengers in motion. A gilded eleva-tor waited to take one straight to the casino's doors, the attendants chirping out *"Ascenseur! Ascenseur!"* On occasion—more frequently than any booster with a stake in the lie of nonstop sun along the Riviera cared to admit—arriving passengers avoided the elevator and the terrace altogether. Instead, they were led through a tun-nel from the station directly to the gaming rooms, safe from any spell-breaking rain.

Under the canopy of iron and glass at the casino's front entrance the "dress police" remained as vigilant as ever, at least according to Americans looking to poke fun at what they considered a vestige of centuries-old European class snobbery. Dorothy Parker quipped in the *New Yorker* about being refused entry to the casino one night in 1926 for having bare legs, saying, "I went and found my stockings, then came back and lost my shirt." Parker's friend Sara Murphy had her own version of this story. As Sara told it, she, and not Parker, was the one barred entry in Monte Carlo, until she outsmarted the doorman by using some eye pencil to draw lines down the backs of her legs to mimic seams. Harpo Marx, in his memoir, twisted the tale another way; he said that he'd tried to get in without wearing a tie until a tuxedoed "goon" blocked his way. So Harpo went round the corner, took off one of his black socks, and tied it in a bow under the collar of his polo shirt. The doorman, all smiles, promptly let him in.

Once admitted, patrons were charged an entry just as they had been in the days of François Blanc. Camille Blanc had not reinstated admission fees after he'd cut them during the war, but Léon preferred the elder Blanc's original policy. Entry now cost 10 francs per day, 100 per month, and 200 for the season. Léon also cribbed another move from the resort's founder, putting his own spin on Blanc's roulette publicity stunts, though with comparatively poor results. Each night, always at a different time and without any warning, Léon had a bell rung, and for the next half hour if the ball landed on the single zero, the round was discounted and no losing bets collected, meaning that the casino had no mathematical advantage over its clients. But the gimmick failed to catch on. Some particularly superstitious gamblers even complained about being denied the right to play their lucky number zero.

Léon, meanwhile, streamlined the SBM's internal operations. The company had grown fat, the legacy of decades of preferential hiring policies for Monégasques combined with the more recent need to give jobs back to men returning from war. Léon fired as many as nonessential employees as he could. He made no secret of his disdain for the older generation of workers that he inherited from Camille Blanc. Explaining the massive layoffs to an American

interviewer, he remarked that the "camaraderie among the old employees . . . approaches the proportions of *banditti*." He made an
offhand joke that in light of subsequent events sounded a deeply
ominous note: "Already they are calling me a reformer. I am going
slowly for I do not wish to start a revolution in the principality of
Monaco. You probably know Prince Louis has an army of only one
hundred soldiers, and the employees of the casino number more
than three thousand."

Even as Léon trimmed his operation, Prince Louis continued to
pressure him to hire more locals. Most of the company's top managers were French and only about a quarter of the croupiers were
Monégasques. Léon fired off angry letters to the prince about how
poorly suited his subjects were to casino work. "No sooner is an
employee hired, than he pleads on his Monégasque status to ask for
preferential treatment: a raise, a change of assignment, a promotion," he wrote; and unlike other SBM staffers, the locals had "great
difficulty" submitting to his discipline. He scoffed at the prince's
notion that he could hire any new employees at all, regardless of
nationality, since the SBM in his opinion already had a surplus of
one-third-too-many employees. His staff at that time so happened
to be roughly one-third Monégasque.

Unsurprisingly, Léon was not a favorite among the locals. Editorialists alleged that he was leading the resort to ruin through
his shortsightedness and the mistreatment of his employees. They
dubbed him Léon-le-saboteur. His critics said that he'd failed to invest in annual events that would attract repeat visitors, that he'd let
the local roads fall into such disrepair that cars were ruined just by
driving over them, and that he was so stingy with the gas supply that
there was hardly enough hot water for a single bath.

There were wistful elegies for how much better things had been
under Camille Blanc. There were also threats of darkness to come.
"The day the omnipotent, tyrannical Administration of the SBM is
faced with . . . a great collection of determined men, and not just

baying sheep, everything will change," wrote one local polemicist. "Then, finally, men will be paid according to their worth." Such complaints often came couched in anti-Semitic rhetoric. When a Monégasque writer criticized Léon for failing to make adequate repairs to a local church, he wrote "you can bet the SBM would take better care of St. Charles if it was a synagogue."

Léon meanwhile had to deal with the usual blackmail attempts and outlandish accusations normally associated with his line of work. In 1925 a California woman sued the casino, claiming that the SBM's medical staff had forced her to take an emetic against her will. She'd been losing steadily at roulette for a few hours, then stood up abruptly and took a vial from her handbag and swallowed a white tablet. Three guards grabbed her and rushed her to the surgery where a female attendant "administered the usual remedy." The woman maintained that she hadn't been trying to kill herself but had only taken an aspirin to soothe her headache.

Léon recognized that it would take more than publicity stunts and austerity measures to rescue the SBM from its doldrums. The key lay, as it always had, in shaping Monte Carlo's social and cultural life to suit the needs and tastes of the era's trendsetters. Not unlike François Blanc a half-century earlier, he wanted Monte Carlo to be a place where strangers feeling no deep or lasting allegiance to any force outside their immediate grasp could still coalesce, however briefly, into some kind of community, where people would feel free to live more boldly than they could at home, a place where, as Evelyn Waugh would later say of Monte Carlo, "No one can feel a foreigner." Faced with growing local unrest, he looked outward. To reinvent Monte Carlo, he first needed to enlist the services of one of the brightest cultural luminaries of the age.

14

A MONUMENT TO FRIVOLITY

Le Train bleu *is more than a frivolous work. It is a monument to frivolity!*

—Jean Cocteau

IN 1924 JEAN COCTEAU wrote a libretto for Serge Diaghilev's Ballets Russes that played to popular fantasies about the Côte d'Azur. He called it *Le Train bleu*. There were costumes by Coco Chanel. There was an overture curtain—two topless women running hand in hand by the water's edge—from Picasso. There was a frothy score by the avant-garde composer Darius Milhaud. There was Bronislava Nijinska dancing with a tennis racket. What there was not much of was a plot. *Le Train bleu* was light, meaningless, even a bit silly. But that was the point. In 1924 the world was light, meaningless, and even a bit silly, at least for the kinds of people who could secure a place aboard the real Blue Train, as well as tickets to see their Riviera amusements presented back to them as art.

On the eve of its debut at the Théâtre des Champs-Élysées in the summer of 1924, a Parisian critic suggested that the work perfectly captured "the color of our times," and when, after its Parisian run the Ballets Russes moved on to London, a reviewer there said that it was "as difficult to get a seat for *Le Train bleu* as it is to get a seat for the thing itself during the height of the Riviera rush." In other words, *Le Train bleu* was very good business for Monte Carlo. This makes sense, since the piece was developed in the resort, while Diaghilev and his Ballets Russes were on the SBM payroll.

The Ballets Russes may have been the most influential dance company of the twentieth century, but it rarely enjoyed financial stability during its twenty-year existence from 1909 to 1929. The company toured for months without pause, forever chasing the money and the applause. Eating was done in restaurants and sleeping in hotels, both usually on credit. Cocteau described Diaghilev "running from patron to patron, from hotel to hotel, from country to country, seeking the means to bring the luxuries he offered the world to life, devising ways to feed and house the multicolored retinue he brought in tow." Lacking the steady support enjoyed by state-funded companies, Diaghilev turned to a revolving network of society patrons—the ones that rival impresario Gabriel Astruc liked to call "*Mes chers snobs*, without whom no new artistic venture would prosper."

Sporting jet-black hair skunked with a streak of white left deliberately undyed ("Chinchilla," his friends called him), luxurious fur coats with opossum collars, and occasionally a monocle, Diaghilev could play the cultured cosmopolitan with ease, switching between French and Russian, peppering sentences with a few words of English for effect, as comfortable with royalty as he was among the grubbiest denizens of bohemia.

His own life had bridged East and West and high and low. He'd gone from a Saint Petersburg house full of servants to reinvention in Paris after his feckless father went bankrupt trying to keep up appearances befitting an officer and member of the gentry, while the income from the family's vodka distilleries dwindled steadily.

Diaghilev understood the importance of appearances, especially among the subset of the elite for whom mere wealth and position proved insufficient. He knew the comfort that came from bathing in the refracted light of art, which assured you that you were as beautiful and ingenious and modern as the works you patronized. Diaghilev saw himself as a kind of midwife to greater talents. In an 1895 letter to his stepmother he wrote: "First of all I am a great charlatan, although one with flair; second I'm a great charmer; third I've great nerve; fourth I'm a man with a great deal of logic and few principles; and fifth, I think I lack talent; but if you like, I think I've found my real calling—patronage of the arts. Everything has been given me but money—*mais ça viendra*."

A quarter century later, Diaghilev was famous but still waiting for the money to come. The year 1922 started off especially badly. He'd fled London to avoid angry creditors and the threat of jail. To keep afloat he borrowed money from the mother of one of his dancers, while trimming his troupe to half of the previous season's size. Igor Stravinsky, numbering among his many unpaid collaborators, wrote Diaghilev: "I realize you're having a hard time of it at the moment . . . I only wish I could help you. But how? If the music can't help you, what can?"

With Prince Louis's ascension to the throne in Monaco, Diaghilev thought he had found an answer to that question. The company's prewar Monte Carlo stops had been lucrative if fleeting, but now, with Princesse Charlotte and Prince Pierre becoming more active in the principality's cultural scene, he sensed an opportunity to set up a more permanent base in Monaco. He knew Charlotte and Pierre shared a passion for ballet and for his company in particular, and that they also harbored aspirations to ascend to the ranks of the great cultural benefactors of their time. It was clear that Pierre, wanting to take a bold first step to publicly establish himself as a serious supporter of arts, wanted to act as Diaghilev's champion and protector. Praising the young couple's fine taste, Diaghilev told his company régisseur early in 1922: "My idea is to establish ourselves at Monte Carlo, as a base for the winter from November to May. Madame de Polignac has promised to help me; and I see no reason why this should not come off."

By Madame de Polignac, Diaghilev referred to Pierre's aunt, Princesse Edmond de Polignac, whom Diaghilev liked to call one of his muses. Born Winnaretta Singer in New York, an heiress to the Singer sewing machine fortune, she'd married into an aristocratic family seeking ballast in difficult times by aligning itself with new American wealth. Reputations were made and broken in her salons. Despite all the forward-thinking energy of the modernist movement, and of the 1920s in general, the business of making art in Europe was then still very much rooted in a nineteenth-century system of patronage. Yet while the salons of Paris were the most vital centers of these networks of influence, there was also a great deal of money to be found along the Côte d'Azur: at tea in the gardens of the Villa Euphrussi de Rothschild in Cap-Ferrat, or among the cubist splendor of the Villa Noailles in the hills above Hyères, or at an outdoor spread at Villa America. Diaghilev knew this well. A list of names in his diary from the early twenties contains "Cunard, de Noailles, Radziwill, Rothermere, Rothschild, the Aga Kahn, the Count E. De Beaumont, the King of Spain, de Polignac." He titled the list: *Patronage M. Carlo*.

The SBM held the potential to be the biggest Riviera patron of all. Booking out the Salle Garnier for a whole season, with two months set aside for vacation, meant only having to fill four more months of the calendar. By the end of 1922, Diaghilev had brokered an agreement with the SBM that would steer the company toward stability, however fleetingly. The Ballets Russes would rehearse and perform rent-free in the Théâtre de Monte-Carlo for six months a year and in return promised not to tour anywhere between Saint-Raphaël and Genoa during that time. The SBM paid Diaghilev a "general grant" of more than two hundred thousand francs for the 1922 contract alone.

The benefits were not only financial. "We were to have a home at last," recalled dancer Lydia Sokolova; "Dancers who had been obliged to leave their possessions scattered in hotels throughout Europe—many since 1913—were at last able to settle down in flats or lodgings which were semi-permanent." By basing itself in Monaco, the Ballets Russes went from being on the periphery of Paris's art world to becoming what the dance historian Lynn Garafola has described as its "southern outpost." Developing new works in the resort built anticipation for their metropolitan debuts, as critics were invited to rehearsals to talk them up to readers back home. Diaghilev, eager to please his patrons, put on a mix of works meant to excite both the trendsetting members of the beau monde and those with more conservative leanings. He offered revived versions of old French operas, and commissioned neoclassical pieces, as well as the more avant-garde fare for which the company is best known. Erik Satie poked fun at his peer's pretensions to make the casino-resort into a cultural center, in one of the Parisian papers. "The state of music? . . . Hmm . . . Monte Carlo? . . . gloriously oversweet . . . A mixture of sex, un-sex, and emetics . . . Syrups of all kinds . . . Musical lemonade aplenty."

Being brought into Monaco's family fold meant performing certain favors. Diaghilev felt obligated to introduce Charlotte and Pierre into his circle and arranged a private visit to Picasso's atelier. He also tried but failed to convince Picasso to paint the couple's portrait. When Charlotte decided to take up ballet shortly after giving birth to Rainier, Diaghilev deployed one of his principal dancers to give her private lessons twice a week. Sokolova remembered the distraction of having Charlotte ("small, dark and pretty") and Pierre ("very tall with fair straight hair and immaculately dressed") drop by rehearsals unannounced. The dancers would stop whatever they were doing, until two high-backed red-and-gold chairs were brought out for the royal pair. These happened to be set up directly in front of the door leading to the dressing rooms. "Although we appreciated the honour of having a visit from our princely patrons," said Sokolova, "we also found it most inconvenient to not be able to disappear or tidy up in between our classes and rehearsals."

———————

At one such rehearsal Cocteau conceived of *Le Train bleu*. A new member, Anton Dolin, had joined the group after a former dancer spotted him in an amateur production in London and recommended him to Diaghilev, always on the lookout for fresh talent. Dolin was born Patrick Kay in Sussex but, following standard Ballets Russes operating procedure, had been rechristened in this more exotic guise. Impresario and dancer were romantically involved and the other company members received Diaghilev's new favorite coldly. Dolin remembered those first days in Monte Carlo as among the loneliest in his life. He tried to win over his colleagues during a break in rehearsals, showing off some fancy acrobatics, walking on his hands, somersaulting and flipping and landing hard on his knees and springing back up into a slick cartwheel.

Meanwhile Cocteau was in Monte Carlo getting over the death of his lover Raymond Radiguet, a recuperation that seems to have consisted mainly of smoking opium in a hotel with some composer friends from Paris. "Voilà—I suffered a great loss, and I ran away," he wrote to an editor friend from the resort. Cocteau later said that after Radiguet's death, "my nervous suffering became so unbearable, so overwhelming, that Louis Laloy [a Parisian critic and friend] at Monte Carlo suggested that I relieve it this way. Opium is a living substance. It does not like to be forced. At first it made me sick. Only after a fairly long trial did it help me." Watching Dolin's acrobatics, perhaps under the influence of what became a lifelong habit, Cocteau had the idea for a piece that would showcase the young man's athleticism while trading on the growing fashion for sporting life on the Côte d'Azur. Cocteau shared with Diaghilev a knack for working the "vulgar" to suit the tastes of the smart set. He gave metropolitan audiences the thrill of the circus, the carnival, and the brothel, sleekly repackaged for the box seats.

While written in an elliptical style, Cocteau's libretto is full of obsessive details that must have driven the choreographer Nijinska crazy.

SCENE II

The door of the cabana opens. A bather (*in a swimsuit*) appears. He poses in the cabana. The tarts [as Cocteau dubbed the female side of the corps de ballet] group themselves to the right in graceful attitudes. (*One points to her breasts; another puts a finger over her mouth; a third lies down and shakes her legs.*) Think of the groups as they finish the quadrille at the Moulin Rouge. The gigolos [Cocteau's term for male members of the corps] come looking for the bather and hoist him up in triumph. (*Look at pictures of boxers carried in triumph after a match.*)

Nijinska—pale face devoid of makeup, bright blond hair pulled back into a severe little bun, eyebrows unshaven in rejection of the prevailing style among the women of the corps—had little interest in the kinds of superfluities Cocteau described. Unlike the work's other principal collaborators, she was decidedly not a Blue Train person. Language barriers worsened matters. Diaghilev tried to act as translator and go-between. "Ask Nijinska how she's feeling about me," Cocteau wrote to Diaghilev. "I am not going to make a move unless I am sure she will listen to me, for ridiculous diplomatic games are useless."

The composer Milhaud finished the score in less than three weeks, but hated its dumbed-down mix of polkas and waltzes. He later said that he'd only been hired because Diaghilev wanted to trot out Dolin as soon as he could, and Milhaud had a reputation for working quickly.

Diaghilev opened rehearsals with a grand speech, telling his dancers: "You are already acquainted with the poetry of machinery, skyscrapers, transatlantic liners; now you must absorb the poetry of the streets, their tempo, and think seriously about it. You must not let the 'banality' of this new music of the future frighten you off. Diaghilev's Russian Ballet, the first ballet in the world, cannot afford to mark time, cannot be content with yesterday, or even the present alone. It must forestall the future, and predict *tomorrow*; must lead the masses and discover what no one has discovered before."

Rehearsals were exhausting. "Working all day and every day on a salary of 1,500 francs per month loses its glamour," remarked one of the dancers. Nijinska, meanwhile, worried about Dolin's unimpressive technical skills. When rehearsals moved from Monte Carlo to the Mogador theater in Paris, the dancers, already on edge, were intimidated by the stars who dropped by to watch them: Misia Sert and Coco Chanel one night, Nijinsky, another. Dolin remembered how in the anxious days leading up to the debut, Princesse Charlotte "would suddenly arrive in the middle of rehearsal, as she did so many times in Monte Carlo. There would be a break—the men would bow and the women curtsey—and then the rehearsal would continue as if they were not there." Nijinska hardly noticed or cared who was in the crowd. A Parisian critic, after describing the stars in attendance at a rehearsal, reported that Nijinska saw "nothing but her dancers, hears nothing but the allegro rhythm of the piano. It is as though her whole being is possessed by some magnificent demon." The principal dancers flubbed the final dress rehearsal, which ended with a screaming fit from Cocteau and Nijinska in tears.

———

Le Train bleu was the only ballet to debut in Paris that summer, which was one of the hottest in the city's history. The timing was good for a work about beachside fun and the body beautiful. When the one-act "danced operetta" (as Diaghilev called it) opened on June 10, 1924, the city was playing host to the Olympic games, whose breakout star, the swimmer and Riviera regular Johnny Weissmuller, later played Tarzan on film. Athleticism, no longer considered 'unfeminine,' was growing into a big business. By the close of the decade, the designers Jeanne Lanvin, Coco Chanel, Jean Patou, and Edward Molyneux had all opened sportswear boutiques, with locations in Paris and along the Côte d'Azur.

Nervously, from the back row, Diaghilev watched the opening night unfold. The piece began with a short fanfare from Georges Auric, as Picasso's curtain parted to reveal the sculptor Henri Laurens's Cubist fantasy of a seaside resort. Picasso never produced another work for Diaghilev, who continued to use the curtain to open other Ballets Russes performances for many years. (Artists gossiped about the perils of being seduced by the "great charmer." Henri Matisse told a friend: "What Diaghilev wants is my name; [he] is very nice when he needs us.") On stage were two lopsided cabanas reminiscent of the ones Gerald Murphy had recently set up at la Garoupe. A pair of oversized fish in mid-dive flanked the scene. Coco Chanel, who may also have put some of her own money into the production, had designed rubber slippers for the dancers. These were totally unsuited for ballet, as were the hand-knit bathing suits she'd also made, which were impossible to grip, but audiences loved them. The striped tricots, also by Chanel, were likely inspired by the uniforms she'd seen the crew wearing aboard the Duke of Westminster's *Flying Cloud*. The dark suede bathing caps and large pearl stud earrings worn by the dancers soon formed part of the decade's must-have resort uniform.

The piece comprised a disjointed series of flirtations shared by a few fashionable tourists during a day at an unnamed Riviera beach in 1924. Dolin's sunburnt "Beau Gosse" (Handsome Lad)—greased hair, daring bathing suit cut high up on the thigh—worked to impress the assorted beachgoers with cartwheels, somersaults, and trampoline work. Sokolova danced as Perlouse, a seaside flapper draped in georgette, while Nijinska danced the role of the Tennis Champion, based on Wimbledon winner and Riviera fashion plate Suzanne Lenglen. Her costume referenced the trademark bandeau Lenglen used to tame her long hair, fastened with a diamond pin. Sokolova's husband, Léon Woizikovsky, danced the part of The Golfer, a nod to the Duke of Windsor. Woizikovsky went on to lose much of his and his wife's salaries at the tables, talking his way into the casino through the kitchen since, being under SBM pay as a member of the Ballets Russes, he was forbidden from playing.

Save for a pleasant waltz, which Nijinska based on a ballroom dancing duo she'd seen at a Monte Carlo hotel, the choreography was stilted and unsettling. It featured much rigorous machinelike movement. Performers ran in place, then stopped sharply to gaze up at imaginary planes flying overhead. At other times they moved as if in a slow motion sequence, before freezing their poses in midaction, as if for a magazine spread. But audiences ate it up. They enjoyed seeing dancers smoking cigarettes and wearing sunglasses and flashy wristwatches. The outfits were tight, the figures toned and lean, the legs bare. One could easily get lost in all the cabana antics and swinging of rackets and clubs.

The point of Cocteau and Diaghilev's story was that there was no point and no story. To be a part of Blue Train crowd was to reject the idea of linear narrative—the love won forever, the opponent bested, the deeper lesson learned. Postwar resort life, at least as imagined in *Le Train bleu,* was a collection of moments, an onrushing flood of pleasures, of posing and of being posed for, of showing off one's body and the things it could do, of getting into and out of dangerous and brief liaisons, of being entertained by the sight of something shiny and new rushing by and then running off to be distracted by the next novelty. On this Riviera beach there were no loves to be won forever, and no opponents to be bested, and the search for meaning was a waste of time.

Wedged between ads for high-end sportswear boutiques, Peugeot automobiles, and Hermès luggage, Diaghilev included an introduction to the program, writing: "The first thing one notes about *Le Train bleu* is that it has no blue train. This being the age of speed, it has already reached its destination and dropped off its passengers. We can see them on a beach that does not exist in front of casino that exists even less. Above will pass an airplane that you won't see, and whose presence is in fact meaningless." With this bit of wit Diaghilev tended to some serious business. With a sly *coup de plume* he slipped in some editorial advertising for the wealthiest patron he ever charmed, the SBM. Indeed, while the casino never appears in *Le Train bleu,* and "exists even less," its influence over the proceedings is undeniable.

———————

While Diaghilev might have enticed a few Parisians and Londoners to come see the coast for themselves, this alone would not be enough for Monte Carlo to reclaim its prewar title of "Jewel of the Riviera," as René Léon knew well. Besides which, Parisians and Londoners were increasingly yielding to newcomers from across the Atlantic as the leading arbiters of taste. Now Léon wanted an American's perspective.

15

ENTER ELSA

Elsa wasn't a vulgar woman. This is hard to explain to someone who never knew her, because she looked vulgar . . . She always dined with kings. Nice kings.

—Diana Vreeland on Elsa Maxwell

SOMETIME IN 1926 PRINCE PIERRE summoned the American publicist and society maven Elsa Maxwell to lunch in Monte Carlo, likely at the urging of René Léon. Maxwell was already a familiar figure in the principality. She'd celebrated her fortieth birthday (which was in fact her forty-second birthday) in the resort in 1923 with a fantastic party, whose guests included the Aga Khan and Serge Diaghilev. It had featured two short pieces by the Ballets Russes, which Maxwell later said were premiered in her honor. Maxwell had known Pierre socially even before his marriage to Charlotte. No noble was too minor for her to befriend, and the de Polignacs were hardly minor. But she suspected the Monte Carlo invitation had something to do with a job. For Maxwell the luncheons and the cocktails and the dinners all ended up being about work in one way or the other.

That in 1926 a European prince should invite the professional counsel of an American woman was unusual, but then Elsa Maxwell was an unusual woman. She established herself as one of the premier press agents in Europe while the public relations industry was still gaining legitimacy on that continent. Of her meeting with Prince Pierre, Maxwell said that when she described herself as a "press agent" he struggled to understand the term; *entrepreneuse* was the closest translation he could summon for her line of work. She wasn't someone easily squeezed into a single job title. Press agent, songwriter, theater impresario, editor, nightclub owner, author, event planner—even strung together such descriptors fail to capture the range of her talents. Still, for all its breadth, each step of her career marked a variation on a single and deceptively simple premise: find out what story people wanted to hear and give it to them. To Maxwell it mattered less how the story got told than that her audience left happy.

Her best public relations work lay in crafting her persona to suit the needs of the popular press. Recognizing that any journalist has a weakness for the exaggerated and the simple, she made sure that everything she did was big and easy to grasp. When Elsa Maxwell spoke about Elsa Maxwell—which was often—she spoke in headlines.

She claimed to have been born in 1883 in Keokuk, Iowa, in the middle of a performance at the local Opera House, where she came out yelling "louder than the dreadful mezzo soprano." A fitting birth for a woman with a big mouth and a keen ability to discern talent in others, but a lie. She had indeed been born in Keokuk, but in the less exciting confines of her grandparents' home, and in 1881, not 1883. And her just-a-plainspoken-girl-from-Iowa routine belied a childhood spent mostly in San Francisco's Nob Hill. The Maxwells left Keokuk a few months after the birth of their only child.

The outsized personality matched an outsized body. Hers was more big than it was soft, a solid and determined bulk. After she took a tumble during a party aboard the Guinness yacht, one waggish columnist assured his readers that the ship was expected to survive. She possessed a round and jowly face, with small dark eyes framed by bushy eyebrows and puffy bags below. Maxwell would be the first to bring attention to her own unattractiveness, so long as a reporter was listening. She liked telling the story of how she'd won a beauty contest as a child, which she offered as a warning to boastful parents. "I'm certainly not vain," she said. "Just look at me—what do I have to be vain about?" Such statements weren't meant to be self-effacing but rather the opposite, more examples of her ability to spin whatever raw material was at hand into the most crowd-pleasing tale possible. She knew what people wanted to read about a woman shaped as she was: Elsa Maxwell is fat and Elsa Maxwell is ugly and Elsa Maxwell does not give a damn what you think of her. "Fat, 40, and Funny," read the headline of a 1930 profile.

She could swing wildly between self-deprecation and egotism. An example, from her ghosted memoir *RSVP: Elsa Maxwell's Own Story* (note the use of the third person, stylistic device of narcissists worldwide): "Clothes? There was a running gag that Elsa Maxwell always traveled with fourteen trunks and a hatbox—the trunks for her clippings and the hatbox for her other dress. A base canard. I didn't own another dress . . . It was just as well that my vanity was as negative as my bank account. I didn't have the figure or the flair for wearing clothes [and] I circulated in a set where chic clotheshorses were a dime a dozen. While they were knocking themselves out trying to look distinctive, I achieved the same effect by making my one suit and dress my trade-marks. Ask the veteran habitués of Paris society who was the best-dressed woman in the early 1920s and you'll get a dozen different answers, but the nomination for worst-dressed woman stops with me."

Such self-mythologizing necessitated a flexible approach to the notion of truth. Maxwell in her autobiography devoted two pages to railing against what she described as "the shocking increase in homosexuality as further evidence of decadence in the top levels of American and European society," yet she lived for half a century with another woman, Dickie Fellowes-Gordon, whom she described in the same book as "a tall, stunning girl who was—and still is—the best and most helpful friend I have ever known." Only an expert fabricator could pull off the public tightrope walk required of someone seeking to portray herself as both the tastemaking doyenne of European high society and a tough-talking American outsider. Yet her tendencies to fabricate and exaggerate did not apply when it came to listing her famous intimates, whom she considered close allies, handpicked because of this or that talent to join her coterie. "I next met Einstein at Charlie Chaplin's home in Hollywood," reads a typical Maxwell sentence. Where someone who enjoyed such proximity to real wealth, influence, and fame might be easily fooled into thinking herself of equal status, Maxwell recognized that she only served as the conduit for currents that started before her and ended somewhere after. She made her living by being a vessel for other people's stories. When she described her friends as her "greatest riches" she wasn't being sentimental.

———————

Maxwell first gained prominence in Paris in the early twenties as a high-society hostess and party planner. To speak of Americans in postwar Paris is to conjure images of young bohemians in the garrets and cafés of the Left Bank, getting by on wine, sex, and art—perhaps the occasional good meal if you were lucky enough to be invited to Gertrude Stein's or had cadged a loan off of Sylvia Beach—the rose-colored Hemingway Paris, in "the early days," as he put it, "when we were very poor and very happy." But Hemingway could self-mythologize on a par with Elsa Maxwell and in truth the expat crowd in Paris was neither as bohemian nor poor as all that. In a piece for the *Toronto Star* in 1922 Hemingway himself described the lush life he was living in Paris, replete with a fine restaurant down the street from his "comfortable hotel in the Rue Jacob," where for roughly fifty American cents diners could enjoy meals of "beef, veal cutlet, lamb, mutton and thick steaks served with potatoes prepared as only the French can cook them."

While Hemingway might have been imagining himself poor and happy in Left Bank Paris, there were more than a few wealthy Americans in the city after the war, as made clear by the presence of Gerald and Sara Murphy ("these rich," as Hemingway poisonously dubbed the couple years later in what would become *A Moveable Feast*). These were the Americans of the Right Bank, the ones who were met with smiles rather than glares as they passed through the gilded lobbies of the American banks on the Place Vendôme. One spotted them having dresses made by the celebrated couturiers of the Rue de la Paix, or dining at the Ritz, or in the loggias of the Opéra, or at nightclubs such as the Boeuf sur le Toit or Zelli's near the Place Blanche. One spotted them also at soirées hosted by Elsa Maxwell.

Not that a Maxwell party was ever an Americans-only affair. She sought out all the boldface names of the era, with a particular fondness for royalty. Attending a Maxwell fête, whether in Paris, London, or Venice, became a favored pastime among the more trend-conscious members of the aristocracy. An American journalist said that in Paris, Maxwell served as "a sort of liaison officer between her fellow countrymen and titled Britons, who liked her zest." She seemed so comfortable in her own body and so full of joy that guests couldn't help but feel at ease in her presence. Even the stiffest upper lips broke into bawdy laughter around her. Look at the photographs of Maxwell from this time and you will find that she's almost always smiling.

Members of the European *grand monde* were drawn to Maxwell's events because they unfolded so differently from those they normally encountered while doing the rounds of the European social circuit. They were like little pieces of theater. Where else could one see a parade of trained seals let loose on the dining hall just as the fish course was served? Or take part in a scavenger hunt (a game Maxwell is credited with inventing) through the streets of Paris in search of "a slipper taken from Mistinguett on the stage of the Casino de Paris; a black swan from the lake in the Bois de Boulogne . . .

three hairs plucked from a redheaded woman . . . a pompon off the cap of a French sailor . . . and a handkerchief from the house of the Baron Maurice de Rothschild?" A good party unfolded like a good story, as Maxwell counseled would-be hosts and hostesses. She encouraged her readers to think differently about how they structured their evenings. They might, for instance, "run the party backwards."

When she suggested that "the best parties are given by people who can't afford them," one might assume she meant to be inspiring, suggesting that anyone could come up with evenings as winning as hers. But in reality she spent great sums on her entertainments and on other ventures, including two failed nightclubs she ran in Paris with the designer Edward Molyneux, who lost a fair amount in the process. Maxwell always made sure that whatever funds she spent came from someone else. She herself "never had a cent," as Diana Vreeland wrote of her friend. "She'd stay in any hotel that would pick up the tab."

In Monaco, Maxwell would again be spending other people's money. Prince Pierre waited until after the garçon had taken their orders before raising the matter, and then, like any good aristocrat, did so indirectly, by asking his guest about her recent work for the city of Venice. Elsa told him how the project had come about. They knew her in Venice in the early twenties as a thrower of wild parties and for being friends with Cole and Linda Porter, who'd rented a three-story palazzo, complete with private gondola, on the Grand Canal. Maxwell and the Porters stood out in Venetian society, as the city was not fashionable among Americans just then. The *podestà* of Venice had asked her advice on how to bring her countrymen to the city, complaining that while women were naturally drawn to its "romantic atmosphere of Byron, Shelley and Browning," men seemed to prefer visiting other places, and no one wanted to be there in the summer. Maxwell suggested that introducing sporting life to Venice would bring the men, Americans in particular, and would keep them there through July and August. They should host motorboat races, aviation displays, waterskiing contests. They could give out trophies. She said she knew of a strip of land a few miles up the coast that would make for a good golf course. The Lido beach, then catering to Italian families on a budget, should be taken upscale. She would continue to host her parties, but now in the service of Venice, and for a fee.

Under Maxwell's watch Venice soon boasted a floating nightclub, known as the *galleggiante*, or 'dance boat,' on a string of barges draped in faerie lights with a jazz band from Paris playing in the moonlight. The *galleggiante* made only one journey out onto open water—people complained about the slippery dance floor and lack of bathrooms—but stayed in use for some time afterward, tethered to a dock. Decades later, Maxwell and Porter each claimed credit for dreaming up the floating club. In a letter to his paramour Boris Kochno, Serge Diaghilev (assumedly with a heavy dose of irony) described how "the whole of Venice is up in arms against Cole Porter because of his jazz and his Negroes. He has started an idiotic nightclub on a boat moored outside the Salute, and now the Grand Canal is swarming with the very same Negroes who have made us flee from London and Paris. They are teaching the 'Charleston' on the Lido Beach! It's dreadful. The gondoliers are threatening to massacre all the elderly American women here. A few years later a writer for *Fortune* reporting on Venice's resurgent tourist trade as part of a larger piece about Italy's economic strides under Mussolini wondered if Maxwell had single-handedly "put the Lido on the map." Maxwell later claimed that Mussolini presented her with a medal for her services, which she returned when she learned "the true nature of fascism."

In her autobiography Maxwell recalled that when she told Prince Pierre about her Venice work, it became apparent that he'd had more than an "academic interest" in rehashing her résumé. "We need a similar effort here," he told her. "Monte Carlo is dying." Pierre couldn't understand why tourists swarmed to every other town along the coast but Monte Carlo. It was as though the resort was a sick patient, quarantined from the rest of the Riviera. He asked Maxwell: "Why are we missing the boat?"

"You're not rendering proper homage to the new king," she answered.

"Which king?"

"*Le Soleil,* the sun. Life has moved outdoors. People come to the Riviera to relax, to get away from formality. They want to play on the beach and in the water. You've got the water. Get a beach if you want tourists."

After which Maxwell immediately laid out detailed instructions on how to bring "the middle-class tourist, the backbone of the business," to Monte Carlo: "Build a new summer casino with facilities for entertainment. Build a hotel, a swimming pool. You don't need much space for tennis courts. Stage an international tournament every year after the Wimbledon matches when all the great players of the world are in Europe." When the prince balked at the cost of such projects, Maxwell answered with a phrase that would have been banal to Americans but less so to a member of the European aristocracy: "You've got to spend money to make money."

Her work for the SBM would make the Venice job look small by comparison. Venice had canals, but here she had the whole Mediterranean to play with. Maxwell could see, as François Blanc had seen decades earlier, that Monte Carlo's natural setting was as important an asset as its gambling laws. With his youthful energy and admiration of American styles and sporting pursuits, René Léon was headed in the right direction, but he hadn't fully capitalized on the sea that rolled right in front of his casino. No one could deny that Monte Carlo had been the great winter resort of the Belle Époque, but the Belle Époque was dead and so was winter.

Maxwell understood, earlier than most, that the tourist trade, as with public relations and party planning, was just another form of storytelling. Monte Carlo's difficulties could be traced to a matter of genre. The Blue Train crowd avoided the resort because they believed it offered them only stuffy Victorian romance. They preferred the lesser-known beach towns along the Riviera for the same reason people were flocking to the theaters to see Douglas Fairbanks as Zorro and Ramón Novarro as Ben Hur. They wanted adventure.

———————

Léon hired Maxwell as a publicist for the SBM, paying her an annual fee of anywhere between $5,000 and $20,000—Maxwell cited different figures at different times. The numbers were never meant to be more than impressionistic, such details serving little purpose in her life; the only reason to define the amount of her pay was to set up yet another self-abasing and self-serving punch line: "As usual, I wound up working for nothing. I promptly lost the money on the roulette wheel." She wrote that she must have escaped the SBM's ban on anyone in its employ from gambling at Monte Carlo, either because "the croupiers didn't know I was on the Société's payroll, or they could not resist the temptation to take a novice for a ride."

This may be true. Or it may be another one of Maxwell's well-spun Monte Carlo stories.

———————

In histories of Monte Carlo, the late 1920s are offered as the most glamorous years in the resort's existence. And they were, thanks in large part to the work of Elsa Maxwell, in terms of the attractions offered, the celebrities who frequented the resort, the amounts of money that flowed into the casino's coffers, and the general sense of postwar abandon that is palpable in the photographs from the time: smiling faces, skimpy bathing suits, bands playing in the sun, tanned men in white dinner jackets serving drinks poolside. Less present in the popular memory of this era are the human costs and conflicts that simmered below this shining surface. For these same golden years were also marked by scandal, violence, and tragedy.

16

THE FAST LIFE

*The one thing that was evident was that all here [in Monte Carlo]
were healthy, vigorous people with the lust of life in their veins,
eager to be entertained and having the means in the large majority
of cases to accomplish this end.*

—Theodore Dreiser, *A Traveler at Forty*

EARLY IN THE SPRING of 1926, René Léon sped through the
small French town of Plainoiseau in his roadster. He lost control of
the car, struck a young girl, and fled the scene. The girl, whom we
know only by her last name of Magnin, survived her serious injuries.
The French police caught Léon and he was sentenced to fifteen days
in jail and fined five hundred francs, though it doesn't appear that
he was ever made to serve his sentence.

The crime and its handling caused a furor. The editor of *Le
Monégasque* said Léon lacked the "dignity" required to oversee an
organization so vital to the people of Monaco and that if he had any
shred of honor he would "pack his bag and leave the principality in
shame." The editor claimed that Léon escaped his penalty thanks
to two influential men: the current French prime minister Louis
Barthou, whose brother held a top SBM post, and Léon Blum, a
future French prime minister, whose brother also worked for the
SBM as director of ballet at the Monte Carlo Opera. That the powerful Blums and René Léon were all Jewish did not go unnoticed;

according to *Le Monégasque*, the SBM boss wielded power with "the Synagogue and the International Bank." The scandal made its way across the ocean. A writer for the *Washington Post*, reporting erroneously that the young Magnin had died from her injuries, told readers that the outrage over the accident gave only small indication of a much deeper unrest in Monaco that had been building for years, and that the Monégasques had "opened war" on the casino. An unnamed representative of the "common people" was quoted saying: "Blow the Casino into the sea and Monaco would be a better place for all." In the aftermath of the accident Léon received threatening, unsigned letters.

Meanwhile the parties and galas went on. Magazines catering to English speakers on the Riviera listed the luminaries seen trading bons mots with René Léon and Elsa Maxwell at the Hôtel de Paris: Suzanne Lenglen, Lord Rothermere, Jascha Heifetz, the Duke of Westminster, Princess Orsini, King Gustav V of Sweden, William Dodd, Mr. and Mrs. Marion Crawford, the Dolly Sisters, the Belmonts, Lord Inchcape. An issue of *Americans on the Côte d'Azur* carried the story of a group of old friends from stateside who had reconnected by chance at one of the local restaurants; they were heard making loud toasts "in protest of prohibition," and spotted, five bottles later, heading to a dance hall. Below the society gossip in the glossy *Continental Life,* SBM-funded advertisements announced various entertainments on offer in Monaco: "Motor-Cycle Hill Climbing; Military Tournament; International Dog Show; Floral Fêtes; Athletic Sports; Golf Competitions; Competitions for Ladies; *Tir aux Pigeons*; Sailing and Rowing Regattas." There were Wednesday-night galas in the Egyptian Hall of the Grand Hôtel, while Thursdays were for the "Mimosa Dinners" and foxtrot contests at the Métropole's restaurant Les Ambassadeurs, where the dancing duo of George and Betty Hope and Nic Fuly's band were so popular they sometimes performed as many as five encores. Marini Miharti's nine-piece band played gypsy-jazz across from the casino at the Café de Paris. New movies played at the resort's two cinemas, La Poste and the Palais des Beaux-Arts.

In the hot summer months of 1926 Monaco fell prey to an outbreak of fevers, which struck hardest in the poorest districts. A few cases proved mortal. *Le Monégasque* launched an investigation and traced the sicknesses to the local water supply. An editorial suggested that the filthy state of Monaco's drinking water had long been a well-kept secret, and that a National Council member had tried discussing the fevers in the terms of a water-borne pandemic at a recent session, but after strong words from the minister of state had grown "strangely disinterested" in pursuing the matter. "It seems that there are words one is forbidden from saying aloud around here," read the story in *Le Monégasque,* "and these words are 'typhoid fever.'" The water supply, overseen by the SBM, had been a contentious issue for decades. As early as 1894 there is record of company managers discussing the threat of waterborne sickness, and of hiring a doctor to devise ways to purify the two water sources then under its control.

Le Monégasque called on Léon to take responsibility for the illnesses and deaths. The casino director instead suggested that the whole affair could be explained by a bad batch of mussels that must have made its way into the food supply. *Le Monégasque* countered that if Léon had any understanding of local customs he would know it wasn't common to eat mussels in the summer, besides which, the poorer Monégasques—those most deeply affected by the fevers—were unlikely to partake of such a delicacy in any season.

On Christmas Eve, 1926, the SBM hosted a party at the edge of one of the local reservoirs to celebrate the adoption of a new scientific breakthrough in sanitation, known as the Bunau-Varilla system. Philippe Bunau-Varilla, a key figure in the construction of the Panama Canal, devised his purification method while serving as an officer at Verdun, where typhoid and other maladies ripped a hole through the French forces. He hit on a system where, with the help of an automatic pump, a small amount of bleach was slowly introduced into a water supply. At the edge of the reservoir, René Léon, the Monégasque minister of state, and other local notables made champagne toasts to health and progress. A writer for *Le Monégasque* interpreted this stunt as the closest thing to an "official recognition" of the SBM's guilt in the typhoid affair that the principality was likely to see, and meanwhile questioned the safety of the relatively unproven Bunau-Varilla method. "When it comes to the health of an entire country," he wrote, "the Gambling House has no right to put its economic interests above all else: a company charged with protecting a community's wellbeing should not go bargain-hunting while doing so."

A week later, the Monte Carlo Palace Hotel hosted one of the biggest New Year's Eve parties ever seen in the resort. For eighty francs, guests dined on:

> *Potage Mock Turtle or Crème de Volaille Sultane*
> *Filets de Sole Mona*
> *Selle de Veau Prince Orloff*
> *Perdreaux Rôtis Impériales*
> *Salade Victoria*
> *Petits Pois à la Française*
> *Soufflé Glace Palphi*
> *Gâteau Breton*
> *Mignardises*
> *Corbeille de Fruits*

Just over three weeks later, Prince Louis awarded René Léon the Order of Saint-Charles, Monaco's highest honor. The *Gazette de Monaco et de Monte-Carlo,* an SBM ally, commended the prince on having recognized the effort of "a man of action and initiative, generous and open-minded, highly cultivated, yet modest." Three days later the principality hosted another of Alexandre Noghès's by-now-famous annual Automobile Rallies. By that point the typhoid story had completely disappeared from the pages of *Le Monégasque* and other local papers, and doesn't appear to have been mentioned again in print. Léon's message to the people of Monaco had been clarion, the prince had received and approved it, and the tourists were too busy eating mock turtle soup and watching the shining cars to care.

———————

At 9:30 in the morning of March 2, 1927, an SBM worker called at the small office at the Sporting Club kept by René Léon's friend, Léon Radziwill, nominal president of the company and, as grandson of François Blanc, one of its main shareholders. Radziwill was slumped over in his chair. The Monégasque authorities first reported an embolism, and then changed the cause of death to an overdose of opiates. One theory, circulated often enough that some American reporters took it as fact, maintained that Radziwill had been drugged by his mistress, the notorious con artist Marthe Dalbane. According to one paper, it had been in the arms of the sultry Dalbane (dubbed "the Death Flower") and not those of his wife that Radziwill spent his last morphine-and-alcohol-fueled night on earth. Even the more sober items concerning Radziwill's death contained allusions to loose living and underworld ties. *Le Monégasque* reported that the police had brought in three young "demi-mondaines" for questioning, just hours after the discovery of the body, and that they'd detained one of these women for several weeks, though the women were eventually released without charges. The same paper advised René Léon to "thank the god of Israel for having rid him so soon of a friend who was fast becoming more and more of a rival."

Radziwill's death marked the start of an especially trying time for René Léon and the SBM. Four days after Radziwill was found dead, a twenty-year-old from the Netherlands shot himself in the heart in the casino's Salle Touzet. The blindfolded dame Fortune decorating one of the room's walls must have been smiling down, as the dejected Dutchman survived his wound. A day later, a writer for *Le Monégasque* claimed that René Léon had committed yet another hit-and-run, this time in Cap-Martin. Léon explained away the accident by saying he hadn't noticed hitting the other car, but only after trying unsuccessfully to pay the owner of the damaged vehicle to keep the matter out of the papers. Then, in July, the body of a woman was found on a back road near the casino. The police suspected a botched robbery, as someone had hacked off four of her fingers, which had presumably been adorned with expensive rings. No record indicates that the crime was ever solved. Finally, in September, Isadora Duncan, one of the shining lights of the Côte d'Azur expat community, accidentally strangled herself to death in Nice when her scarf became caught in the wheel of her speeding car.

———

The SBM meanwhile faced growing competition, as the American Frank Jay Gould, son of the wealthy financier Jay Gould, teamed with a French businessman in a bid to make Juan-les-Pins the Riviera's next great gambling resort. Gould was also building a casino in Nice, the Palais de la Méditerranée, which was to be ten times larger than the Monte Carlo casino. Gould and other casino operators grew more vociferous in their calls for the legalization of roulette in France. Even without that game, receipts from gambling at the French casinos along the coast came in at more than 400 million francs in 1928 alone. To Monaco's east, the Fascist government also overturned laws restricting games of chance and by the end of the decade the San Remo casino would be offering table limits higher than those in Monte Carlo.

Léon addressed these threats by shoring up the resort's infrastructure. The multimillion-dollar Monte Carlo Country Club opened in February of 1928. It was built right into a hill, with its three layers of courts descending like staircases, while giant columns trellised with rambler roses separated each of the twenty clay courts from the other. Myrtle and cypress shielded the clubhouse from the ocean winds. The Duke of Connaught, third son of Queen Victoria, inaugurated the club by throwing a tennis ball out onto center court from high up in the grandstand, surrounded by a host of grandees, including Prince Louis, Prince Nicolas of Greece, the prince of Montenegro, and King Gustav V of Sweden.

The Monte-Carlo Beach hotel opened shortly afterward. Located a quarter mile to the east of the principality in Roquebrune, relatively far, at least by Monaco standards, from the casino, and enclosed by a deep pine forest, the SBM used the hotel's opening as one more way to announce that Monte Carlo meant more than just its famous casino. Elsa Maxwell launched the venue in grand style, opting for an ancient Roman theme and arranging for the Ballets Russes to lend out some of its costumes for revelers to wear. The evening's highlight was a parade of speedboats towing waterskiing gladiators into the small bay in front of the hotel. Guests chatted and sipped cocktails by the giant turquoise pool at the edge of the sea while a band played light rumbas.

A few months before the opening of the Monte-Carlo Beach hotel, Maxwell had floated a story to reporters that has become part of venue's lore, and is still often repeated as fact despite its being a complete fabrication. As Maxwell recalled in her memoir: "I got such a kick out of engineering the [Monte Carlo] revival that I continued to promote it after my contract expired. When I returned to America two years later, I told the reporters who interviewed me on the boat that Monte Carlo soon would have the finest beach in the world. I spoke simply to get a plug in the papers for an old client, but one reporter outsmarted me. He had been to the Riviera but knew that there wasn't any spot along the rocky Mediterranean that could compare with America's magnificent beaches on the Atlantic Ocean. When he continued to press me for details, I boldly announced Monte Carlo was building a 'rubber beach' over the rocks. That stopped the reporter, and the more I thought about the screwball scheme the more it intrigued me. Why couldn't we pour tar and rubber over the rocks, then cover it all with sand? Dickie Gordon gave me the answer. 'The tide will wash away the sand faster than you can dump it on the surface, idiot,' she said scornfully. That killed the rubber beach, but the story couldn't have gotten a better play in the papers if the stunt had been practical."

Many were fooled, including a reporter from the *Daily Express* who in 1927 wrote how "Miss Maxwell caught my imagination when she described the private beach she and her associates are going to build. The rubber will be renewed every year. All day long people will be able to lounge on clean sand, swim, and then take a sun bath, then plunge into the sea again—in and out, in and out, all day long." American readers were hungry for stories about these kinds of frivolities along the Riviera and reporters working the European desks were happy to oblige them. As a sign posted in the Paris offices of the *New York Herald* in the 1920s read: IT NEVER RAINS IN NICE. THERE'S ALWAYS SNOW IN SWITZERLAND. ALL RESORT GEESE ARE SWANS.

———————

On June 8, 1928, Léon woke to the news that someone had littered Monaco with anti-SBM posters, wheat-pasted to lampposts and walls during the night. Cheaply printed, with bold black text set crudely against a solid red background, they read:

MONÉGASQUES STAND UP! The most repugnant insult has been sent to the Monégasque people, on behalf of a foreigner who has exploited us for years, the administrator of that gambling hell. Our freedom is not meant to be controlled by these wretched characters, these shady racketeers. We shall take that which they owe the Monégasque people. It is vital, once and for all, to rid ourselves of the absentee-managers from who-knows-where, and we will succeed in cutting them down. We have had enough of this octopus with its many tentacles! Enough of this plague of invaders! The Monégasques must be the Masters of their own land!

It hadn't been the work of some lone crank: the posters were seen the same day in Nice, Cannes, and Juan-les-Pins. The campaign came as little surprise to Léon. Three days earlier, a Detective Duchamp of French intelligence in Nice had contacted the principality's top security official with a tip that a Niçoise printing house had produced a large run of anti-SBM posters authored by a figure already well-known to the local police: a Monsieur Noah, self-proclaimed director of a group called The Four Devils. Detective Duchamp had been tracking Noah's movements and sent his reports to Léon. He had spotted Noah meeting with an SBM employee, also believed also to be a member of The Four Devils. He later saw Noah in Beausoleil, planning the posters' diffusion with another contact; then in a tramway, showing the poster to fellow passengers. This Noah had even visited the detective's own house while he was out, telling a frightened Madame Duchamp that he had an "axe to grind" with the SBM. Tracking the plate of a car seen parked outside the print shop led to another accomplice, a French-born ice-cream vendor living in Monaco. Duchamp promised to round them all up as soon Léon gave the word, but the SBM boss asked that no action be taken.

Léon couldn't keep the matter *intra muros* for long. By the end of the summer of 1928 the foreign press had picked up the story that Monaco stood poised "on the verge of serious internal trouble."

A piece in the *Washington Post,* describing a raucous general meeting of several hundred Monégasques held in August, suggested that there was even more "revolutionary agitation" in the principality than could be seen, since many casino employees had skipped the meeting lest they be fired for attending. Local editorialists joined in on skewering Léon and the SBM; a writer for *L'Écho Monégasque* suggested that all of Léon's expensive building projects had only served "to destroy, and make ugly," and that by buying up so many independently owned hotels in Monaco the company veered toward monopolization. A writer for the normally pro-SBM *L'Avenir de Beausoleil et de Monte-Carlo* chided Léon for thinking himself somehow above local political concerns, suggesting that the casino director had "enclosed himself in an ivory tower and does not desire any contact with the locals . . . [he seemed to want] to disappear, when he should be doing precisely the opposite." A writer for the same paper suggested that foreign workers and speculators were squeezing out middle-class families with deep roots in Monaco, who could no longer afford the cost of living.

Late in December of 1928, all twenty-one members of Monaco's National Council resigned in protest over what they claimed was the SBM's failure to provide adequate water, electricity, and sanitation services, and its inability to properly advertise the resort. They demanded more rights for workers, the guarantee of jobs for all Monégasques and their children, better retirement benefits, and a clearer separation between private and public interests. American journalists covering the story were hesitant to sympathize with a population that demanded representation without taxation, and items about this "Tempest in a Teapot" took on a jokey tone.

Prince Louis worried about the negative publicity. From his château in Marchais he issued the following statement: "Already the events of recent weeks have been greatly exaggerated and bruited abroad, and it is time we put an end to these regrettable rumors. On the eve of the season most essential to Monaco's prosperity, Prince

Louis calls the people of Monaco, in the name of and by the affection they hold for their country to an appreciation of their sane and essential duties." On New Year's Day, 1929, the prince returned by train to Monaco and was shocked to find that his subjects greeted him at the station not with the customary fanfare but with hisses and jeers. Meanwhile, the SBM quietly announced profits of 98 million francs for the year, the best in its history.

———————

In January 1929 the head of the resigned National Council, a Monaco-born architect named Eugène Marquet, helped to found a new paper, *L'Écho Monégasque*. Marquet was a beloved figure in the principality and on friendly enough terms with the Grimaldi family that a few years earlier Prince Pierre had visited Marquet at home to console him on the passing of his wife. Marquet and other Monégasques filled the pages of *L'Écho* with angry rhetoric about the foreign presence in the principality, much of which was directed at Léon and the Jewish-owned banking firm of Daniel Dreyfus, the new alleged majority shareholder in the SBM. "The Jew Daniel Dreyfus has ensured the reelection [as head of the SBM] for six years of the Jew René Léon," wrote one unnamed contributor; "More than ever, the Monte Carlo casino remains the great Ghetto of the Littoral." Another anonymous author alleged that the "Shylock" Léon had told his "co-religionists" that although he realized he would soon lose his hold on the SBM, he still intended to leave Monaco "with a fat wallet." *L'Écho* even suggested that René Léon was a fake name, used to disguise the director's true "foreign" identity. The paper dubbed him "Van der Put," and "Van den Push," names presumably meant to imply a hidden Germanic and aristocratic background. Someone at *L'Écho* had fun taunting Léon by regularly sending him copies of the latest edition; these were promptly returned.

The Monégasque authorities kept a close watch on the people

involved with the paper. Marquet and his cronies returned the favor, publishing details about the principality's top security official: "Last Monday, the 28th of January, at 1:44 p.m., M. Michel, head of the *Sûreté,* took the number 24 train. He was carrying a light suitcase. He seemed to have a sad air about him. No one saw him off to his train."

Midway through January, Prince Pierre met with local representatives to address complaints about the SBM's providing public utilities and to discuss a more liberal interpretation of the constitution. It would be the first of many such meetings. Commenting on the futility of discussing democratic reforms with a prince, a Niçoise journalist teased the Monégasques for failing to see that only republican democracy could bring them the autonomy they desired. Referencing one of Aesop's fables, he said that in seeking reform rather than revolution they were like "frogs who want to change their king."

———————

In February Monaco was hit by the biggest snowstorm it had seen in more than fifty years. Whenever there was a break in the fall, SBM workers in blue overalls dashed out to shovel and scrape away as much of the snow as they could before the storm picked up again. They climbed ladders and shook out trees. They replaced damaged flowers with ones fresh from the hothouse. They piled up the brownish slush that had gathered in the gardens, to be carted away in wheelbarrows. Evelyn Waugh, passing though when the storm hit, made note of how quickly the casino workers cleaned things up and interpreted this a sign of how delightfully upfront Monte Carlo was about its own phoniness. "This triumph of industry and order over the elements seems to me typical of Monte Carlo. Nothing could be more supremely artificial," wrote Waugh. "But there is a consistency and temperance and efficacy about the artificiality of Monte Carlo . . . The immense wealth of the Casino, derived wholly and directly from man's refusal to accept the conclusion of mathematical proof; the absurd political position of the state; the newness and neatness of its buildings; the absolute denial of poverty and suffering in this place, where sickness is represented by fashionable invalids and industry by hotel servants, and the peasantry in traditional costume come into town to witness in free seats at the theatre . . . all these things make up a principality which is just as real as a pavilion at an International Exhibition."

In the spring of 1929 a panicked Louis suspended the constitution. The scheduled municipal elections were canceled. *L'Écho* deemed this a "permanent rupture" between the prince and his subjects, a break that had been "a long time coming." On March 24, the resigned members of the National Council called a General Assembly of the Monégasque People, whose nominal purpose was to discuss the issue of another refusal by Prince Pierre (who acted as the main representative of Prince Louis) to meet with a delegation of Monégasques that had asked for a public reaffirmation of the values of the constitution. Things escalated after Marquet gave an angry speech delivered in the local Monégasque dialect, which *L'Écho* printed the next week in French "for the benefit of our foreign friends and for Prince Peter [referring to Pierre by the English version of his name, assumedly intended as an insult] who has not been able to take the time to familiarize himself with our language."

Amid shouts of "To the Palace!" six hundred angry Monégasques poured out onto Rue Grimaldi, one of the principality's busiest streets and retail centers. With Marquet at the front, the crowd headed southeast toward the Grimaldi palace. It reached the police station in the Condamine district where Rue Grimaldi meets the narrow avenue leading to the palace. Roughly two dozen policemen were waiting. The "cortège" (so described in *L'Écho Monégasque*) tried to press through the police cordon. Marquet, in an exchange of words with the head of security, Michel, said: "I am surprised to learn that we have closed the streets of Monaco to the Monégasques." Michel informed the crowd that he had orders to use force, if necessary.

Accounts differ over what followed. Some newspapers reported that the police fired into the mob, while others reported that a protestor had fired first, wounding a policeman amid cries of "Vive la République Monégasque!" *L'Écho Monégasque* claimed that a police officer shot into the air, and that there had been no critical injuries. All accounts agreed that after a tussle the protestors managed to breach the palace gates, some climbing over a police car that had been parked to block their entry, and that an even greater defensive force waited behind the gates. Eventually, after some heated back-and-forth, a delegation led by Marquet was allowed inside the palace, where they aired their grievances to a reportedly sympathetic Prince Pierre. *L'Écho* described how after the meeting there were cries of "Vive la Constitution! Vive la President Marquet! Vive le peuple Monégasque!" Prince Pierre briefed his father-in-law on the meeting and Louis publicly agreed to address demands for constitutional reform, scheduled elections for June, and assured his subjects that a delegation would look into the issues of utilities and employment of Monégasques. Marquet later told the press that the majority of Monégasques loved and supported the Grimaldi and were not in favor of a republic. The "3-Hour 'Revolution,'" as the *New York Times* called it, was over.

Prince Louis made some cosmetic concessions, but Monaco experienced no great shift in power. The local workers gained little. It was obvious that control of the casino would never be turned over to the people. For all of their revolutionary talk the Monégasques accepted that SBM profits were more important to their livelihoods than any kind of princely decree. By the end of the spring of 1929, the point was moot. Any of the last cries calling for a different future in Monaco were soon drowned out by the sounds of howling motorcars and cheering crowds.

17

ONE-WAY STREET

Motors in all directions, going at all speeds. I was overwhelmed, an enthusiastic rapture filled me. Not the rapture of the shining coachwork under the gleaming lights, but the rapture of power. The simple and ingenuous pleasure of being in the centre of so much power, so much speed.

—Le Corbusier, *The City of To-morrow and Its Planning*

YOU FELT THE NOISE as much as you heard it, a low substantial rumble. For many in the crowd, the sound of sixteen engines amplified by the semicircle of cliffs that make Monaco a natural amphitheater would have been the loudest they'd ever heard outside of wartime. Those few people in the gambling resort who'd chosen to avoid the spectacle would have heard the engines and the cheers from their rooms. They would have smelled the acrid fumes as well. It was April 14, 1929, on the Boulevard Albert I, next to the harbor. The starting line of the inaugural Monaco Grand Prix lay less than a hundred feet from where Eugène Marquet and six hundred protestors had launched their own procession three weeks earlier.

Sitting high up in their boxy machines, the drivers evoked riders on horseback. Like so many medieval jousters and ancient charioteers, who had been equally eager to show their mastery of horsepower, many of the Grand Prix entrants hailed from the European nobility. There was the Italian count Goffredo Zehender in his Alfa Romeo 6C, and the Baron Philippe de Rothschild (fooling nobody by having entered under the pseudonym "Philippe") in his Bugatti Type 35C. "I am a great driver," Rothschild wrote in his memoir, "a born driver, my buttocks were designed to fit a driver's seat."

Other competitors represented the European gentry's increasing shift into the realm of merchant capitalism. One driver, Marcel Lehoux, had been born in a French château but now ran a trading company in Algeria; another, the marquis Raoul de Rovin, was steadily burning through his family's fortune with his motorcycle company. Some prosperous bourgeois drivers also mixed among the aristocracy in the starting grid, just as they had in Monte Carlo. Rudolf Caracciola, the son of German hoteliers, cut an imposing figure in his huge Mercedes-Benz SSK. He was flanked by the French wool wholesaler Philippe Étancelin.

Finally came the professionals. There was René Dreyfus, a Niçoise Jew whose repeated defeats of German racers would become a sore spot for Hitler. There was also a mysterious driver who listed his nationality as British though he spoke perfect French, and registered only as "W Williams." He drove a sleek Bugatti painted in a distinctive hue that motorsport fans soon started calling British Racing Green. His real name was William Grover-Williams, and before dedicating himself full-time to competitive driving, he'd made his living as a Riviera chauffeur. (He later put his driving skills to use as a secret agent in the Résistance). Now Williams was preparing to battle the same kinds of people he used to serve, for the grand prize of one hundred francs.

That a collection of men from varied national and social backgrounds competed in a car race in 1929 was not in itself exceptional. Motorsport was by then an international pursuit and professional drivers had started to dominate the sport, once the exclusive purview of wealthy amateurs. The 1929 Monaco Grand Prix stands alone in the history of motorsport because it was the first race run directly through city streets, rather than on an enclosed track. It was assumed that running cars at speed through Monaco's narrow and winding roads would lead to serious injuries, if not fatalities. As one reporter covering the race put it, "Any respectable traffic system would have covered the track with <DANGER> sign posts left, right and centre."

A year earlier, a young Monégasque, Antony Noghès, had gone to Paris to lobby the International Association of Recognized Automobile Clubs (IARAC) on behalf of the Automobile Club de Monaco. He was the club's general commissioner, a position that carried much weight in Monaco, which at the time trailed only America in cars per capita, with a car for every eighteen residents. Noghès also oversaw the state-held monopoly on the distribution of tobacco and matches, an appropriately lucrative sinecure for someone hailing from one of Monaco's most esteemed families. Antony's father, Alexandre, founded Monaco's famous Auto Rally as well as the Auto Club the younger Noghès now headed. The locals regarded the family as the ideal Monaco success story—father and son had distinguished themselves in fields having nothing to do with gambling. Antony's son later married Princesse Antoinette, granddaughter of Prince Louis II.

So prominent a Monégasque would have wanted his peers to understand that his homeland offered more than just a casino and a castle. It was vital that the officials in Paris recognize the ambitions of his humble club. But the IARAC directors scoffed at his application, saying that an auto club in a place with a dozen miles of drivable roads at best was hardly an "internationally relevant" organization. Noghès pointed to the Monte Carlo Rally, but the officials countered that its success was due to other auto clubs and the roads of other nations; Monaco merely provided a pretty finish line. Noghès—at least as he remembered that meeting a few decades later—promised on the spot that Monaco would hold a race that would be of "world-wide interest."

Funding the event wasn't likely to be an issue. The Monte Carlo casino was enjoying record profits and the principality was flush. Space, however, presented a more difficult problem. In tiny Monaco, one couldn't build a dedicated track on some empty patch of land, as the people of Le Mans had done a few years earlier. It was this restriction that led Noghès to the idea of staging what he called the "Race Within the Town." He remembered how, for days on end, he walked Monaco's streets until he "hit on the only possible circuit. This skirted the port, passing along the quay . . . climbed the hill of Monte Carlo, then passed round the Place de Casino, took the downhill zigzag near [the] Monte Carlo [train] station to get back approximately to sea level and from there, along the Boulevard Louis II and the *Tir aux Pigeons* tunnel, the course came back to quayside."

But Noghès's claim to have discovered the only possible route in Monaco is misleading. Small though it was, the principality could have offered any number of alternate routes. Noghès himself described the impracticality of his particular choice. "Today the roads comprising this circuit look as though they were made for the purpose," he told a journalist several decades after that first race. "But then! Some of the obstacles seemed to be insuperable—the steps near the Bureau de Tabac, for example, had to be replaced by an inclined plane connecting the Quai des États-Unis with the Quai Albert Premier." Noghès also conceded that the very idea of "letting loose speeding cars in a city challenged good sense."

Yet it was an idea that met with enthusiasm at the highest levels in Monaco. Noghès first shared his vision with the Monégasque racecar driver Louis Chiron, one of the principality's most illustrious sons, and with Prince Pierre, who spoke of it in glowing terms to his father-in-law. Noghès said later that the race was run under Prince Louis's patronage, "while the public services gave of their best to make effective contribution." Again, his memory seems a bit muddy, as it was the Monte Carlo casino that financed the bulk of the event and would continue to do so, sometimes resulting in heavy financial losses.

Why was Noghès so set on his impractical circuit—from port, to casino, to train station and back, passing the Bureau de Tabac along the way? And why, given all the far-fetched ideas for novelties and events that René Léon fielded and dismissed, did he agree to fund this expensive idea, which even its originator admitted "challenged good sense"?

There is something else at play here. Another Monte Carlo story being spun. A story about speed and power and place.

———————

All casino owners trade on the idea that there is such a thing as social mobility. They profit from the collective madness that leads us to believe that fundamental economic realities can somehow be upended in an instant. It's an illusion that has given comfort to countless denizens of society's bottom rungs—the promise of Fortune's wheel, which can make the rich man poor and the poor man rich. Much of why Monte Carlo stood so far ahead of its competitors for so long was due to how well its managers paired that promise of social mobility at the casino with the glamorization of physical mobility in the resort that surrounded it. The gambling boomtown that went up seemingly overnight at the edge of the Mediterranean with the help of an international collection of highly mobile speculators, workers, and clients, celebrated, above all, freedom of movement. "True to its Phoenician origin, everything that is connected with locomotion, be it on land or sea . . . finds favour at Monaco," wrote a British journalist in 1912. "The moment a new means of locomotion is discovered it meets with encouragement." That new means of locomotion found favor in Monaco, however, had less to do with the principality's ancient past than with how vital these technologies were to its emergence as a tourist destination in the nineteenth century, and to its continued success in the twentieth. For six decades the resort's boosters had been promoting the message that the best kind of life was the fast life—that the highest reward for the financial gains awaiting at the casino would be that such wealth allowed you to move around quickly, skillfully, and wherever you pleased.

One could see this message wherever one looked in Monaco: In the bay where pleasure craft bobbed gently; out front of the casino, where the finest carriages and then cars were parked; in the skies where aviators delighted audiences with their casino-funded displays; in mass-produced posters, and postcards, and photographs, and in films. Theodore Dreiser understood this the first time he set foot in the principality in 1912: "It struck me here [in Monte Carlo] . . . that the difference between the person who has something and the person who has nothing is one of intense desire and . . . a capacity to live . . . Some people can live more, better, faster, more enthusiastically in less time than others."

At the Monte Carlo casino there was only the movement and the moment, the tumbling dice and the spinning wheels. Gamblers have remarked on the ways that the practice seems to speed up the pace of time. The nineteenth-century writer Edouard Gourdon spoke of how "a series of lucky rolls give me more pleasure than a man who does not gamble can have over a period of several years . . . I live a hundred lives in one." Walter Benjamin, himself an avid gambler, suggested that "a game passes the time more quickly as chance comes to light more absolutely in it, as the number of combinations encountered in the course of play . . . is smaller and their sequence shorter. In other words, the greater the component of chance in a game, the more speedily it elapses." If, as Benjamin proposed, small sequences of numbers increased the component of chance and so accelerated the pace of the game, then Monte Carlo's roulette wheels, with their single-zero tables offering the most favorable odds in Europe, passed time more "quickly" than in any other casino.

Another writer, Francis de Miomandre, made the link between gambling and speed explicit in a short "Gentleman's Guide" to casinos, which he penned around the same time Antony Noghès was making his final preparations for the Monaco Grand Prix. De Miomandre advised his readers: "Whether it be smoking a good cigar, selecting a fine wine, driving a car in a gentlemanly fashion, profiting at the Casino, or permitting oneself the pleasure of a pretty woman, it is the art of doing all these things with ease and grace that defines the sophisticated man . . . The domestic sphere is destroyed, aided by the advent of the automobile . . . and so modern man must be constantly on the move. But where to? The casino is open all day and night and responds to a basic need of modern man: to escape."

Driving a car in a gentlemanly fashion, and profiting at the casino: here were two ways to flirt with destruction and "live a thousand lives in one."

———————

The Grand Prix began at 1:25 in the afternoon, with Prince Pierre taking a ceremonial first lap in a chauffeured Voisin Torpedo. In keeping with Monte Carlo's embrace of anything related to chance, starting positions in the grid had been decided not with the standard prerace speed trials but by drawing lots. At 1:30 the yellow flag waved and Williams, the former chauffeur, shot out from the middle of the pack. While Marquet and the Monégasque protesters had a few weeks earlier headed in a southwesterly direction toward the traditional seat of power in Monaco, the Grand Prix drivers plotted their course northeast toward the casino.

Williams and the others headed from the edge of the harbor—near the sea-bathing facilities that evoked Monte Carlo's early pretensions as a spa resort, and where speedboat and water-skiing races reinforced the resort's more recent aspirations as a center of summertime sporting life—and then up the Boulevard Albert Ier. They passed by the Sainte-Dévote Chapel, burial ground of Monaco's patron saint and a key site for socializing in this predominantly Catholic territory. Having climbed the hill to Monte Carlo, the drivers navigated between the Hôtel de Paris and the casino, the race's halfway mark as well as the Mount Olympus of Monaco's social world. Almost anyone of note who had ever visited the resort would have either dined, drank, or slept there. The drivers next descended the Avenue des Beaux Arts, passing underneath the Monte Carlo train station and the *Tir aux Pigeons*. Exiting the tunnel, they had to execute a key turn in front of the Bureau de Tabac—perhaps a coincidence, or perhaps a conscious decision by the tobacco-rich Noghès.

The point was clear: Noghès's racing circuit adhered closely to all the key sites in the principality's social circuit. The hundred-lap course drummed out a story about Monte Carlo's past and—circled again and again, year after year—would itself become the story of its future. The course followed a path that kept Monaco's working classes conveniently out of sight. Of Monaco's five districts, the drivers passed through only two, Monte Carlo and La Condamine, the two centers of tourist life and retail business.

Williams carried the day. To René Léon, that outcome would have mattered far less than the fact that the crowds and the press corps had seen Monaco looking well scrubbed and full of action under a clear blue sky. Sixteen young men had passed by the major sites in the resort, while expertly maneuvering the most charged signs of luxury and privilege the era had to offer. Few, if any, reporters would have filed their stories on the event without mentioning the casino.

The inaugural Monaco Grand Prix was less a race than it was

a parade. Where the Great War had not long before shown the devastation that could be wrought by a mix of blind nationalism and modern technology—millions relocated, displaced, and repatriated—the Grand Prix suggested a more benign form of machine-based battle, a pleasant rather than terrifying movement of bodies. Men could win glory for their nations by collectively taking possession, if temporarily, of "neutral" and "international" territory. At the Grand Prix ground was neither won nor lost, but only circled, again and again, an endless loop of self-regard.

A stretch of the circuit has since been renamed Boulevard Louis II, and one of its most difficult turns is known among motorsport enthusiasts as the Virage Antony Noghès. By contrast the failed demands of Monégasques driven by quasi-nationalist chauvinism and hateful xenophobia are largely forgotten. The scene of princely subjects walking from the center of local commerce toward a fortified palace to seek an audience with the descendant of one of the longest-reigning dynasties in Europe was downright medieval in comparison to the forward-looking image of Monaco that Noghès, the SBM, and the Grimaldi hoped to project with their international race meant to spark "worldwide interest."

While a statue of the foreign-born William Grover-Williams today greets tourists and commuting workers as they emerge from the principality's ultramodern subterranean train station, a few dozen feet from where both the race and the protest began, no marker in Monaco specifically commemorates the uprising of March 25, 1929, that started on the same site, nor is there any mention of it in any histories of the other procession through the streets of Monaco that followed so closely on its heels.

Antony Noghès, Prince Pierre, Princesse Charlotte, René Léon, Elsa Maxwell, Serge Diaghilev—these people possessed (or were hired to advance) a particular vision of Monaco. Like them, Monaco would be modern, cosmopolitan, privileged, and efficient—a place whose international appeal was heightened precisely by its own lack of any distinct national identity. Eugène Marquet and the hundreds of Monégasques who joined him in failed protest had another vision for their homeland. They wished it to be a place marked by tradition, and by pride in the local working and middle classes, a place where outsiders might be begrudgingly tolerated, but never fully welcomed.

Ultimately it came down to who could tell their story the loudest.

FAITES VOS JEUX

ON A SPRING DAY in 1930, a man entered the Monte Carlo casino, using an alias when filling out his entry card. The members of the "dress police" who worked the doors that day were unable, later, to remember anything specific about his appearance other than that he wore a sleek tailcoat.

The man played roulette and lost steadily. Then, too quickly to be spotted by the guards, he took a grenade from the pocket of his coat, pulled the pin, and tossed it into one of the spinning wheels. He bolted for the exit and was never caught. There was a small explosion, followed by the sounds of screams and of shattering crystal as one of the room's giant chandeliers fell to the floor. Unlike the last time the casino had been bombed—fifty years earlier, nearly to the day—nothing here indicated that robbery had been the motive. There seemed to be no clear reason behind the act at all, though some speculated that the man must have been a disgruntled loser seeking revenge against the SBM.

No one was hurt. The roulette table had been so solidly built that it had absorbed the force of the blast and projected it up toward the ceiling. Less than an hour after the explosion all the glass had been swept away. The scraps of table were hauled off, and the dust wiped from the shoulders of dinner jackets, and the drinks refilled, and the crowds reassembled, and the wheels were back spinning again. Then, just as before, one heard the croupiers and their familiar refrain: *"Mesdames, Messieurs, faites vos jeux! Rien ne va plus!"*

ACKNOWLEDGMENTS

This book began as a doctoral dissertation, "Spinning Wheels: Cosmopolitanism, Mobility, and Media in Monaco, 1855–1956," which I defended at the University of Southern California in 2013. I thank USC's department of History and the Visual Studies Research Institute for providing research funding as well as an exciting intellectual home for many years.

In Los Angeles: the members of my dissertation committee, Elinor Accampo, Phil Ethington, Vanessa Schwartz, and Nancy Troy deserve a special thank-you. Daniela Bleichmar, Leo Braudy, William Deverell, Richard Fox, Karen Halttunen, Paul Lerner, Peter Mancall, Richard Meyer, and Steve Ross each contributed a great deal to helping me along in my research. Lori Rogers, Joe Styles, Laverne Hughes, and Sandra Hopwood kept things running smoothly. A heartfelt thanks to Deb Harkness for being a mentor and friend. I count myself as especially fortunate to have matriculated alongside Matthew Fox-Amato. Matt read and reread several drafts of the dissertation, and in dozens of coffee shops from Venice Beach to Miracle Mile put up with many hours of my riffing on all things Monaco. A person could not ask for a more engaging academic peer or a more decent human being. Matt and Kate are valued friends.

No single person had a greater influence on the research that went into this book than my graduate adviser and the head of my dissertation committee, Vanessa Schwartz. Vanessa was the first person to believe in the idea that a history of Monaco could make for a valuable research project, and she spent more time hearing and reading about this subject than any one person should ever have to in one lifetime. A formidable intellectual mentor and a cherished friend, to whom I say *merci*.

In New York: I'm still realizing the full influence of the brief year spent completing NYU's interdisciplinary French studies master's program. George Trumbull, Herrick Chapman, and Stéphane Gerson were wonderful academic guides during my time there. Thanks to my NYU chum, the brilliant Vanessa Agard-Jones. Zack and Amanda Silverman were gracious hosts when I returned to New York for research. This book simply would not have been possible without the help and counsel of Ken Silver. The influence of Ken's *Making Paradise: Art, Modernity, and the Myth of the French Riviera* on this project is profound. Thanks also to Amy Fine Collins and to Luc Sante. Erik Larson offered some great tips to this first-timer (and complete stranger) who reached out for some "Yoda-like" advice. David Kuhn, Grant Ginder, Billy Kingsland, Becky Sweren, and Jessie Borkan believed in this project from the beginning and were instrumental throughout. William LoTurco and Chelsey Heller have been great new additions to the team. Many thanks as well to Linda Lichter and to Steve Fisher. Webster Younce and Dominick Anfuso got this all going. Sarah Knight has been a savvy editor and an absolute joy to work with. Many thanks to Jonathan Cox for seeing this through to completion. Thanks also to Kaitlin Olson for additional edits and comments on the manuscript, to Isolde Sauer for her sharp eyes, and to everyone else involved in this project at Simon & Schuster.

In Paris: Dominique Kalifa pointed me to some especially valuable sources at the BNF. Thank you to Elise Jamet, Alix Mounou, Marion Pinson, Louise de Nicolay, Aline d'Ormesson, and Delphine Tagger for helping me to learn Paris and with securing accommodation in Nice.

In Nice: thank you to Nik Jenkins and Jennifer Morone for making us feel as though Nice was home, if only for a short while.

At Stanford: thanks to Dan Edelstein for helping me on my way as a researcher and lecturer. Thanks also to Nick Bausch, Giovanna Ceserani, Nicole Coleman, JP Daughton, Paula Findlen, Richard Meyer, Reilly Brennan, Erik Steiner, and Nancy Troy (again). I must single out Zephyr Frank, who read a draft of the final manuscript and offered sound advice. Giorgio Caviglia helped me understand that in many ways this is a book about design. He is, not coincidentally, a great designer and a great friend.

Allison Morehead kindly shared her work on Edvard Munch in Monte Carlo. Thanks also to Mary Hunter, Ann Fabian, Russ Smith, Jacob Soll, and Priya Swaminathan. Many colleagues have heard me present this material in various forms at conferences and workshops, especially at the annual meetings of the Society of French Historical Studies, the Western Society for French History, the Nineteenth-Century Studies Association, and the Nineteenth-Century French Studies Association, and I appreciate all the questions and critiques they offered.

In Vancouver: Alejandra Bronfman and Chris Friedrichs, at UBC, were those passionate and generous professors every undergraduate hopes for. Graham Hindson, Josh Linde, the Malchiks, Zack Silverman (again), and Marc Weber: thanks a million for all the good times. Love and gratitude to my brother Jon Braude, who knows more about Formula One (and most other things) than I ever will. Daylan Braude is the best sister-in-law someone could have. Ayelet and Poppy Jane Braude make the days bright. My parents, Eleanor and Jeremy Braude, have encouraged and supported this book in innumerable ways and I will be forever grateful for their love and guidance. I thank my two great teachers, my grandmothers, Rita Klein and Esther Braude. Most of all, I thank Laura Marie Braude—first reader, sharpest critic, greatest inspiration, and love of my life.

ARCHIVAL SOURCES

Many thanks to the staffs of the archives listed below. I must single out Charlotte Lubert, archivist of the SBM.

MONACO

Archives of the Société des Bains de Mer et du Cercle des Étrangers à Monaco (SBM)

Folders: 1838–1943 (Each folder contains all available archival data for a given year.)

Correspondence, Budgets, Company Statutes, Contracts, Bills of Sale/ Receipts, Minutes of Shareholder Meetings, Hiring and Human Resources Documents, Security Intelligence, Operations Reports, Press Clippings, Guidebooks.

SBM Image Collection

Folders: Casino, Café de Paris, Hôtel de Paris, Hôtels de Monaco, Sporting d'Hiver, Sporting d'Été, Monte-Carlo Beach, Opéra, Cartes Postales.

Photographs, Press Clippings, Illustrations, Architectural Blueprints and Sketches, Postcards, Promotional Materials, Posters, Newspaper Advertisements, Reproductions of Paintings inside the Monte-Carlo Casino, Reproductions of Betting Chips, Stamps, Maps, Ballet, Theatrical, and Musical Programs.

Automobile Club de Monaco

Bibliothèque Louis Notari

Exhibition of His Serene Highness The Prince of Monaco's Vintage Car Collection

Fonds Régional de Monaco

The Museum of Stamps and Coins of Monaco

The Museum of Vieux Monaco

The Oceanographic Museum of Monaco

NICE

Archives Départementales des Alpes-Maritimes (ADAM)

Fonds de la préfecture: Accords / Monaco; Consulats étrangers; Coupures de journaux illustrés, 1856–1947; Coupures de presse locales: Monaco.— Administration, constitution, 1948–1960; Évacuation de la Principauté de Monaco; Dossiers individuels des étrangers expulsés; Lutte contre le régime fasciste; Monaco, mouvements révolutionnaires de 1910–1911; Relations avec la Principauté de Monaco, 1856–1913; Police des Ports; Relations Avec Monaco WW2; Spectacles et Jeux; Surveillance de la presse, 1886–1900; Surveillance de la vie politique italienne; Vie politique et économique monégasque, 1902–1924; 1910–1911; 1931–1939.

Fonds Virgile Barel: Monaco.—Situation des Français vivant à Monaco, 1946–1964.

Fonds Donadeï—Martinez—Szkolnikoff

Fonds Gassin

Documents isolés: Brochures publicitaires sur communes des Alpes-Maritimes et Monaco

Bibliothèque nationale de France (Mitterrand and Richelieu)

Bibliothèque nationale de France (Opéra)

Fonds Kochno

Bibliothèque Historique de la Ville de Paris (BHVP)

Bibliothèque Forney

Forum des Images

COLLEGE PARK

National Archives, College Park

Records of the Office of Strategic Services

Records of the Foreign Service Posts of the Department of State

Records of the Federal Reserve System

OSS Records Pertaining to Safehaven Operations and Related Matters, COI/OSS Central Files

Records Relating to Resistance History

Records of the Foreign Exchange Depository Group of the Office of the Finance Adviser

Records of the Office of Alien Property

Records of the War Department General and Special Staffs

CIA Select Documents of the OSS

OSS Washington Secret Intelligence/Special Funds Records

LOS ANGELES

Margaret Herrick Library, Academy of Motion Pictures Arts and Sciences

To Catch a Thief Production Files

University of California Los Angeles, Film, Television, and Theatre Archival Collection

Herbert Baker Papers; Hearst Image Vault

University of Southern California, Cinematic Arts Library

NEW YORK

Jerome Robbins Dance Division, New York Public Library

Sergei Denham Papers

Serge Diaghilev Papers

David Libidins Papers

NOTES

PREFACE
MONTE CARLO STORIES

1   *In the same era, the color poster gained favor*: The use of the color poster for mass advertising reached critical mass by the early 1880s. See Marcus Verhagen, "The Poster in *Fin-de-Siècle* Paris: That Mobile and Degenerate Art," in Leo Charney and Vanessa Schwartz (eds.), *Cinema and the Invention of Modern Life* (University of California Press, 1995).

2   *"real, subtle, subterranean, but omnipresent power"*: "Riviera Notes," *Guardian*, February 6, 1905.

3   *"held up work until a clause was inserted"*: Elsa Maxwell, *R.S.V.P.: Elsa Maxwell's Own Story* (Little, Brown, 1954), 189.

1
THE CUNNING AND THE EASILY DUPED

5   *When the gambling impresario François Blanc arrived*: Charles Graves, *The Big Gamble: The Story of Monte Carlo* (Hutchison and Co., 1951), 57.

6   *"a crime which has been forgotten"*: Honoré de Balzac, Olivia Mc-
    Cannon, trans., *Old Man Goriot* (Penguin Classics, 2011), 104.

7   *And someone with François's facility with numbers*: On professional
    gamblers, see Ann Fabian, *Card Sharps and Bucket Shops: Gambling
    in Nineteenth-Century America* (Routledge, 1999); John Findlay,
    *People of Chance: Gambling in American Society from Jamestown to
    Las Vegas* (Oxford University Press, 1986); Karen Halttunen, *Con-
    fidence Men and Painted Women: A Study of Middle-Class Culture
    in America, 1830–1870* (Yale University Press, 1982); Jackson
    Lears, *Something for Nothing: Luck in America* (Penguin, 2004).

9   *The Parisians sent more than 100 packages*: The details of the
    Blancs' scheme come from a report on their trial, in *Gazette des
    Tribunaux,* no. 3552, January 28, 1837; no. 3590, March 13–14,
    1847; no. 3592, March 16, 1837; and no. 3593, March 17, 1837.
    All quotations pertaining to the case come from these issues of the
    Gazette des Tribunaux.

10 *"an infamous gambling-hell"*: As quoted in Stanley Jackson, *Inside
    Monte Carlo* (Stein and Day, 1975), 25.

11 *It had served as the Parisian residence*: Thomas M. Kavanagh, *Dice,
    Cards, Wheels: A Different History of French Culture* (University of
    Pennsylvania Press, 2005), 132.

12 *"the paper on the walls is greasy"*: Honoré de Balzac, *The Wild Ass's
    Skin (Le Peau de Chagrin)* (Oxford University Press, 2012), 7.

12 *People joked about how perfectly these hells were located*: The narra-
    tor of the *Wild Ass's Skin* briefly contemplates such a jump.

13 *This had been the most popular of the* enfers *in the time of Bona-
    parte*: "'Déterville,'" *Le Palais-Royal ou les filles en bonne fortune*
    (Paris, 1815), 24; Victor Champier, *Le Palais-Royal: d'après des
    documents inédits, 1629–1900* (Société de propagation des livres
    d'art, 1900).

13 *It is testament to his great charm*: David G. Schwartz, *Roll the Bones:
    The History of Gambling* (Gotham Books, 2006), 192.

13 *"held their breath when his name was mentioned"*: Adolphe Smith,
    Monaco and Monte Carlo (Grant Richards, 1912), 282.

13   *It was a controversial move*: Kavanagh, *Dice*, 133.

13   *The Palais-Royal may have had special meaning for Bonaparte*: "Note from Hotel de Cherbourg, Paris, November 22, 1787," as collected in John Eldred Howard (ed.), *Letters and Documents of Napoleon*, vol. 1, *The Rise to Power* (Oxford University Press, 1961).

14   *A few hours later another man shot himself*: Smith, 269.

15   *"Nous avons détruit"*: As quoted in Xan Fielding, *The Money Spinner: Monte Carlo and Its Fabled Casino* (Little, Brown, 1977), 42.

2
THE ART OF MISDIRECTION

17   *François met an Alsatian woman*: Egon Corti, *The Wizard of Homburg and Monte Carlo* (Thornton Butterworth, 1934), 100–103, refers to François Blanc's marriage to Marie Hensel as his second marriage, while Jackson, 26, refers to a Luxembourg "mistress by whom [François Blanc] sired two sons, Camille and Charles."

17   *François had seen a newspaper advertisement*: For details on Bad Homburg, I am indebted to Everett John Carter's "The Green Table: Gambling Casinos, Capitalist Structure, and Modernity in Nineteenth Century Germany" (PhD diss., University of Illinois at Urbana–Champaign, 2002).

18   *In exchange for the right to the concession*: The contract granting the concession was signed in the summer of 1840, but the official act offering them the concession only took effect nearly a year later on May 23, 1841. See Carter, 36.

19   *People settled in at their favored sites*: Eric T. Jennings, *Curing the Colonizers: Hydrotherapy, Climatology, and French Colonial Spas* (Duke University Press, 2006), 41–42.

19   *Since neither the journey*: Douglas Mackaman, *Leisure Settings: Bourgeois Culture, Medicine, and the Spa in Modern France* (University of Chicago Press, 1998), 129.

19   *Yet, while expensive to reach*: Alain Corbin, *The Lure of The Sea:*

The Discovery of the Seaside in the Western World 1750–1840 (Penguin, 1995), 254.

19 *Instead, this wagering formed part of a larger and more elaborate social ritual*: Kavanagh makes this argument, both in *Dice* and *Enlightenment and the Shadows of Chance* (Johns Hopkins University Press, 1993). Also pertinent to discussion of performative displays of wealth is Marcel Mauss, I. Cunnison, trans., *The Gift: Forms and Functions of Exchange in Archaic Societies* (Cohen and West, 1954).

19 *By playing for high stakes*: Kavanagh, *Dice*, 18.

20 *For a fading class*: Kavanagh, *Shadows*, 51.

20 *Parents even hired "gaming masters"*: Gerda Reith, *The Age of Chance: Gambling in Western Culture* (Routledge, 2002), 65.

20 *"Being a gambler gives a man position"*: Charles-Louis de Secondat Montesquieu, trans., C. J. Betts, *Persian Letters* (Penguin, 1977), 119.

20 *The future lay in economies of scale*: Reith, 74.

21 *A reputable spa casino*: Kavanagh, *Dice*, 192.

21 *Rather than setting out to battle their peers*: Reith, 72–78.

23 *With Bad Homburg gaining a reputation*: Douglas Mackaman has similarly argued that many bourgeois visitors to nineteenth-century French spa towns enjoyed the regimented medical routines associated with spa life because they allowed them to justify their vacations as hard work rather than mere frivolity. Mackaman, 9.

23 *They did make sure that no one shareholder*: Carter, 37.

24 *Blanc often gave Kisselev cash advances*: Bad Homburg today pays the countess homage with its Kisseleffstraße, which runs just past the original *Kursaal* and on which stands the Hotel Villa Kisseleff.

25 *Freud believed Dostoyevsky*: Sigmund Freud, "Dostoevsky and Parricide," in *Dostoevsky: A Collection of Critical Essays*, Reni Wellek (ed.) (Prentice-Hall, 1962).

25 *"The fascination of danger"*: Walter Benjamin, Rolf Tiedemann

(ed.), Howard Eiland, and Kevin McLaughlin, trans., *The Arcades Project* (Harvard University Press, 2002), 499.

25 *In the crowded gaming rooms*: Carter, 42.

25 *"a more colorful confusion"*: Johann Christian Glücklich, as quoted in Carter, 43.

27 *Even though the numbers*: Carter, 37.

27 *"showed himself to be a master"*: "Letter from Eynaud to the Prince," February 23, 1863, SBM Archives, Folder 1863. Hereafter sources from the SBM archives will be attributed as "SBM" followed by the year, indicating their corresponding folder (these are sorted by year) in the archives.

3

THE ANTECHAMBER OF DEATH

29 *Historians of nation-building*: The seminal work here is Benedict Anderson's *Imagined Communities* (Verso, 1991).

29 *Yet despite having little*: CIA World Factbook: Monaco. www .cia.gov/library/publications/the-world-factbook/geos/mn .html. Accessed September 2014. See also Vincent Peillon and Arnaud Montebourg, *Monaco et le Blanchiment: un territoire complaisant sous proctection française; Mission de l'Assemblée nationale sur la déliquance financière* (Assemblée nationale/Édition 1, 2000), 39.

30 *Monaco lies roughly halfway*: For general histories of Monaco, see Marc Bourgne, *Histoire de Monaco* (Dargaud, 1997); Corti; Fielding; Graves; Jackson, L. H. Labande, *Annales de la Principauté de Monaco* (Archives du Palais, 1939); Didier Laurens, *Monaco* (Hachette, 2007); Gilbert and Olivia Marangoni-Navello, *L'Identité Monégasque* (Monaco, 2007); Ethel Coburn Mayne, *The Romance of Monaco and its Rulers* (John Lane, 1910); Henri de Métevier, *Monaco et ses princes* (Imprimerie E. Jourdain, 1865); Pierre Polovtsoff, *Monte Carlo Casino* (Hillman Curl, 1937), and Smith.

32   *"I am Monaco upon a rock"*: As quoted, in the Monégasque dialect, in Corti, 134:

> *Son Monaco sopra uno scoglio,*
> *Non semino e non raccoglio;*
> *Ma pur mangier voglio.*

32   *"Menton and Roquebrune paid"*: As quoted in Fielding, 11.

34   *"an unhappy little sovereign"*: Victorien Sardou, *Rabagas: comédie en cinq actes, en prose* (1872).

34   *"spent money there like water"*: As quoted in Corti, 139.

35   *"The bathing establishment"*: As quoted in Corti, 140.

35   *The document outlining the SBM's founding statutes*: "Projet de Cahiers des charges redigé par M. Eynaud," September 15, 1855, SBM 1855.

4
COMPLETE DISORDER REIGNS

37   *"It would be such a doubtful venture"*: As quoted in Corti, 85.

38   *"distractions of all kinds"*: "Ier cahier des charges de la S.B.M.," April 26, 1856, SBM 1856. See also "Bains de Monaco Acte de Société," July 13, 1856, Archives Départementales des Alpes-Maritimes (hereafter ADAM), 1M0432.

39   *The SBM bought up land*: "Achat des Spélugues," June 7, 1856, SBM 1856.

39   *Hearing of these developments*: D. Schwartz, 300.

39   *A quarter of the net profits*: "Bains de Monaco Acte de Société," July 13, 1856, ADAM, 1M0432.

39   *"virtually ready"*: As quoted in Fielding, 22.

40   *The act codifying*: "Bains de Monaco Acte de Société," July 13, 1856, ADAM, 1M0432.

41   *"On the ground floor"*: "Bains de Monaco," Report of January 15, 1857, SBM 1857.

41 *"it is impossible to verify"*: Ibid.

41 *Had the inspector commissioner been granted access*: Fielding, 74.

41 *Of the few visitors who did reach*: D. Schwartz, 299.

42 *Between March 15 and March 20*: After another slow week when only two gamblers visited, the prince's commissioner reported: "though the rooms were opened for play fourteen times during the week, gambling took place only five times. Neglected publicity and lack of communications with Nice are to blame." As quoted in Fielding, 27.

42 *Eventually one of them decided to install a telescope*: Smith, 301.

42 *Instead, he and Eynaud pushed the pair to find another buyer*: Fielding, 28.

42 *With the Monaco concession*: Schwartz, 299.

43 *One cost-saving strategy*: Anthony Burgess, "The Ball Is Free to Roll," from *One Man's Chorus: The Uncollected Writings* (Carroll and Graf Publishers, 1998).

43 *The head architect*: Fielding, 30.

43 *"For three months"*: "Letter from Eynaud to Daval," August 11, 1858, SBM 1858.

43 *They were met by the threat of cannon fire*: Fielding, 30.

43 *The SBM was more than 2 million francs in debt*: "Situation approximative des comptes de la SBM," January 20, 1859, SBM 1859.

5

WE DO NOT APPROVE OF GAMING HOUSES

45 *"He is mad"*: As quoted in Corti, 158.

46 *There was a quick hint of brightness*: Corti, 161.

46 *"The disappointment of those coming"*: As quoted in Fielding, 32.

46 *By the end of 1860 the SBM had suffered a net loss*: Fielding, 33.

46 *"always nervous about the future"*: As quoted in Corti, 162.

46 *He refused to advertise*: Corti, 164.

47 *Eynaud had to pester*: "Letter from Eynaud to Prince Charles III," February 5, 1862, SBM 1862.

47 *"such a gathering"*: "Letter from M. Lefebvre to the Prince," December 12, 1861, SBM 1861.

47 *Over a few weeks in March 1862*: "Letter from M. de Payan to the Governor General," March 1, 1862; "Letter from M. de Payan to the Governor General," March 8, 1862; "Letter from M. de Payan to the Governor General," March 29, 1862; Report from M. de Payan to the Governor General," August 23, 1862, SBM 1862.

47 *Monaco's governor general*: "Letter from the Governor General of Monaco to the Prefect of the Department of the Alpes Maritimes," circa November, 1862, Fonds de la préfecture: Relations avec la Principauté de Monaco, 1856–1913, ADAM 1M 0432. The letter is undated but is almost certainly in response to an inquiry written by the French minister of the interior on November 10, 1862, housed in the same folder. The tone of this and later communications with the French state were almost always deferential and Monégasque authorities evidently shared some information with the French police.

48 *Many of them started their days*: Fielding, 33.

48 *Valmy put his men to work*: Jackson, 20.

49 *"Monsieur Blanc is enormously rich"*: As quoted in Corti, 171.

50 *"most troublesome disability"*: Ibid.

50 *"one of the most frequented winter stations"*: "Letter from François Blanc to the Prince," January 12, 1863, SBM 1863.

50 *"It is enormously to Your Highness's interest"*: As quoted in Corti, 178.

50 *"only a pretext"*: Ibid., 179.

51 *Blanc had also apparently managed*: Jackson, 30.

51 *"Though Blanc may appear"*: As quoted in Corti, 179.

52 *"Think the matter over"*: As quoted in Jackson, 32.

52 *On All Fools' Day 1863*: "Granting of Gambling Privileges to

François Blanc," April 2, 1863, SBM 1863. The agreement was made on April 1, but codified the following day.

52 *"while the old town"*: "Letter from Eynaud to the Prince," February 23, 1863, SBM 1863.

53 *Though he'd been up as much as seventy thousand francs*: Corti, 182.

53 *"We do not approve of gaming houses"*: Métevier, *Monaco et ses princes*.

6
A WHOLE TOWN REMAINS TO BE BUILT!

55 *"The new management will do great things"*: As quoted in Corti, 183.

55 *"From an existence of dreaming inaction"*: Ibid., 187.

57 *"growing rumors that Germany"*: Ibid., 189.

58 *This is why the already wealthy Blanc*: In 1865, for instance, when the casino took in just over 800,000 francs and devoted nearly 750,000 francs to operating costs, Blanc spent more than 2,000,000 additional francs on infrastructure-related projects, such as the construction of additional sea-bathing facilities, renovations to the Hôtel de Paris, the building of roads, the establishment of a gasworks, and the planting of gardens. See "Letter from de Payan to the Governor General" January 13, 1866, SBM 1866.

59 *"spoken of as a marvel"*: Corti, 186.

59 *It became unofficial policy*: Jackson, 33; "'J.O.,'" "'Monaco,'" in George Smith and William Makepeace Thackeray, *The Cornhill Magazine*: 10, (1864), 182.

59 *He bought four steamers*: *Monte-Carlo 150: SBM* (Monaco, 2013), 85.

59 *"shaded, artificially lighted rooms"*: Theodore Dreiser, *A Traveler at Forty* (The Century Company, 1913), 387.

59 *The idea was simple*: Jon Sterngass, *First Resorts: Pursuing Pleasure at Saratoga Springs, Newport, and Coney Island* (Johns Hopkins University Press, 2001), 152.

60   *Historians of the Côte d'Azur*: Mary Blume, *Côte d'Azur: Invent-*
     ing the French Riviera (Thames & Hudson, 1994), 38; Kenneth
     E. Silver, *Making Paradise: Art, Modernity, and the Myth of the*
     French Riviera (MIT Press, 2001), 63; Jean-Bernard Pouy, "Des
     Symboles à la Dérive," in Brigitte Ouvry-Vial, René Louis, and
     Jean-Bernard Pouy (eds.), *Les Vacances: Un Rêve, un Produit, un*
     Miroir (Autrement, 1990).

60   *Blanc also installed outdoor*: In 1865, for example, the SBM spent
     nearly twenty thousand francs on lighting alone. "Letter from de
     Payan to the Governor General," January 13, 1866, SBM 1866.
     Maurice de Seigneur's *Le Théâtre de Monte-Carlo* (Paris, 1890),
     contains the earliest mention I have seen of electric lighting in
     Monte Carlo.

61   *"never regarded as a rival"*: Polovtsoff, 35.

61   *The shoot also fostered a cottage industry*: "Bertall," *La Vie hors de*
     chez soi (E. Plon, 1876), 81.

61   *Construction began*: Smith, 121.

61   *The SBM hired an esteemed spa doctor*: "SBM advertisement," *Le*
     Journal de Nice, January 5, 1867.

62   *Inside, gamblers paid a small fee*: Labande, 42. For an example of
     individuals denied entry to the casino, see "Untitled Report," Sep-
     tember 27, 1884, SBM 1884.

62   *Officially, if not always in practice, entry was forbidden to*: Fielding,
     105.

62   *Some of the SBM's clients*: Marcel Silvy, *À la colonie étrangère.*
     Casse-Cou, considérations sur les cartes d'entrée de la maison Blanc et
     Compagnie (De Caisson, 1874).

62   *Gold leaf trimmed most of the fixtures*: "General Inventory of Gam-
     ing Rooms no. 26," circa 1923, SBM 1923.

63   *A twenty-four-piece band*: " 'J.O,'" 181.

63   *Croupiers answered to sous-chefs*: Polovtsoff, 126.

63   *Then, quietly, and with the help of a few guards*: Smith, 332.

63   *"A Mlle. Pichon"*: "Letter from Vidal to the Commissioner,"

February 14, 1883, SBM 1883. This and some other reports used in this chapter date from after the François Blanc era but are included here for the sake of thematic continuity. Secondary sources point to similar events taking place during the François Blanc era.

64   *A former Monaco croupier claimed*: Villy, 56, 89.

64   *An SBM security report*: "Letter from Camille Blanc to M. Wicht," November 9, 1908, SBM 1908. See also "Letter from M. Guere-choff de Salismon," June 20, 1907, SBM 1907, and "Untitled Report," September 18, 1891, SBM 1891.

64   *"the casino never forgets"*: Polovtsoff, 237.

64   *Employees divvied up these tips*: D. Schwartz 308. Schwartz points out that originally croupiers were allowed to receive tips in the early years but that this practice changed at some point. Schwartz also writes that after worker action in 1948 the policy was changed and croupiers kept 70 percent of the tips. See also Smith, 345, 440–444, and Graves, 95, 145.

66   *A croupier would drape a shroud of black crepe*: Graves, 90.

66   *"so gracefully as the old* noblesse*"*: Paul de Ketchiva, *Confessions of a Croupier* (Hurst & Blackett, 1928), 17.

67   *The Prince of Wales*: Jackson, 43.

67   *"lounging and smoking"*: As quoted in Polovtsoff, 105.

67   *Gross receipts*: Fielding, 57; Corti, 187.

7

THIS LITTLE PARADISE

69   *"I am convinced"*: As quoted in *Monte-Carlo 150*, 27.

69   *The rail company directors*: "Convention privée entre la Société des bains et la Cie. des Chemins de Fer P.L.M," March 10, 1865, SBM 1865. See also "Déclaration de Commande par M. F. Blanc en faveur de la Cie. des Chemins de Fer P.L.M.," December 12, 1866, SBM 1866.

69   *A few years later, a French muckraker*: Louis Boisset, *Monaco—
     Monte-Carlo, Grandeur et Decadence d'une Maison de Jeu* (Gau-
     thier et Cie, 1884), 37.

69   *His timing in Monaco could hardly have been better*: Kavanagh,
     Dice, 193.

70   *With rare exception*: Ibid.

70   *Mentions of the casino*: "Folder 1901," in the SBM Archives con-
     tains a great deal of information regarding the company's press
     strategies over the years, including amounts paid to individual
     newspapers.

70   *MONACO SEA BATHING*: "Untitled SBM Advertisement," *Le
     Journal de Nice*, January 1, 1864.

70   *The skill with which the charade*: Such editorial advertising was
     especially common in the French press, where the practice of in-
     sidious publicity was known as *réclame*. See Hazel Hahn, *Scenes
     of Parisian Modernity: Culture and Consumption in the Nineteenth
     Century* (Palgrave MacMillan, 2009).

70   *"no direct or indirect attacks"*: "Letter from Wagatha to Administra-
     tors of the *Journal de Nice*," December 19, 1863, SBM 1863.

70   *In a single fiscal year*: "SBM Earnings Report up to 1880–81,"
     SBM 1881. Note that this heavy spending on publicity also took
     place in a year where much of that year's operating capital was
     devoted to major construction projects. Mention of the SBM's
     publicity budget is also made in "Letter from M. de Payan to the
     Governor General," April 24, 1880, SBM 1880.

71   *He sold a prime plot*: Corti, 194.

71   *"Monaco is an earthly paradise"*: "Figaro en Voyage," *Le Figaro*,
     February 23, 1865.

71   *She deemed the newspaperman coarse*: Jackson, 36.

71   *"What does M. de Ste. Suzanne"*: "Letter from M. Alziary de Roque-
     fort to M. Wagatha," November 1, 1880, SBM 1880. Though
     this incident took place three years after the end of the François
     Blanc era, I have included it here because it offers key archival
     evidence of the kind of culture fostered among SBM managers in

relations with the press in the company's first decades, following the tone set by François Blanc.

72 *In 1866, a petition*: "Monaco; A Letter On The Moral and Material Injury caused by the Gambling Establishment of Monte Carlo Addressed to the French Senators and Deputies," credited to "A Few Inhabitants of Nice, Cannes, and Mentone" (Nice, 1866). This and other documents pertaining to anti-Monaco petitions in Nice are housed in ADAM Folder 33J 423, "Spectacles et Jeux," subfolder "Petition contre la maison de jeu de Monaco 1866–1869." A later version of the petition appears as "La Suppression des Jeux de Monte-Carlo-Monaco. Mémoire à l'appui de la pétition presentée aux chambres françaises" (Nice, 1881), Bibliothèque nationale de France (hereafter BNF), 8-V Piece-3355 L.3.34-A.

72 *Ultimately, the Niçoise petition failed*: "Letter from the French Minister of the Interior to the Prefect of the Department of Alpes-Maritimes," April 20, 1866; "Letter from the Governor General of Monaco to the Prefect of the Department of Alpes-Maritimes," January 20, 1867. ADAM, 1M0432, subfolder "Monaco, Maison de Jeu (Affaires Diverses) 1866–1867."

72 *After much pestering from Blanc*: "Letter from de Payan to Prince Charles," July 22, 1865, SBM 1865.

73 *Advertisements recommended*: Jackson, 30.

73 *This coincided neatly*: Jean-Marie Lhôte, *Histoire des jeux de société: géometries du desire* (Flammarion, 1994), 320–321.

73 *Where in the early years*: On the placement of trains stations see, Wolfgang Schivelbusch, *The Railway Journey: The Industrialization of Time and Space in the Nineteenth Century* (University of California Press, 1987), 174.

73 *"the sad reflection"*: Cope Devereux, *Fair Italy, the Riviera and Monte Carlo* (Kegan, Paul, Trench, and Co., 1884).

74 *Blanc personally reimbursed*: Jackson, 34.

74 *Nearly two hundred thousand visitors*: Monte-Carlo 150, 45.

74 *Especially offensive*: Jackson, 37.

74   *Blanc fought for his foreman*: In addition to Jackson's description of
      this event, there is mention of Doineau in SBM correspondence
      dated December 22, 1866, but the document is mostly illegible.
      "Letter from De Payan," December 22, 1866, SBM 1866.

74   *French and Italians made up the bulk*: "Letter from François Blanc to
      the Governor General," May 16, 1863, SBM 1863. See also P. de
      Saint-André, *Monte-Carlo et la guerre* (Imprimerie de Monaco, 1916),
      which lists following breakdown of national origin for SBM workers
      before the outbreak of the First World War: French, 1,296; Italians
      1,1236; Monégasques, 414; Belgians, 218; Germans, 8; Various, 26.

74   *A list of casino supervisors*: The complete list reads "Fouilleroux;
      Gindreau; Lavitonnière; Engremy; Fillhard; Lanek; Zwerner;
      Babel; Yungmann; Bergeand; Kohl; Hein; Schmidt; Guédon;
      Chomprek; Fontenoy; Lecocq; Schlein; Jacquemain." See "État
      du Personnel Supérieur des Jeux," December 1883, SBM 1883.

75   *The eighty-four-member chorus*: Smith, 429.

75   *Within months, land values*: Jackson, 34.

75   *"veritable Californian Gold Rush"*: As quoted in Elaine Denby,
      Grand Hotels: Reality and Illusion (Reaktion Books, 2004), 92.

75   *"bower of oranges"*: *Annuaire officiel de Monaco*, 1878, as quoted in
      Jackson, 45.

75   *One historian claims*: Jackson, 38.

75   *Whatever his motivations*: The Monégasques would still pay taxes
      on the purchase of tobacco, matches, and stamps, and duties were
      levied on all foreign goods coming into the principality as well,
      but these kinds of indirect taxation were mostly meant to keep
      Monaco in line with French practices and discourage smugglers
      from plying their trade in principality; the revenue collected was
      minimal. See Smith, 125.

76   *"as though a fairy wand"*: As quoted in Polovtsoff, 111.

76   *Just over 215,000 rail passengers*: Smith, 310.

76   *"Opposite to the palace"*: As quoted in Ted Jones, *The French Riv-
      iera: A Literary Guide for Travelers* (Tauris Parke, 2007), 150.

76 *Guests at the wedding*: Corti, 261.

77 *"Nobody loses in Monte Carlo"*: As quoted in *Monte-Carlo 150*, 54.

77 *He died on July 27, 1877*: D. Schwartz, 303. The calculations of francs to 1877 dollars are Schwartz's.

77 *He'd overseen the construction*: Denby, 92.

8
KARL MARX'S COUGH

79 *"great influence over Blanc"*: As quoted in Corti, 234.

79 *He said that his title*: Corti, 274. It is worth noting that Corti, too, claimed noble heritage and published under the name Count Corti.

79 *He also claimed*: Concerning Bertora, see Marcel Turbiaux, "Marie Bonaparte, princesse Georges de Grèce et de Danemark (1882–1962): Portrait d'une femme engagée," *Bulletin de psychologie* 6, no. 510 (2010), 481–488; Frédéric Masson, *Napoléon et sa famille* (1907), 425. "Bertora" is listed as part of Napoléon III's retinue, as "aides des cérémonies, secrétaires à l'introduction des ambassadeurs," in *Annuaire Statistique du département de l'Yonne* (1869), 31. Count Bertora is listed as "a representative of the Order of Saint Charles" during the funeral procession of Charles III, in Ludovic Colleville, *Albert de Monaco Intime* (Paris: Félix Juven, 1908), 60. Bertora listed himself as Chevalier of the Legion of Honor in an 1882 contract with the SBM. See "Procuration," January 1882, SBM 1882.

80 *One historian suggests that Bertora proposed*: Jackson, 48.

80 *Regardless of the romantic arrangements*: See, for instance, "SBM Report from the Government Commissioner," April 24, 1880, SBM 1880; "SBM Report from the Government Commissioner," May 1, 1880, SBM 1880.

80 *Bertora worked mostly in the shadows*: I make this claim based on my research into the SBM archives, yet it is worth noting that

the recently published SBM-sponsored history of Monte Carlo by contrast suggests Marie Blanc played a far more active role in running the company. See, for instance, *Monte-Carlo 150*, 48. Two historical novels, Philippe Saint-Germain's *La Grande dame de Monte-Carlo* (1981) and Stéphane Bern's *Plus Belle sera la vie* (2007), also portray Marie Blanc as being very directly involved in the daily operations of the casino after the death of François. Regarding Wagatha, see Corti, 188; Fielding, 57, 80; Graves, 59. The SBM archives lend credence to these claims of nepotism. For instance, a company report mentions a "M. Ferdinand Hensel" (Marie's maiden name was Hensel) as a top SBM manager. See "SBM report," July 30, 1881, SBM 1881.

80   *But she mostly avoided the resort*: Marie Blanc's Parisian address is listed in "Contact between Marie Blanc and the SBM," June 28, 1880, SBM 1880.

80   *Less than three years after her husband's death*: Ibid.

80   *"Artists, I have gathered palms"*: As quoted in Smith, 321.

81   *This concert hall*: Concerning Garnier's Monte Carlo architecture, I have consulted Jean-Lucien Bonillo et al., *Les Riviera de Charles Garnier et Gustave Eiffel: Le rêve de la raison* (Imbernon, 2004); P. Joanne, *Guide Diamant: Stations d'hiver de la Méditerranée* (Hachette et Cie, 1881); Labande; Michel Steve, *La Riviera de Charles Garnier* (Demaistre, 1998); De Seigneur; Philippe Thanh, *Opéra de Monte Carlo: Renaissance De La Salle Garnier* (Éditions le Passage, 2005).

81   *Not coincidentally, the French government*: Corti, 259.

81   *Garnier dutifully borrowed from the tropes*: Garnier's widow wrote that his work in Monte Carlo was "the result of the studies he conducted for the Opéra [de Paris]" and marked "the apogee of his genius." As quoted in Steve, 37. The architect repeated many of the styles and themes that he had recently used for the Opéra de Paris, including his use of oversized oculi, moldings, and color. Garnier also modeled the foyer of the Monte Carlo concert hall directly

on that of his Paris building, while commissioning mosaics by an Italian artist that evoked similar pieces in the Opéra de Paris. See Steve, 36.

81 *As one guidebook writer noted*: De Seigneur, 1.

82 *She allegedly lost one hundred thousand francs*: Monte-Carlo 150, 120; I have also consulted Raoul Mille, *Sarah Bernhardt et Monaco* (Éditions du Rocher, 2005).

83 *As in the brightly lit casino*: When a Niçoise paper reported (erroneously) that Queen Victoria planned to attend a concert, the show quickly sold out. "Report from Jalivot to the Governor General" (numbered 1069), circa 1882, SBM 1882.

83 *"when decent sort of people confess"*: The London *Times* piece is quoted in "Attractions Of Monte Carlo: The Music, The Show, The Gayety," *New York Times,* April 28, 1879.

84 *"justified or seemed sincere"*: Quotations and details concerning the explosion come from "Untitled Report," May 1, 1880, SBM 1880. The explosion is also described at length in Charles Limouzin, "Quittes pour la peur," *Le Monégasque,* January 10, 1927.

84 *"enabled him to appreciate"*: "Mme. Roland Bonaparte," *New York Times,* August 21, 1882.

85 *Bertora, who may have arranged the union*: See Turbiaux. According to "Two Weddings in Paris," *New York Times,* April 10, 1882, it was Roland's sister Jeanne, and not Bertora, who played matchmaker.

85 *It was in front of this church on 13* Vendémiaire: The "whiff of grapeshot" comment is often attributed directly to Bonaparte, but seems to have originated with Thomas Carlyle's putting the words in Bonaparte's mouth in *The French Revolution.* See chapter 3.7.VII, "The Whiff of Grapeshot".

85 *While Bertora represented her mother*: "SBM Report 1099," circa 1882, SBM 1882.

85 *She grew up to be a student of Freud's*: Celia Bertin, *Marie Bonaparte: A Life* (Harcourt Brace, 1983).

85 *In the reports filed by the palace representative*: "Untitled SBM Reports," July 30, 1881; August 6, 1881; October 1, 1881. SBM 1881.

85 *Her jewels went on the block*: Corti, 267.

86 *The SBM granted Wagatha a pension*: "SBM Report 1075," circa 1882, SBM 1882. Wagatha's job fell to a man named Dupressoir, who had served the Blanc's old mentor Bénazet in Baden-Baden. Again, Bertora likely organized this shift behind the scenes. "Report 1075," circa 1882, SBM 1882.

86 *In company reports following Marie's death*: "Letter from Jalivot to the Governor General" (numbered 1074), circa 1882, SBM 1882. Presumably this was written before Marie-Félix's death in August of that year. A document in 1885, after the split in shares, lists the following shareholders: His Serene Highness 1600 shares 8 votes; M. Edmond Blanc 13,900 shares 69 votes; M. Leduc 3200 shares 16 votes; Mme La Princesse Radziwill 17,800 shares 89 votes; Mme La Princesse Bonaparte [assumedly Marie-Félix and Roland Bonaparte's daughter, represented by her legal guardian] 15,600 shares 78 votes. Bertora makes the list with 200 shares and 1 vote. Oddly, neither Charles nor Camille Blanc appears on the list. "Undated SBM report," circa 1885, SBM 1885.

86 *The Marie Blanc–Count Bertora years*: Figures for 1879, for instance, can be found in "SBM Report from the Government Commissioner," April, 24, 1880, SBM 1880. Figures for 1877–1880 are available in "Rapport," circa 1881, SBM 1881. The 1880 financial report shows how heavily gambling provided for the receipts: 14,450,107 of the 14,534,260 francs in total receipts came from the tables, the rest from hotels owned by the SBM. The breakdown of table profits lists roughly 8,500,000 francs coming from trente et quarante and the rest coming from roulette, which indicates that those were the only two games offered at the casino. Note that Corti's claims of profits check against those in the SBM archives, which lends credibility to the rest of his research. See Corti 273 vs. the 1878 SBM balance sheet. During this moment of transition, the board moved to double the SBM's capital from

15,000,000 to 30,000,000 francs, splitting the existing 30,000 shares into 60,000. See "SBM Report," April 23, 1883, SBM 1883.

86 *An 1879 report noted the presence*: " 'Letter from Jalivot to the Governor General.'" September 6, 1879, SBM 1879.

86 *M. D'ubexi, Judge from Épinal*: " 'Letter from M. de Payan to the Governor General,'" April 24, 1880, SBM, Folder 1880.

87 *"magical gardens on barren rocks"*: "Letter from Marx to Jenny Longuet," May 8, 1882, *Karl Marx and Friedrich Engels: Collected Works,* vol. 46 (International Publishers, 1992), 255. Marx's recuperation in Monte Carlo is also mentioned in "Letter from Marx to Engels," May 8, 1882, Marx and Engels, 253, and "Letter from Engels to Sorge," March 15, 1883, Marx and Engels, 460. All quotes here are from the May 8 letter..

88 *"holders of these shares"*: "Untitled SBM Report," December 16, 1893, SBM 1893.

88 *"Mme. la princesse Radziwill"*: "Untitled SBM Report," circa 1894, SBM 1894.

9

PRODIGAL SONS AND WAYWARD DAUGHTERS

89 *François left him only 100*: Corti, 272.

89 *His name appeared*: An SBM report from the 1880 annual shareholders meetings does make note of the absence of Camille Blanc, along with his brother Charles and half brother Edmond, but also asserts that their limited "number of shares held do not require representation for this Meeting to be valid." "SBM Report from the Government Commissioner," April 24, 1880, SBM 1880.

90 *But Edmond loved the horses*: D. Schwartz, 305.

90 *He also won election*: Jean Jaurès, Edmond Claris, "La Corruption Électorale," *Discours Parlementaires* (Cornély, 1904).

90 *"the more spectacular"*: As quoted in Ralph Tegtmeier, *Casinos* (Vendome Press, 1989), 39.

90 *By the time Camille Blanc began his tenure*: "Untitled Report," circa 1884, SBM 1884. The reports lists the number of entry cards issued per year, which I have rounded to the nearest thousand: 87,000 in 1880–1881, 108,000 in 1881–1882, 122,000 in 1882–1883, and 127,000 in 1883–1884.

91 *"the dearest bed"*: As quoted in Patrick Howarth, *When the Riviera was Ours* (Century, 1988), 39–40.

91 *Camille had an elevator*: The first mention of the elevator and escalator I have found are in Léon Honoré Labande, *Guide Pratique de Monte Carlo* (Nice: 1908), 1, 42. But this 1908 account, though highlighting that these amenities were offered free of charge (implying their relative novelty) does not make any special reference to these amenities as being especially new in that year, which leads me to think that they appeared at least a few years earlier.

91 *While across the ocean Coney Island operators*: Ibid. Concerning elevators and escalators in Coney Island, see Rem Koolhaas, *Delirious New York: A Retroactive Manifesto for Manhattan* (New York: Monacelli Press, 1997), 29–80.

91 *It was stocked with Limoges porcelain*: *Monte-Carlo 150*, 46.

91 *One night at the restaurant*: Ibid., 87.

92 *The restaurant's director*: Victor Bethell, *Ten Days at Monaco at the Bank's Expense* (William Heinemann, 1898), 101.

92 *Escoffier created a few dishes*: Blume, 58.

92 *"displaying the smartest frocks"*: Bethell, 102–103.

93 *"After a cigar"*: Ibid., 48.

93 *Camille had parceled the SBM's operation*: D. Schwartz, 305.

94 *At that time Monte Carlo didn't use the colored chips*: Graves 113. The company started to phase out the practice of accepting any kind of currency after a casino inspector noticed a rash of small denomination silver pieces from Mexico, Chile, and Peru, which he figured was the result of an illicit money laundering scheme. See "Untitled SBM report," May 1, 1880, SBM 1880.

94 *The British journalist Adolphe Smith*: Smith, 351–354.

95   *Smith wrote that the SBM spied*: Smith, 359.

95   *"Charles Bauscher, croupier"*: "Untitled SBM report," February 23, 1893, SBM 1893.

95   *These kinds of infractions*: D. Schwartz, 306.

95   *"In reality, the great majority of gamblers"*: Marx and Engels, 255.

96   *Guides described another "infallible" betting system*: This was known as the d'Alembert scheme—named for the eighteenth-century French polymath Jean-Baptiste le Rond d'Alembert, though it is unclear whether he actually devised the system. See Jackson, 42.

96   *In the 1890s a song*: "Hero of Once Widely Famous Song Dies in Abject Poverty," *Washington Post*, July 30, 1922.

99   *Smith recounted meeting a woman*: Smith, 453. Much of my writing on superstitions at Monte Carlo below is drawn from D. Schwartz, 307–208 and Smith, 453–462.

99   *Chaplains at the principality's Saint Paul's Anglican Church*: Clair Price, "A Roulette Battle Resounds in Europe," *New York Times*, March 4, 1934.

100   *After surviving the ordeal*: Fielding, 88.

100   *Another favorite tale was that of Sir Arthur Sullivan*: Polovtsoff 45–46.

100   *Yet while three hundred people died in a San Remo church*: Jackson, 52.

100   *"We can imagine the sensation"*: As quoted in Fielding 88.

100   *Casino profits remained strong*: See, for instance, "Untitled SBM report," April 1, 1892. SBM 1892; Smith, 323.

101   *"all discussion of a political or religious nature"*: "Undated Statutes of International Sporting Club," circa 1905, SBM 1905.

101   *Aside from the Romanovs, there was King Leopold II of Belgium*: Jackson, 58.

101   *Perhaps at the Sporting*: Ibid. See also Michael Nelson, *Queen Victoria and The discovery of the Riviera* (Tauris, 2007), 102–103.

101   *Charles M. Schwab*: Robert Hessen, *Steel Titan: The Life of Charles M. Schwab* (University of Pittsburgh Press, 1990), 133. All quotations related to this incident are from Hessen, 133–135.

102 *By the 1880s SBM managers found they could no longer count on the newspapers*: "Report from Jalivot to the Governor General" (numbered 1064), circa 1882, SBM 1882.

103 *The Monte Carlo suicide story was a favored trope*: The following by-no-means-exhaustive list of news items about suicide in Monte Carlo should serve as some indication of the frequency of such stories: *L'Ami des arts* (Nice): June 27, 1885; *Guardian*: May 23, 1881; August 1, 1888; March 22, 1889; June 27, 1893; April 4, 1896; February 6, 1905; January 21, 1908; April 16, 1925; March 15, 1926; November 24, 1928; *New York Times*: "Attractions of Monte Carlo," April 28, 1879; "At Monte Carlo," June 26, 1881; "Monaco's Nine Centuries," June 19, 1882; "Monte Carlo's Den of Evil," July 20, 1884; "A Story from Monte Carlo," December 12, 1884; "A Bride's Suicide at Monte Carlo," March 27, 1885; "Gamblers No Suicides," June 1, 1885; "Current Foreign Topics," June 23, 1885; "Current Foreign Topics," August 23, 1886; "The Monte Carlo Record," June 6, 1887; "The Decline of Monte Carlo," November 27, 1888; "Tragedies of Monte Carlo," March 25, 1889; "Monte Carlo," May 12, 1889; "Is Monte Carlo Doomed?," September 14, 1889; "A Desperate Female Gambler," April 28, 1891; "An American's Suicide," April 23, 1892; "Superb Genoa and Nice," March 24, 1895; "Behind the Scenes at Monte Carlo," November 24, 1895; "Monte Carlo As a Business," July 25, 1897; "Casino a Boon to Monaco," December 26, 1897; "Monte Carlo and Monaco," March 13, 1898; "Monaco, A Venerable City," April 3, 1898; "Lost, Then Killed Himself," May 10, 1904; "American Suicides Abroad," August 7, 1907; "Woman Suicide An American," August 9, 1907; "Probably No One Covets the Little Kingdom, But It Is Said to be in Need of Discipline," September 1, 1907; "Suicide at Banquet's Close," March 14, 1909; "Riviera Cold Spell Nips Americans," April 12, 1925; "Sues Monaco Over Emetic," April 26, 1925; "American Baroness Says she was Tricked," January 24, 1926; *Observer*: October 30, 1892; February 23, 1908; *Le Petit Journal*: March 11, 1869; April 8, 1869; February 24, 1870; May

18, 1870; November 3, 1871; March 18, 1873; April 14, 1875; February 24, 1876; May 21, 1876; *La Stampa*: June 22, 1884; December 29, 1887; August 16, 1888; March 25, 1888; December 1, 1895; April 7, 1889; May 28, 1892; September 17, 1899; December 2, 1902; October 21, 1902; March 17, 1903; *Washington Post*: "Dividends Dripping With Blood and Tears," R. S. Fendrick. June 3, 1928.

103 *"a Spaniard, recently arrived from New York" and other quotations*: *Le Petit Journal*, May 21, 1876; "La cronaca nera di Montecarlo," *La Stampa*, March 25, 1888; "Riviera Notes"; *Guardian*, February 6, 1905; "At Monte Carlo," *New York Times*, June 26, 1881.

104 *A sign posted by the train station*: Edvard Munch reported seeing such a sign in his 1891 journals, according to Silver, 126.

104 *So did this anti–Monte Carlo pamphlet*: "Monaco; A Letter On The Moral and Material Injury caused by the Gambling Establishment of Monte Carlo Addressed to the French Senators and Deputies, by A Few Inhabitants of Nice, Cannes, et Mentone" (Cauvin, 1876).

105 *People whispered about casino security guards*: See, for example, "Riviera Notes," *Guardian*, February 6, 1905, and William Le Queux, *Mademoiselle of Monte Carlo* (Macaulay Company, 1921); Émile de Saint-Auban, in *L'Histoire sociale au palais de justice*. T. II. *Le Silence et le secret* (A. Pedone, 1898) counted one hundred and twenty eight suicides in Monte Carlo in 1891; Louis Boisset's *Monaco, Monte-Carlo, Grandeur et Decadence d'une Maison de Jeu* (Gauthier, 1884) contains an entire chapter dedicated to suicide in Monaco, contending that the police and press were paid to cover up the frequent suicides; "Un homme politique," in *Monte Carlo Devant L'Europe* (Paris: Alacan-Lezy, 1884), claims to have found twenty reports of suicide in Monte Carlo between January and March of 1884, though he or she suggested that the SBM covered up most of the suicides. "One suicide a month," a London paper estimated in 1879. A decade later, *La Stampa* counted forty-nine suicides in a ten-week period. And by 1902, a Niçoise

paper was providing a detailed list of over 100 recent Monte Carlo suicides. See the London report referenced in "Attractions of Monte Carlo," *New York Times,* April 28, 1879; "La cronaca nera di Montecarlo." *La Stampa,* March 25, 1888; "Untitled Article," *Littoral Mondain,* May 4, 1902.

105 *By the 1890s reporters covering Monte Carlo*: "The Gambling at Monte Carlo," *Guardian,* April 4, 1896, noted "a falling off in the number of suicides;" while "Foreign and Colonial Affairs;" *Observer,* October 30, 1892, counted "only five suicides this year.".

105 *While there is no evidence suggesting that suicides were more frequent*: An 1880 SBM report, for instance, detailed how "the body of a suicide was found in the casino gardens during the night." "Report from Javilot to the Governor General," August 28, 1880, SBM 1880. See also the threatened suicide of Mme. Pichon, detailed in "Letter from Vidal to the Commissioner," February 14, 1883, SBM 1880. I analyze suicide statistics in relation to stories about suicide in Monaco at length in my doctoral dissertation.

105 *In the spring of 1901, Enrico Testa*: Details concerning Enrico Testa's death and its handling are drawn from the following documents in the SBM archives: "Enrico Testa Letter to Camille Blanc," May 10, 1901, SBM 1901; "Surveillance of the Gaming Rooms, Inspector's Report of 7 October 1902: The Testa Affair," SBM 1902; and "Letter from M. Delalonde, Director of Public Safety," October 20, 1902, SBM 1902.

106 *"husbands thoughtlessly encourage" and "hardly the place for ladies"*: J. H. Barnett, "Monte Carlo's Den of Evil," *New York Times,* July 20, 1884; "Scenes at Monte Carlo," *New York Times,* July 8, 1881.

107 *"femmes publiques" and "the fatal beauty of a glorious courtesan"*: Louis Boisset, *Monaco, Monte-Carlo, Grandeur et Decadence d'une Maison de Jeu* (Nice: Gauthier, 1884); Robert Service, *The Poisoned Paradise* (New York: Mead, 1922), 320.

107 *Contemporary observers suggested that prostitutes plied their trade openly*: Boisset, 57.

107 *"Who they are, how they love"*: 'J.O,'" 182.

107 *"evil, rather glorious"*: Dreiser, 393.

107 *"What does one come to Monte Carlo for"*: As quoted in Blume, 58.

107 *According to the SBM account, the company rescued Otéro*: SBM *Monte-Carlo 150*, 66.

108 *In happier times*: Jackson, 57.

108 *In a 1903 French police register*: "List of expulsions from Monaco, 1866–1903," ADAM, 04M 0581.

108 *Prostitutes were regarded as the ultimate arrivistes*: Joanna Richardson, *The Courtesans* (1967), 3.

108 *So too did associating the resort with venal sex*: As the art historian T. J. Clark has suggested, nineteenth-century critics treated prostitution as "the site of absolute degradation and dominance, the place where the body became at last an exchange value, a perfect and complete commodity, and thus took on the power of such things in a world where they were all powerful." T. J. Clark, *The Painting of Modern Life: Paris in the Art of Manet and His Followers* (Princeton University Press, 1999), 100–121.

108 *Prostitution transforms pleasure into a financial transaction*: See Benjamin, 489–515.

109 *Prince Albert was attacked for his second marriage*: "Prince et Chevalier," *La Libre Parole*, July 21, 1896.

109 *"plundering one's neighbors"*: Edward Legge, "The Truth About Monte Carlo" (London, circa 1900), 3.

109 *Novelists spun pathetic scenes*: Paulian, "A Visit . . ."

109 *"the unwholesome lethargic fantasy"*: Mrs. Campbell Praed, "The Casino at Monte Carlo," *The Graphic*, November 8, 1890.

109 *"the habitation of some romantic witch" and "cosmopolitan pandemonium"*: As quoted in Jackson, 36; Paul Bourget, *Une idylle tragique: Moeurs cosmopolites* (A. Lemerre, 1896).

109 *"countries of reality"*: "Monaco," *New York Times*, April 23, 1873.

110 *"Honest families"*: Edmond Lému, *La Semaine Sanglante de Monte-Carl.*, BNF, Gr-Fol-K, circa 1890s.

110 *Novelists and playwrights picked up the thread*: Hall Caine, *The*

Prodigal Son (William Heinemann, 1904); E. Phillips Oppen-heim, *Prodigals of Monte Carlo* (Little, Brown, 1926).

110 *"Listen to these names"*: As quoted in Silver 126.

110 *"Once you've penetrated the enchanted castle"*: Ibid., 128.

111 *"fertilized with the blood of thousands"*: Edvard Munch, MM T 2760, *The Violet Journal,* fol. 24r. Translated by Francesca M. Nichols. Accessed at: emunch.no/TRANSMM_T2760.xhtml# .U96LaYBdV22.

112 *Outside at the train station*: I have recreated this scene by drawing directly from Munch's writing about Monte Carlo in his journals, a particular folio from 1891–1892 that is known among Munch scholars as the Violet Notebook. It is unclear to me how much of this is drawn exactly form his own experience and how much of these scenes he has fictionalized or at least poeticized, but I feel they offer an accurate representation of what he might have seen and felt at the casino. Allison Morehead's "'Are There Bacteria in the Rooms at Monte Carlo?': The Roulette Paintings, 1891–1893," in *Munch blir "Munch" / Munch becoming "Munch"* (exhibition catalog Munch Museum, Oslo, 2008) has also been an invaluable source.

112 *Just as Munch was settling into Nice*: Silver, 126.

112 *Rendered in an unearthly glow*: As Silver, 128, notes, the tableau makes obvious "how completely captivated all the players are by the table itself, aglow in the light from the overhead lamp.".

113 *"This table is like a living thing"*: As quoted in Silver, 128.

113 *The* Observer *reported*: See Richard Ellmann, *Oscar Wilde* (Knopf, 2013).

113 *"At a time when I should have been in London"*: Oscar Wilde, *De Profundis and Other Prison Writings* (Penguin, 2013).

113 *"never had the pluck"*: Lord Alfred Douglas, *Oscar Wilde and Myself* (Duffield & Company, 1914).

114 *"truly sinful"*: Theodore Dreiser, *A Traveler at Forty* (New York: Century Company, 1913).

114 *The Goolds were both found guilty*: *Le Petit Journal,* August 25, 1907; Fielding 112–113.

116 *More than a hundred gaming houses*: Smith, 464.

116 *He refused to allow the kinds of no-limit versions*: Schwartz, 317–319.

10
MONACO AT WAR

119 *"The scientist builds up"*: "Monaco Ruler Lands," *Washington Post*, September 11, 1913.

119 *His first ship, the* Hirondelle: "Prince of Monaco Dead," *Times of India*, June 28, 19; "Prince of Monaco Has Two Kinds of Sharks and Suckers," *New York Tribune*, September 21, 1913; "Monaco and its Prince," *Observer*, December 5, 1920.

120 *Whether in Marchais or Monaco*: Pierre Abramovici, *Un rocher bien occupé: Monaco pendant la guerre, 1939–1945* (Seuil, 2001), 13.

120 *While Albert's subjects were exempted*: Saint-André, 4.

120 *"The Oasis of Europe"*: Whythe Williams, "The Oasis of Europe—Monte Carlo: Where Royalty Goes to Forget the War by Gambling Away Small Fortunes Daily and Where Opera and Pleasure Rule," *New York Times*, May 2, 1915.

120 *"le prince Roulette"*: Colleville, 5.

121 *"the meeting place"*: De Ketchiva, 24.

121 *An 1884 exposé*: See Boisset; and "Report for Camille Blanc," June 16, 1896, SBM 1896; "Letter to Camille Blanc," June 18 1896, SBM 1896.

121 *In 1916 a Monégasque publishing house produced*: De Saint-André, 5–7.

121 *In E. Phillips Oppenheim's 1915 Mr. Grex of Monaco*: E. Phillips Oppenheim, *Mr. Grex of Monaco* (Little, Brown, 1915).

121 *"If you only knew the underground workings"*: Robert Service, *The Poisoned Paradise* (Mead, 1922), 117, 162.

122 *The writer Charles Graves*: Graves, 136.

122 *Other than the date of its production*: Mary Ann Caws and Sarah Bird Wright, *Bloomsbury and France: Art and Friends* (Oxford University Press, 1999), 165. John Maynard Keynes visited the

same villa in February of 1919, a break from his diplomatic duties at the Paris Peace Conference; the villa's owner Dorothy Bussy wrote to her sister-in-law that "Maynard had been gambling heavily at Monte Carlo with no luck." As quoted in Caws, 101.

123 *He did participate in at least one key mission*: Abramovici, 15.

123 *"a reminder"*: "Prince of Monaco Urges Co-operation of U.S. and Europe," *New York Tribune*, April 8, 1921.

124 *She was born in 1898*: Abramovici, 1820.

125 *"in complete conformity"*: See "Ordonnance du 09/08/1919 promulguant le traité fixant les rapports de la Principauté avec la France" and "Traité du 17/07/1918." www.legimonaco.mc /305/legismclois.nsf/db3b0488a44ebcf9c12574c7002a8e84/ cf98c1484c39d9eac125773f003778d0!OpenDocument&Highlight=0,1919, accessed September, 2014.

125 *"for lack of a direct"*: Ibid.

125 *"In the absence of a direct heir"*: Jackson, 119.

125 *Later, in a solemn ceremony*: Ibid.

126 *"amazingly dull"*: Dreiser, 293.

126 *He also supported several charities*: Albert also rallied support for the defense of the falsely accused officer Alfred Dreyfus, and organized a conference to promote international cooperation among police officials, a meeting that played an important part in the later establishment of Interpol.

126 *The exact amounts of his annual payments*: *The Washington Post*, for instance, reported that Albert had received $2 million in 1913 in exchange for renewing the SBM's right to the gambling concession in Monaco for another fifty years and another $3 million in 1914. The paper suggested that the prince received an annual stipend of $300,000 plus 8 percent of the gross receipts of the tables beyond $5 million. "Pope Asks Ruler of Monaco to End Monte Carlo Gambling," *Washington Post*, September 10, 1916. *The Times of India* said he was paid £70,000 annually, and received

£4 million in 1899 for the extension of the concession. "Prince of Monaco Dead," *Times of India*, June 28, 1922.

127 *Stories circulated about his longtime mistress*: "Poor Camille!," *Time* magazine, January 2, 1928.

127 *Although the company stayed profitable*: Casino profits totaled 36 million francs in 1914, but by the war's end, profits were down to 12 million. See Fielding, 118.

127 *"the continued existence"*: "Letter from French Employees of the Monte Carlo Casino," November 14, 1918, SBM 1918.

127 *"In Monaco, only two men matter"*: From an April 1918 issue of *Le Rabelais*, as quoted in "La Question Monégasque," no. 1 19, April, 1918, SBM 1918.

11

THE MERCHANT OF DEATH

129 *They were adorned with pretty flower boxes*: "Sir Basil Answers Cable," *Wall Street Journal*, September 18, 1923; "Zaharoff, European Wizard, Dies," *Los Angeles Times*, November 28, 1936; "The World's Window," Pierre Van Paasen, *Atlanta Constitution*, March 2, 1928.

129 *According to several Zaharoff biographers*: For Zaharoff's biography, my main sources have been: Richard Lewinsohn, *The Mystery Man of Europe: Sir Basil Zaharoff* (Lippincott, 1929); Anthony Allfrey, *Man of Arms: The Life and Legend of Sir Basil Zaharoff* (Weidenfeld & Nicolson), 1989; Robert Neuemann, *Zaharoff, the Armaments King*, R. T Clark, trans. (Allen & Unwin, 1938); Guiles Davenport, *Zaharoff, High Priest of War* (Boston: Lothrop, Lee and Shepard Co., 1934). Jean-Marie Moine's "Basil Zaharoff, le "marchand de canons," in *Ethnologie française*, t. 36, no.1, (Janvier–Mars 2006), 139–152, was an essential source. The following news items list Zaharoff as owner or part owner of the Monte Carlo casino: "'Richest Man in World": Mysterious Zaharoff," *Boston Globe*,

September 3, 1922; "New "Richest Man in World": Sir Basil Zaharoff, Man of Mystery," *New York Times*, August 27, 1922; "Brit-
ish Busy in Monaco; French Are Apprehensive," *Washington Post*,
July 15, 1923; "Is Sir Basil Zaharoff World's Richest Man?," *Balti-
more Sun*, October 26, 1924; "Europe's '"Man Of Mystery'" Now
Becomes A Bridegroom," *New York Times*, September 28, 1924;
"But God Disposes," *Los Angeles Times*, March 14, 1926; "Mighty
Man Of Mystery, Zaharoff Now A Cripple," *Boston Globe*, De-
cember 8, 1929; "Sir Basil Zaharoff Not Ill: Monte Carlo Casino
Stockholder Seen at Luncheon in Hotel," *New York Times*, Feb-
ruary 1, 1931; "Zaharoff Fights France For Monaco," *New York
Times*, February 3, 1923; "Blanc, Who Grew Rich in Monaco,
Dies at 81," *New York Times*, December 23, 1927.

130 *Albert asked Zaharoff for the loan*: Fielding, 119; Jackson, 125;
Laurent, 64.

131 *"vampire . . . born in Bulgaria"*: *Tout Va*, September 13, 1926, as quoted
in Frédéric Laurent, *Le Prince sur son rocher* (Fayard, 2003), 66.

131 *Drawing from the most rigorous sources*: I have traced this account
from biographies about Zaharoff, histories of Monaco, and press
items from his time, cited above, or, as needed, below. I have tried
as much as possible to avoid prefacing each sentence with 'reportedly' or 'rumor had it' or 'journalists alleged,' which would
become tiresome.

131 *Settling in Odessa*: Lewinsohn, 17.

131 *Returning to Turkey in the 1840s*: Lewinsohn, 14. Zaharoff's birth-
date has also been listed as October 8, 1849, in "Sir Basil Zaharoff
Believed Near Death," *Atlanta Constitution*, October 20, 1929;
October 7, 1850, in 'Zaharoff 83 Years Old," *Wall Street Journal*,
October 7, 1933; and October 20, 1850, in "Zaharoff, European
Wizard, Dies," *Los Angeles Times*, November 28, 1936.

131 *Basil attended one of the city's best English schools*: "But God Disposes," *Los Angeles Times*, March 14, 1926.

131 *While anyone with business aspirations*: Lewinsohn, 18.

131 *By some accounts he supplemented his income*: "Mystery Man of Millions Retires to European Palace," Ralph Heinzen, *Atlanta Constitution*, November 4, 1929.

132 *After three years of labor unrewarded*: "Is Sir Basil Zaharoff World's Richest Man?," *Baltimore Sun*, October 26, 1924.

132 *Sevastopoulos promptly broke down*: Lewinsohn, 38.

132 *Zaharoff pledged himself to the Allied cause*: "Sir Basil Zaharoff Honoured," *Manchester Guardian*, May 15, 1919.

132 *In 1923 the Wall Street Journal*: *Wall Street Journal*, May 22, 1923.

133 *In her youth she had been known*: "Zaharoff, Europe's Man of Mystery, is married at 78," *Chicago Daily Tribune*, September 23, 1924.

133 *"so wishes to keep hidden"*: "New "Richest Man in World": Sir Basil Zaharoff, Man of Mystery," *New York Times*, August 27, 1922.

133 *Some biographers and journalists have suggested that Zaharoff planned to take over Monaco*: This theory appears in many sources, but see, for instance, Laurent, 64: "Zaharoff wanted the throne, not for himself but for his duchess.".

133 *In some accounts, while Camille Blanc was conveniently out of the principality*: See for instance Jackson, 131.

134 *In other versions the arms dealer simply revealed*: D. Schwartz, 322; Herald and Radin, 115.

134 *Camille's nephew Léon Radziwill*: Jackson 131; Corti, 279–280.

134 *"the famous casino upside down"*: "Monte Carlo Is Shaken Up," *Los Angeles Times*, April 25, 1923.

134 *Zaharoff named a figurehead*: Graves, 139.

134 *Zaharoff also wisely tapped Léon Barthou*: Jackson, 131.

134 *"knows only one head"*: As quoted in Fielding, 122.

134 *"since everything here belongs to you"*: Fielding 121; Graves, 139; Herald and Radin, 105.

135 *"inherited the softest job"*: "Heir to Monte Carlo, $3,900,000 A Year Income," *Evening World*, June 29, 1922.

135 *There were reports of the London pretender*: "Ex-Butcher May Ask Throne of Monaco," *New York Times*, July 4, 1922; "Former

Butcher Appears as Pretender to Monaco Throne and Owner of Monte Carlo Casino," Henry Wales, *San Francisco Chronicle,* July 4, 1922.

135 *The locals called him "The Bear"*: "Woman to Rule Monaco," Nina Eastbrook, *Los Angeles Times*, June 11, 1922; "Monte Carlo Ruler Dies in France," *Baltimore Sun,* June 27, 1922.

135 *He kept full-length versions of this portrait*: Anne Edwards, *The Grimaldis of Monaco* (William Morrow, 1992), 195–197.

135 *When he did come to Monaco he often dined alone*: Ibid.

135 *His official title read as follows*: See "Royal Family," in the "Official Monte Carlo Guidebook," 1927–1928, Fonds Régional, Monaco.

136 *News items on the wedding*: "Woman to Rule Monaco," Nina Eastbrook, *Los Angeles Times*, June 11, 1922.

136 *once we'd passed through"*: Lucinge, *Gentilhomme* (Perrin, 1990), 206.

137 *"of their day and generation"*: "Woman to Rule Monaco," Nina Eastbrook, *Los Angeles Times*, June 11, 1922.

137 *"no one doubts as being the true power"*: "British are Busy in Monaco," *Washington Post,* July 15, 1923.

137 *"The superstitious are suggesting"*: Ibid.

137 *A photograph snapped shortly afterward*: "Sir Basil and Lady Zaharoff, Monte Carlo, 1924," uncredited photograph in Lewinsohn, 228.

138 *Riding in one of the cars*: "Lady Zaharoff Dies at Monte Carlo," *New York Times,* February 26, 1926; "Zaharoff a Wreck at Wife's Funeral," *New York Times,* February 27, 1926; "Sir Basil Zaharoff Believed Near Death," *Atlanta Constitution*, October 20, 1929.

138 *Days after the funeral of Lady Zaharoff*: See, for instance, Laurent, 66. Note that Graves, 140, lists the sale as taking place in 1925 and alleges that Zaharoff kept control of the Hôtel de Paris even after the sale, though this seems doubtful.

138 *Some writers have interpreted the sale*: Laurent, 66; Herald and Radin, 119.

138 *"six Hindoo [sic] attendants"*: "Zaharoff, European Wizard, Dies," *Los Angeles Times,* November 28, 1936.

138 *"Once, kings, Prime Ministers"*: "Mighty Man Of Mystery, Zaharoff Now A Cripple," *Boston Globe,* December 8, 1929.

138 *"dry-eyed"*: "Zaharoff Dies," *Chicago Tribune,* November 28, 1936; "Zaharoff, European Wizard, Dies," *Los Angeles Times,* November 28, 1936.

138 *His body was taken to Balincourt*: "Zaharoff is Buried with Strict Privacy," *New York Times,* November 30, 1936.

139 *They emerged empty-handed:* "Marauders Enter Crypt of Zaharoff," *New York Times,* January 23, 1937.

139 *"I had strongly recommended you"*: "Letter from Zaharoff to Bethell," April 26, 1918, SBM 1918. This letter only speaks in general terms of Bethell's "candidature," but another letter in the same folder front the Aga Khan to Bethell spells out more explicitly that this candidature pertains to being on the board of directors for the SBM. See "Letter from Aga Khan to Bethell," May 15, 1918, SBM 1918. The Aga Khan says that he will lend his support to Bethell, though, "In fact, I am not an important shareholder. But whatever votes I have will be cast in your favor."

140 *But he says that this happened in 1932*: Lucinge, 210.

140 *"to impress his beautiful duchess"*: *Monte-Carlo 150,* 87, 150.

140 *"this moment when we pass through a crisis"*: "Undated SBM memo to Camille Blanc," circa 1923, SBM 1923. The names of individual board members are not listed.

141 *"Sir, You conclude the obituary"*: "Letters to the Editor; Sir Basil Zaharoff and Monte Carlo," *Times,* March 2, 1926.

141 *Léon also mentioned, in a postscript*: "Letter from René Léon," July 2, 1923, SBM 1923.

12

SALVATION BY EXILE

143 *When René Léon started out in Monte Carlo*: Despite René Léon's relatively prominent position in the history of Monaco, I have

struggled to find detailed biographical information about him. There is record of a René Georges Léon, born in Paris's third arrondissement on June 24, 1886, and also of a René Georges Léon (assumedly the same person) registering as a conscript in the same arrondissement twenty years later. The René Léon who directed the SBM was said to be Jewish and Parisian, so it would make sense that he would have been born and reached adulthood in the Marais, the city's historically Jewish quarter of which the third arrondissement forms part. The record of René Georges Léon's joining the army in 1906 would also line up well with claims that the casino boss fought for France in the First World War. And an 1886 birth would put René Georges Léon in his late thirties by the time he came to prominence in Monte Carlo, if he is indeed the same man. Yet, the birth record of René Georges Léon also includes an amendment from 1911 that documents a marriage to a Jeanne Biard, while what little writing there has been done about the SBM's Léon usually mentions some variation of his being a bachelor, with little social life outside of work. There is also mention of a René Léon in America in the 1930s, a financier and adviser to Roosevelt, but it is very unlikely that the same René Léon could have been heading the Monte Carlo casino and helping to craft American financial policy at the same time. There have also been claims that the Monte Carlo Léon ended his career as the director of the Garden of Allah hotel and nightclub complex in Los Angeles. This would have been a fitting next chapter for the casino boss, but in my research into the Garden of Allah I have found no trace of his name. For biographical data concerning René Georges Léon, see the digitized archives of the Mairie de Paris: Naissances, 3e arr. 1860–1882, 27, entry 949. http://canadparchivesenligne.paris.fr/archives_etat_civil/1860 _1902_actes/aec_visu_img.php?registre=V4E_05510&type =AEC&&bdd_en_cours=actes_ec_1883_1892&vue_tranche _debut=AD075EC_V4E_05510_0004&vue_tranche_fin =AD075EC_V4E_05510_0034&ref_histo=670&cote=V4E%20 5510. Accessed September 2014.

143 *Some historians posit that Léon served*: See, for instance, Jackson.

143 *Those less convinced by speculation*: See, for instance, Graves.

144 *He would cross-check the company's prewar list*: Jackson, 127.

145 *Antibes at the time*: Calvin Tomkins, *Living Well Is the Best Revenge* (Viking, 1971), 96; Amanda Vaill, *Everybody Was So Young* (Broadway Books, 1999), 122. In using this particular sentence structure to describe Antibes I am consciously echoing the language of Tomkins and Vaill, who, I believe, were in turn drawing directly from the Murphys' own description of the place in an interview with Tomkins.

145 *This had been the arrangement*: Tomkins, 34; Vaill, 121. Mary Blume claims that Sella was actively trying to bring a summer season to the Riviera even before the Murphys arrived, but, in a work that is extremely well researched and well-documents, she offers no footnote to support these particular claims. See Blume, 75. I am more convinced by the direct statements of Gerald Murphy concerning Sella, as relayed in Tomkins's book.

145 *"always had great originality"*: As quoted in Tomkins, 34.

145 *"considered crazy"*: As quoted in William McBrien, *Cole Porter: A Biography* (Alfred A. Knopf, 1998), 83; the villa is described in Robert Kimball, *Cole* (Holt, Rinehart, & Winston, 1971), 53.

146 *"dug out a corner"*: As quoted in Tomkins, 34. It should be noted that this and other quotations from the Murphys are rendered slightly differently in other sources, in this case, in Vaill, 109, and Deborah Rothschild, "Masters of the Art of Living," in Deborah Rothschild (ed.), *Making It New: The Art and Style of Sara & Gerald Murphy* (University of California Press, 2007) 47.

146 *"You had the feeling"*: As quoted in Tomkins, 21.

147 *Americans made great machines*: Frederick J. Hoffman, *The Twenties: American Writing in the Postwar Decade* (Free Press, 1965), 30.

147 *"the simplest, bottomest things"*: Sara Murphy to Gerald Murphy, undated, 1915, as quoted in Rothschild, "Art" in Rothschild, 25.

147 *"the 1914 Cadillac"*: Gerald Murphy to Sara Murphy, 9 April, 1914, as quoted in Vaill, 381. The Murphys' daughter, Honoria,

wrote that though her parents loved their home country, their "discontent had to do with an absence of cultural stimulation in America." Honoria Murphy with Richard N. Billings, *Sara and Gerald* (Holt, Rinehart, and Winston, 1982), 1.

147 *"a defect over which"*: Gerald Murphy to Archibald MacLeish, January 22, 1931, as quoted in Vaill. See Kenneth E. Silver, "The Murphy Closet and the Murphy Bed," in Rothschild, *Making It New.*

147 *"I wonder if I shall ever"*: Gerald Murphy to Sara Murphy, June 21, 1915, as quoted in Vaill, 67.

147 *"feeling like aliens"*: Malcolm Cowley, *Exile's Return* (The Bodley Head, 1951), 6, 74.

148 *"Europe frightened her less"*: Edmund Wilson, Leon Edel (ed.), *The Twenties* (Farrar, Straus, Giroux), 92.

148 *Given the postwar inflation*: For American exchange rates versus the franc, see Hoffman, 46.

148 *Americans were also helped*: Paul Fussell, *Abroad: British Literary Traveling Between the Wars* (Oxford University Press), 72.

148 *"Foreigners were not romantic"*: Gertrude Stein, *Paris France* (1940), 17.

149 *"Every day was different"*: As quoted in Tomkins, 30.

149 *"were among the first Americans"*: As quoted in Tomkins, 8.

149 *"the sort of little virgin port"*: John Dos Passos, *The Best Times: An Informal Memoir* (New American Library, 1966), 148.

149 *Near the end of their two-week stay in 1922*: Tomkins, 35.

150 *"Do you like it here—this place?"*: F. Scott Fitzgerald, *Tender Is the Night* (Penguin, 1934), 26. Fitzgerald, it should be noted, begged his editor Max Perkins not to use the word " 'Riviera'" in any advertising copy from the book, writing "Not only does it sound like the triviality of which I am so often accused, but also the Riviera has been so thoroughly exploited by E. Phillips Oppenheim and a whole generation of writers and its very mention invokes a feeling of unreality and insubstantiality." See Robert Sklar, *F. Scott Fitzgerald: The Last Laocoön* (Oxford University Press, 1967).

150 *"Person after person"*: As quoted in Tomkins, 6–7.

150 *"All your friends wanted"*: As quoted in Rothschild, 1.

151 *But Picasso clearly appreciated the region's mythic qualities*: Silver, *Making*, 110.

151 *"It's strange, in Paris I never draw fauns"*: As quoted in Silver, *Making*, 56.

151 *good for them to get the sun"*: As quoted in Tomkins, 35.

151 *"A young woman lay under a roof"*: Fitzgerald, *Tender*, 6.

151 *"real home"*: As quoted in Honoria Murphy, 15.

151 *"Even when you were broke"*: F. Scott Fitzgerald, "Echoes of the Jazz Age" (1931).

151 *"It wasn't parties"*: As quoted in Tomkins, 41.

151 *The Americans brought to the coast*: Blume, 72.

152 *"whatever is said and done"*: Baldassare Castiglione, *The Book of the Courtier* (1528).

152 *Sara would set up picnics on the beach*: Silver, *Paradise*, 115; D. Rothschild, 82.

152 *That same summer Coco Chanel*: Blume, 74.

152 *"I think she [Chanel] may have invented sunbathing"*: As quoted in Blume, 74.

153 *"There was no one at Antibes this summer"*: Ibid., 77.

153 *"everything that a man needed"*: Ernest Hemingway, *A Moveable Feast* (Simon & Schuster, 2009), 159.

153 *"This island"*: As quoted in Jones, 15–16.

154 *"I am not a bucket but a sieve"*: As quoted in Martine d'Astier and Mary Blume, *Lartigue's Riviera* (Flammarion, 2001), 24.

154 *"The era stands alone"*: As quoted in "The Real Nicole and Dick," Aaron Latham, *New York Times*, February 13, 1983.

154 *"cocktails that hit fast and hard"*: Blume, 72.

154 *"It's like magic"*: As quoted in Silver, *Making*, 95.

155 *"Is the engine working?"*: "Postcard Addressed to M. Joseph Costatino, Villa 'La Tunisienne,' Rue des Écoles, Bandol," circa 1920s, SBM Archives, Image Collection, Folder "Cartes Postales."

13
THE BLUE TRAIN

157 *"The great and beautiful Blue Train"*: As quoted in Howarth, 43.

157 *When they wanted to gamble*: Tomkins, 96. Hemingway mentions a party at the Juan-les-Pins casino with the Murphys and the Fitzgeralds in *A Moveable Feast*, 159.

157 *In photographs from the time*: See photographs of Léon in *Rives d'Azur*, no. 187, April 15, 1924, and in a review of Charles Graves, *The Big Gamble*, in *Nash's Pall Mall*, December 1934.

158 *With this same lack of sentimentality*: Monte-Carlo 150, 172.

158 *"It's high time"*: As quoted in Graves, 141.

159 *As with Monte Carlo's founder*: Jackson 131.

159 *Léon was helped in this capacity*: For Blue Train descriptions, see "Riviera Train De Luxe: The Inaugural Trip," *Times of India*, January 9, 1923; "The "Blue Trains": Trial Trip to Riviera," *Times of India*, January 8, 1923; "The Beauty of the Blue Train," Frank Swinnerton, *Chicago Tribune*, June 19, 1927; "Monte Carlo Past and Present," Mordaunt Hall, *New York Times*, December 31, 1922; "At Monte Carlo," F. Britten Austin, *Los Angeles Times*, September 12, 1926; Blume, 88; Fussell, 132–135; Howarth, 41–43; Jim Ring, *Riviera: The Rise and Rise of the Côte d'Azur* (John Murray, 2004), 2–5. I have deduced the schedule for the Blue Train, which differs slightly from those in other secondary sources, from an advertising brochure reproduced in Philippe Collas and Eric Villedary, *Edith Wharton's French Riviera* (Flammarion, 2002), 77.

160 *"Happiness untrammeled"*: As quoted in Fussell,133.

160 *"sleep [their] way"*: Ibid., 132.

160 *"clearly derived from the pleasurable character"*: Sigmund Freud, *The Standard Edition of the Complete Psychological Works of Sigmund Freud*, trans. James Strachey, vol. 7 (London, 1953), 202.

161 *"Titian hair, with languorous brown eyes"*: Graves, 142.

161 *The great panorama*: On the variety of Riviera destinations, see Silver, 23–24.

161 *"as mysteriously colored"*: Fitzgerald, *Tender,* 24.

161 *The trade in fragrance*: Hal Vaughn, *Sleeping With the Enemy: Coco Chanel's Secret War* (Knopf, 2012), 28–29.

163 *"I went and found my stockings"*: Dorothy Parker, "The Garter," *New Yorker,* September 8, 1928.

163 *As Sara told it*: Vaill, 251.

163 *The doorman, all smiles*: Harpo Marx and Rowland Barber, *Harpo Speaks* (Limelight, 2004), 243–244.

163 *Entry now cost 10 francs*: Fielding, 120.

163 *"camaraderie among the old employees"*: As quoted in the *Berkeley Daily Gazette,* January 12, 1925.

164 *"No sooner is an employee hired"*: "Letter from René Léon to Prince Louis," April 7, 1928, SBM 1928.

164 *He scoffed at the prince's notion*: Ibid.

164 *"The day the omnipotent"*: *Le Monégasque,* February 7, 1927.

165 *"you can bet the SBM"*: *Le Monégasque,* January 31, 1927.

165 *"administered the usual remedy"*: "Sues Monaco Over Emetic," *New York Times,* April 26, 1925.

165 *"No one can feel a foreigner"*: Evelyn Waugh, *Labels* (Gerald Duckworth, 1974), 9.

14

A MONUMENT TO FRIVOLITY

167 *"Le Train bleu is more than a frivolous work"*: As quoted in Alex Ross, *The Rest Is Noise: Listening to the Twentieth Century* (Picador, 2008).

167 *"the color of our times" and "as difficult to get a seat"*: See "Une répétition chez Diaghilev," Joseph Kessel, *Le Gaulois,* May 25, 1924, and an unnamed London article, as quoted in Gay Morris, "'Le Train Bleu' Makes a Brief Stopover," *New York Times,* March 4, 1990.

168 *"running from patron to patron"*: Jean Cocteau, in Detaille and Mulys, with foreword by Cocteau, *Les Ballets de Monte-Carlo,* 9.

168 *"Mes chers snobs"*: As quoted in Francis Steegmuller, *Cocteau: A Biography* (Nonpareil, 1970), 68.

169 *"First of all I am a great charlatan"*: Diaghilev to Diaghileva, October 1895, as quoted in Sjeng Scheijen, *Diaghilev: A Life* (Oxford University Press, 2010), 74.

169 *To keep afloat he borrowed money*: Scheijen, 374.

169 *"I realize you're having a hard time"*: Stravinsky to Diaghilev, February 11, 1922, as quoted in Scheijen, 375.

169 *It was clear that Pierre*: Scheijen, 379. Judith Chazin-Bennahum, *René Blum and the Ballets Russes: In Search of a Lost Life* (Oxford University Press, 2011), 80, also discusses Prince Pierre's influence, as does Lynn Garafola, *Diaghilev's Ballets Russes* (Da Capo Press, 1998), 237.

170 *"My idea is to establish"*: As quoted in Sergei Grigoriev, *The Diaghilev Ballet 1909–1929* (Constable, 1953), 179.

170 *By Madame de Polignac*: Concerning Princesse Edmond de Polignac and the Ballets Russes, see Garafola, 237, and Lifar, 127, 259. See also Sylvia Kahan, *Music's Modern Muse: A Life of Winnaretta Singer, Princesse de Polignac* (University of Rochester Press, 2003).

170 *Despite all the forward-thinking energy*: Ross, 108.

170 *"Cunard, de Noailles, Radziwill"*: "Carnets de Diaghilev, 1921," BNF Opéra, Fonds Kochno, pièce 156.

170 *Booking out the Salle Garnier for a whole season*: Lydia Sokolova and Richard Buckle (ed.), *Dancing for Diaghilev: The Memoirs of Lydia Sokolova* (John Murray, 1960), 202.

170 *The Ballets Russes would rehearse*: See, for instance, "Contract between René Léon of the SBM and Serge Diaghilev, 1926," BNF Opéra, Fonds Kochno, pièce 136.

170 *The SBM paid Diaghilev*: See "Contract between Diaghilev and Camille Blanc, administrator of the SBM, 1922," Jerome Robbins Dance Division of the New York Public Library, C-20-20.4.

For other examples of contacts, see "Contract between René Lon of the SBM and Serge Diaghilev, 1926," which outlines paying 420,000 francs for performances in January, April, and May 1926, plus 25,000 francs in travel expenses. See also the various SBM-Diaghilev contracts, too numerous to list individually, housed in the Fonds Kochno at the BNF Opéra, as well as at the Jerome Robbins Dance Division of the New York Public Library. See also Garafola, 238, 263. My research into the financial connections between the Ballets Russes and the SBM has also been informed by Chazin-Bennahum's and Garafola's respective works, as well as Jennifer Homans, *Apollo's Angels: A History of Ballet* (Random House, 2011). As Garafola points out, it is difficult to ascertain exactly how much money came from which patron and how it was used, given a relative lack of archival material specifically pertaining to financial figures.

171 *"We were to have a home at last"*: Sokolova, 202.

171 *"southern outpost"*: Garafola, 252.

171 *"The state of music?"*: "The Russian Ballets at Monte Carlo," Erik Satie, *Paris Journal,* February 15, 1924.

171 *Being brought into Monaco's family*: The archives of the Opéra de Paris hold a letter from a palace adviser to Diaghilev, informing him that His Serene Highness had "taken an interest" in a local Monégasque artist and that he "would be happy if you will receive him and, eventually, help him." "Letter from Prince of Monaco to Diaghilev," September 11, 1927, Paris, BNF Opéra, Fonds Kochno, Piece 63. This was not the only letter he received from Louis asking for special favors: "Letter from Prince of Monaco to Diaghilev," September 9, 1923 Paris," BNF Opéra, Fonds Kochno, Piece 63. In similar fashion, Louis's father Prince Albert had in 1914 expressed to Raoul Gunsbourg his desire that the Opéra present a little-known work from one of his favorite composers, Amilcare Ponchielli. See "Opéra de Monte-Carlo: Premiere representation, *les Maures de Valence,* de Ponchielli," March 23, 1914, BNF Arts et Spectacles, Folder RF 81808.

171 *He also tried but failed*: "Letter from the secretary of Prince Pierre," May 29, 1924, BNF Opéra, Fonds Kochno, pièce 63; see also Buckle, 407.

171 *When Charlotte decided*: Sokolova, 219.

171 *"Although we appreciated"*: Ibid., 206.

172 *A new member*: Graves, 137.

172 *Impresario and dancer*: Scheijen, 389–390.

172 *Dolin remembered those first days*: Anton Dolin, *Autobiography* (Oldbourn, 1960), 30.

172 *"Voilà—I suffered a great loss"*: As quoted in Steegmuller, 321.

172 *"my nervous suffering"*: Jean Cocteau, *La Difficulté d'être* (Éditions du Rocher, 1947), 45.

173 *"The door of the cabana opens"*: As quoted in Garafola, 109.

173 *"Ask Nijinska how she's feeling"*: As quoted in Kochno, *Diaghilev and the Ballets Russes*, 216.

173 *He later said that he'd only been hired*: Darius Milhaud, *My Happy Life*, 124.

174 *"You are already acquainted"*: As quoted in Lifar, 267.

174 *"Working all day and every day"*: As quoted in Buckle, 428.

174 *"would suddenly arrive"*: Dolin, 37.

174 *"nothing but her dancers"*: Kessel, *Le Gaulois*, May 25, 1924.

174 *The principal dancers flubbed*: Buckle, 433.

175 *"What Diaghilev wants is my name"*: As quoted in Scheijen, 391-393.

175 *Coco Chanel, who may also have put some of her own money*: Garafola, 254. Princesse Edmond de Polignac may also have helped to finance the piece.

176 *Woizikovsky went on to lose*: Sokolova, 211.

176 *Save for a pleasant waltz*: Anton Dolin, *Ballet Go Round* (M. Joseph, 1938), 67.

177 *"The first thing one notes"*: As quoted in Nicole Wild and Jean-Michel Nectoux, *Diaghilev, les ballets russes* (BNF, 1979), 125. Of note are the various Monte Carlo programs from the 1920s, digitized by the BNF and available for online viewing through BNF Opale Plus. Especially striking were "Programme général de la

saison de Monte Carlo 1923–1924, texte de Louis Laloy," BNF, IFN- 8415073 and "Théâtre de Monte-Carlo. Saison de ballets par la troupe de M. Serge de Diaghilew [sic], Janvier 1927, programme M. et J. de Brunoff (Paris)," BNF, IFN-8415085.

15
ENTER ELSA

179 *Sometime in 1926*: Maxwell, RSVP, 187–188; Sam Staggs, *Inventing Elsa Maxwell* (St. Martin's, 2012), 153–158; Jackson, 146–147. Quotations from Maxwell's conversations with de Polignac all come from Maxwell, RSVP, 187–188.

179 *She established herself as one of the premier press agents*: Concerning the history of public relations, see Stuart Ewen, *PR! A Social History of Spin* (Basic Books, 1996). To suggest that the public relations industry was in its relative infancy in Europe in the 1920s is not to discount the influence of publicity and advertising agencies, such as the Havas Agency. See Hahn; Marie-Emmanuelle Chessel, *La publicité. Naissance d'une profession (1900–1940)* (CNRS Editions, 1998).

180 *Maxwell said that when she described herself*: Maxwell, RSVP, 187–88.

180 *"louder than the dreadful"*: Ibid., 29. In tracing Maxwell's biography I also draw on Elsa Maxwell, *How to Do It* (Rizzoli, 2005); Elsa Maxwell, *The Celebrity Circus* (Appleton, 1963); and especially Staggs. I have also consulted various newspaper and magazine pieces about Maxwell, too numerous to list, though I do cite whenever I quote from any specific piece. I have also paraphrased or quoted some sentences from my own piece, "Elsa Maxwell, the Kingmaker," *Daily Beast*, November 1, 2012.

180 *She had indeed been born in Keokuk*: Staggs, 9.

180 *After she took a tumble*: Staggs, 6.

181 *"I'm certainly not vain"*: As quoted in "Elsa Maxwell Turns 80 Today; To Celebrate at a Small Party," Peter Grose, *New York Times*, May 24, 1963.

181 *"Fat, 40, and Funny"*: "Expert Tells How to Throw Parties That

Won't Go Dead: Fat, 40, and Funny, Miss Maxwell Makes a Business of Avoiding Dull People, Dull Times," *Boston Globe,* December 12, 1930.

181 *"Clothes? There was a running gag"*: Maxwell, RSVP, 143–144.

181 *"the shocking increase in homosexuality"* and *"a tall, stunning girl"*: Ibid., 246–247, and 79.

182 *"I next met Einstein"*: Ibid., 35.

182 *"the early days"*: Ernest Hemingway, *A Moveable Feast* (Scribner's, 1964), 211.

182 *"comfortable hotel in the Rue Jacob"*: "A Canadian with $1,000 a Year Can Live Very Comfortably and Enjoyably in Paris," Ernest Hemingway, *Toronto Star,* February 4, 1922. "Roughly fifty American cents." Hemingway wrote that the meals he described could be had for "2.40 francs an order," and that the current rate of exchange then had "the U.S. dollar worth twelve and a half francs.".

183 *One spotted them having dresses made*: Here I draw on the "landmarks" where one could sport wealthy Americans listed by Malcolm Cowley, in *A Second Flowering* (Viking, 1956), 55.

183 *"a sort of liaison officer"*: "Life of the Party," Ishbel Ross, *Baltimore Sun,* May 30, 1937.

183 *She seemed so comfortable*: She was helped in her capacity as a hostess by what Simon Doonan has called her "Falstaffian corpulence." Simon Doonan, foreword to Maxwell, *How to Do It*.

183 *"a slipper taken from Mistinguett"*: Maxwell, RSVP, 165.

184 *"run the party backwards"*: As quoted in Staggs, 97.

184 *"the best parties"*: Maxwell, RSVP, 148.

184 *Maxwell always made sure that whatever funds*: As Staggs has noted, Maxwell "thrived on control, and she specialized in spending other people's money." Staggs, 93.

184 *"never had a cent"*: Vreeland, *D.V.,* 116.

184 *They knew her in Venice*: Maxwell, *RSVP*, 182–184; McBrien, 86–117; Ishbel Ross; Staggs, 145–152.

184 *"romantic atmosphere"*: As quoted in Maxwell, *RSVP*, 183.

185 *"the whole of Venice"*: As quoted in Kimball, 75.

185 *"put the Lido on the map"*: As quoted in McBrien, 86.

185 *Maxwell later claimed that Mussolini*: Maxwell, *RSVP,* 182.

186 *"You've got to spend money to make money"*: Ibid., 187–188.

187 *Léon hired Maxwell as a publicist for the SBM*: Staggs, 154.

187 *"As usual, I wound up working for nothing"*: Maxwell, *RSVP,* 188–189.

16

THE FAST LIFE

189 *The French police caught Léon*: The 500-franc fine is mentioned in an article in *Le Franc Parleur,* December 2, 1926. The *New York Times* and *Washington Post* carried versions of a similar piece that mentioned that Léon received fifteen days of jail time from the French court at Besançon, while other sources fix the first case at Lons-le-Saunier, where the sentence was handed down. "Citizens Open War on Monte Carlo Casino, Starting a Paper to Expose Gambling Evils," *New York Times,* April 7, 1926; "Drive Begun to Rid Monaco of Casino," *Washington Post,* April 7, 1926; "Principality Of Monaco Bites Its Feeding Hand," *China Press,* May 27, 1926; "Grâcié . . . ," *Le Monégasque,* January 17, 1927.

189 *"pack his bag and leave"*: "Grâcié . . . ," *Le Monégasque,* January 17, 1927.

189 *The editor claimed that Léon escaped his penalty*: Ibid. See also "Untitled Editorial," *Le Monégasque,* January 24, which quotes from an undated article in the *Nouveau Journal* concerning Barthou.

190 *"the Synagogue and the International Bank"*: "Grâcié . . ."

190 *"Blow the Casino into the sea"*: "Drive Begun to Rid Monaco of Casino," *Washington Post,* April 7, 1926.

190 *In the aftermath of the accident*: Graves, 141.

190 *Magazines catering to English speakers*: See various issues of *Continental Life,* for instance, February 13, 1926, February 27, 1926, and March 6, 1926, BNF JO-46302. See also various issues of *Americans on the Côte d'Azur,* BNF JO-61780, such as February 15, 1927, and March 5, 1927.

190 *"in protest of prohibition"*: Americans on the Côte d'Azur, March 5, 1927.

190 *"Motor-Cycle Hill Climbing"*: Continental Life, February 13, 1926.

190 *There were Wednesday-night galas*: Continental Life, February 6, 1926; February 13, 1926, *Les Échos mondains de Monte-Carlo*, March 1927.

190 *Marini Miharti's nine-piece band*: Les Échos mondains de Monte-Carlo, January 1927.

191 *In the hot summer months of 1926*: Regarding the water affair, see *L'éclaireur de Nice*, December 26, 1926; "Eau de Javel," *Le Monégasque*, January 3, 1927; *Le Monégasque*, January 10, 1927.

191 *"It seems that there are words one is forbidden from saying"*: "Eau de Javel."

191 *The water supply, overseen by the SBM*: Jackson, 42.

191 *As early as 1894 there is record of company managers*: "Untitled SBM report, no. 1700," April 21 1894, SBM 1894.

191 Le Monégasque *countered that if Léon had any understanding*: "Eau de Javel."

191 *At the edge of the reservoir*: On the Bunau-Varilla method, see "1926: Bunau-Varilla et la Verdunisation," *La Dépêche du Midi*, January 17, 1999, Bleach itself was a French invention. The French called it *eau de Javel*, after the district in which it was first created by a French scientist. I have been unable to deduce the exact location of the SBM party. While *Le Monégasque* makes clear reference to a reservoir in Beausoleil, I have not in my research been able to find a suitable site where it might now or once have been located in that town.

192 *"When it comes to the health"*: Le Monégasque, January 3, 1927.

192 *A week later, the Monte Carlo Palace Hotel*: As advertised on the back page of *Le Monaco-Monte Carlo* (formerly *Petit Monégasque*), December 20, 1926.

192 *"a man of action"*: La Gazette de Monaco et de Monte-Carlo, January 17, 1927.

193　*At 9:30 in the morning*: *Le Monégasque,* March 7, 1927.

193　*According to one paper, it had been in the arms of the sultry Dalbane*: "Mlle Dalbane, The Death Flower, Whose Lovers All Meet Tragic Ends," *Milwaukee Sentinel,* February 5, 1928.

193　Le Monégasque *reported that the police*: *Le Monégasque,* March 14. At the time of the story's publication, twelve days after the death, the woman remained in custody, but as I have found no further mention of her being detained in any subsequent reports, we can assume she was released not long afterward.

193　*"thank the god of Israel"*: *Le Monégasque,* March 7, 1927.

194　*The blindfolded dame Fortune*: As reported in *Le Monégasque* on March 7 and March 14, 1927.

194　*A day later, a writer for* Le Monégasque *claimed that René Léon had committed yet another hit-and-run*: *Le Monégasque,* March 7, 1927.

194　*Gould was also building a casino in Nice*: Blume, 90.

194　*Gould and other casino operators*: Schwartz, 319.

194　*Even without that game*: "Pour conjurer la crise des stations thermales, climatiques et balnéaires," *Le Petit Niçois,* December 2, 1931.

194　*To Monaco's east, the Fascist government*: "French, Italian Casinos Open 'Sucker War,'" *Chicago Tribune,* January 24, 1929.

195　*It was built right into a hill*: Graves, 144.

195　*The Duke of Connaught*: Ibid.

195　*Elsa Maxwell launched the venue*: *Monte-Carlo 150,* 172.

195　*"I got such a kick"*: Maxwell, *RSVP,* 190.

196　*"Miss Maxwell caught my imagination"*: As quoted in Staggs, 157.

196　*"IT NEVER RAINS IN NICE"*: As quoted in Harvey Levenstein, *We'll Always Have Paris: American Tourists in France since 1930* (University of Chicago Press, 2004), 15.

196　*"MONÉGASQUES STAND UP!"*: SBM 1928, subfolder "Crise Monégasque."

197　*Three days earlier, a Detective Duchamp*: "Letter from M. Duchamp to 'Mon Capitaine,'" June 5, 1928, SBM 1928, and "Police Intelligence," June 10, 1928, SBM 1928.

197 *"on the verge of serious internal trouble"*: "Monaco Sees Danger Of Internal Trouble," *Washington Post,* August 12, 1928.

198 *"revolutionary agitation"*: Ibid.

198 *"to destroy, and make ugly"*: *L'Écho Monégasque,* January 19, 1929.

198 *"enclosed himself in an ivory tower"*: *L'Avenir de Beausoleil et de Monte Carlo,* April 20, 1928.

198 *A writer for the same paper suggested that foreign workers*: *L'Avenir de Beausoleil et de Monte Carlo,* July 5, 1928. According to the *Times,* Monaco's population around this time stood at 24,927 and could be broken down along the following national lines: Italian: 9,626; French: 9,126; English: 2,262; Monégasques: 1,574; Swiss: 384; Americans: 323; Germans: 193; Dutch: 177; Russians: 171; Czechoslovaks: 86; Hungarians: 55; Turks: 53; Danes: 50; Greeks: 23; Yugoslavs: 21; Persians: 13. (The article does not account for 790 residents, presumably of various nationalities.) 'The Land of Chance," *Times,* April 9, 1929.

198 *They demanded more rights*: *L'Écho Monégasque,* January 19, 1929.

198 *American journalists covering the story*: See for instance: "Monaco Parliament Resigns in a Body," *New York Times,* December 16, 1928; "Monacans [sic] Seeking Rights From Prince," *New York Times,* December 23, 1928; "Monte Carlo Ends Tempest in Teapot," *New York Times,* December 23, 1928; "Six Picked to Solve Monte Carlo Crisis," *New York Times,* December 27, 1928; "A Prince at Loggerheads with his Subjects," *Manchester Guardian,* December 28, 1928; "Ask Brighter Lights to Lure our Rich," *New York Times,* December 30, 1928; "Monte Carlo is Shaken by Wind of Change," *New York Times,* December 30, 1928; "Monaco Ignores Return of Prince," *New York Times,* January 2, 1929; "Prince of Monaco," *Manchester Guardian,* March 19, 1929.

198 *"Already the events of recent weeks"*: As quoted in "Monte Carlo Calm Restored by Prince," *New York Times,* December 18, 1928.

199 *On New Year's Day, 1929*: Graves 145.

199 *Meanwhile, the SBM quietly announced*: Graves, 146.

199 *In January 1929 the head of the resigned National Council*: This is not to be confused with the existing *Le Monégasque*. See various issues of *L'Écho Monégasque*, especially 1929–1930, BNF, JO-94798.

199 *Marquet was a beloved figure*: *Le Monégasque*, March 21, 1927.

199 *"The Jew Daniel Dreyfus"*: *L'Écho Monégasque*, April 27, 1929.

199 *"with a fat wallet"*: *L'Écho Monégasque*, May 3, 1929.

199 L'Écho *even suggested*: *L'Écho Monégasque*, February 16, 1929, and May 3, 1929.

199 *Someone at* L'Écho *had fun taunting*: *L'Écho Monégasque*, February 2, 1929.

200 *"Last Monday, the 28th of January"*: Ibid.

200 *"frogs who want to change their king"*: The unnamed Niçoise news item is quoted in *L'Écho Monégasque*, January 19, 1929.

200 *In February Monaco was hit*: *L'Écho Monégasque*, February 2, 1929; February 16, 1929.

200 *"This triumph of industry"*: Waugh, 27–28.

201 *"permanent rupture"*: *L'Écho Monégasque*, March 2, 1929.

201 *On March 24, the resigned members*: My description of the events of March 24, 1929 and its aftermath is based on information gathered from various contemporary news reports, including "3-Hour 'Revolution' Stirs Monte Carlo," *New York Times,* March 25, 1929; "Riot in Monte Carlo," *Manchester Guardian,* March 25, 1929; "Revolting Populace Storms Prince of Monaco's Palace," *Washington Post,* March 25, 1929; "The Crisis Over in Monaco," *London Times,* April 3, 1929; "A New 'Dictator'," *Manchester Guardian,* March 30, 1929; "Peace in Monaco," *London Times,* April 9, 1929; "Monte Carlo, Bereft Of Its Rich Gamblers, Mourns '"Great Days,"'" *Washington Post,* May 5, 1929; "Monaco and its Crisis," *Observer,* April 7, 1929; "Monte Carlo Earnings Decreased," *The Wall Street Journal,* May 4, 1929. A lengthy

description of the day's events in *L'Écho Monégasque* on March 29, 1929, was especially useful, though I have approached this account with a great deal of caution given the direct involvement in the events of those who produced this description.

201 *"for the benefit of our foreign friends":* *L'Écho Monégasque,* March 30, 1929.

202 *"3-Hour 'Revolution'":* "3-Hour 'Revolution' Stirs Monte Carlo," *New York Times,* March 25, 1929.

17

ONE-WAY STREET

205 *They would have smelled the acrid fumes:* For histories of the Monaco Grand Prix, I have consulted Jeffrey Ashford, *Grand Prix Monaco* (Berkley Books, 1969); Arnaud Chambert-Protat, *Grand Prix de Monaco: les coulisses* (E-T-A-I, 2003); Robert Daley, *Cars at Speed: Classic Stories from Grand Prix's Golden Age* (Motorbooks, 2007); David Hodges, *The Monaco Grand Prix* (Temple Press Books, 1964); Michael Hewett, *Monaco Grand Prix: A Photographic Portrait of the world's Most Prestigious Motor Race* (Haynes Publishing, 2007); Yves Naquin, *Le Grand Prix Automobile de Monaco Histoire d'Une Legende 1929–1960* (Editions Automobilia Monaco, 1992); Alex Rollo, *Monaco Grand Prix* (Ian Allan Publishing, 1987); Rainier Schlegelmilch, *Grand Prix De Monaco: Profile of a Legend* (Motorbooks, 1998); Philippe De Rothschild, *Milady Vine: Autobiography* (Jonathan Cape, 1984) was also instructive.

205 *Sitting high up in their boxy machines:* For drivers in the 1929 Monaco Grand Prix evoking riders on horseback, see Daley, 53.

206 *"I am a great driver":* Rothschild, *Milady.*

207 *"Any respectable traffic system":* *La Vie Automobile,* April 25, 1929.

207 *He was the club's general commissioner:* According to the United States Commerce Department in "Autos Crowding World, Federal Figures Show," *Washington Post,* June 29, 1928.

207 *So prominent a Monégasque*: Note that Antony Noghès (also rendered as Noghes in some sources) was born in France, not Monaco, but his ties seem to have been stronger to the principality than to France, hence my use of "his homeland."

207 *"internationally relevant"*: As quoted in Hodges, vii. The Automobile Club of Monaco formed in 1925 as an offshoot of the Cycling and Automobile Sport Club of Monaco, which had overseen the Monte Carlo Rally since 1911. Founded in 1890, the Cycling and Automobile Sport was before 1907 known as the Cycling Sport Club of Monaco.

208 *"world-wide interest"*: Ibid.

208 *The Monte Carlo casino was enjoying record profits*: Fielding, 127.

208 *"Race Within the Town"*: As quoted in Hodges, viii.

208 *"hit on the only possible circuit"*: Ibid.

208 *"Today the roads"*: Ibid., vii–viii.

209 *"while the public services"*: As quoted in Hodges, viii.

209 *Again, his memory seems a bit muddy*: According to Hodges's 1964 history of the event, the Monaco Grand Prix by that point had "never been a profitable race for the organizers, whose loss up to now has been guaranteed annually by the town." Hodges, 2. By "town," one presumes that Hodges means the SBM, which for the greater part of Monaco's history has financed almost all of the principality's operations, from sewage to electricity. According to the SBM's history of Monte Carlo, "Noghès sought a patron. He approached the Société des Bains de Mer. Although Camille Blanc had died the previous year, the company continued to sponsor and finance sporting events. After the rally, why not the Grand Prix? An agreement was reached and the Grand Prix scheduled for the following year." See *Monte-Carlo 150*, 156.

209 *"True to its Phoenician origin"*: Smith, 443.

210 *"It struck me here"*: Dreiser, *Traveler*.

210 *"a series of lucky rolls"*: Edouard Gourdon, *Les Fâcheurs de Nuit* (Paris, 1860). Walter Benjamin, who includes this quote in the

Arcades Project, echoed Gourdon by positing that gamblers practiced "the art of collecting into a single instant the emotions dispersed throughout the slot-moving existence of ordinary men." Benjamin, 499.

210 *"a game passes the time"*: Benjamin, 512.

211 *"Whether it be smoking a good cigar"*: Francis de Miomandre, *Le Casino* (Paris, 1928), 16.

211 *In keeping with Monte Carlo's embrace*: Hodges, x.

212 *The point was clear*: Because of this particular routing, drivers rarely got the chance to get into top gear, and they had to make countless small shifts and adjustments over the course of one hundred laps. It became known as the Race of a Thousand Corners; the top speed reached in that inaugural race was roughly fifty miles an hour.

213 *While a statue*: Eugène Marquet is presumably the namesake of the Avenue Marquet that delineates the border of Monaco and France at the west end of the principality, though if this is the case it is still not a specific reference to the protest he led in 1929, as he served as a major figure in the principality in private and political capacities for several years.

POSTSCRIPT
FAITES VOS JEUX

215 *On a spring day in 1930*: "Monaco: Roulette Bomb," *Time,* May 19, 1930.

INDEX

ABOUT THE AUTHOR

Mark Braude is a lecturer in history at Stanford University, where he has also been a postdoctoral research fellow. He has written for the *Daily Beast*, the *Globe and Mail*, and other publications. Born in Vancouver, Braude lives in San Francisco with his wife. This is his first book.